BIBLIOGRAPHY
of
COLORADO MOUNTAIN ASCENTS,
1863 - 1976

JOSEPH D. KRAMARSIC

for
Brett and Jeff

CONTENTS

INTRODUCTION

The Bibliography of Colorado Mountain Ascents, 1863 - 1976 is a compilation of materials of interest to Colorado mountaineering. Only references of an actual mountaineering value are listed - articles, notes, illustrations, maps, or any other item judged to contain information of a mountaineering nature. The following mountaineering journals and magazines were used in compiling the bibliography:

Alpine Journal, 1863 -

American Alpine Journal, 1929 -

Appalachia, 1876 -

Ascent, 1967 -

Canadian Alpine Journal, 1907 -

Chicago Mountaineering Club Newsletter, 1945 -

Climbing, 1970 -

Harvard Mountaineering, 1927 -

Iowa Mountaineers Journal, 1945 -

Mazama, 1896 -

#Mountain, 1969 -

The Mountaineer, 1907 -

The Mountaineering Journal (British), 1932 - 1938

Off Belay, 1972 -

Sierra Club Bulletin, 1893 -

Summit, 1955 -

Trail and Timberline, 1918 -

#Compiled through 1975 only.

The bibliography is arranged in the following format:

1. All the mountain names are arranged alphabetically as are the journal and magazine titles under each name. The references are arranged in chronological order under the journal and magazine titles. Articles, notes, and illustrations that contain information on more than one mountain are noted with an asterisk.

2. Each mountain is named as it appears on the topographic quadrangle map of that area. A mountain name that is placed in quotation marks indicates an unofficial name that will not be found on its topographic map. Some names may differ slightly from the references to those on the topographic maps, such as the juxtaposition of the words mountain or peak.

3. The elevation of each mountain name is given as that found on the topographic map of that area. It may be the specific elevation figure or the highest contour line associated with that mountain name. In the case of a few aiguilles and pinnacles where the elevation locations cannot be found, the elevation figures are taken from a journal or magazine reference.

4. Each mountain name is identified with the physiological division of mountain ranges as found in Robert Ormes, Guide to the Colorado Mountains, seventh edition.

5. Each mountain name is identified with the U.S.G.S. topographic quadrangle map that it appears on. A mountain name that is an unofficial name will be indicated as (Unnamed) next to the topographic map name. All topographic maps are 7½ quadrangles unless indicated as 15M.

6. Significant ascents are noted under many references. These

notations are not complete for all references that refer to first ascents, new routes, etc., and in either case the reader will have to refer to the reference itself for complete information contained therein.

The bibliography was compiled from the reference holdings of the American Alpine Club Library, the Chicago Mountaineering Club Library, the Colorado Mountain Club Library, and the Denver Public Library. I wish to express my appreciation to Frank de la Vega, George Pokorny, Marion Peterson, and several members of the staff of the Denver Public Library for providing access to the materials found in the respective libraries and used in compiling this bibliography.

MT. ABRAMS, 12,801'   San Juan Mountains   Ironton 1955
   Trail and Timberline
      Illustration, "Mount Abrams and Million Dollar Highway,"
      No. 407, November 1952, p. 166.

"ACADEMY PEAK", 9,385'   Rampart Range   (Unnamed) Cascade 1961
   Trail and Timberline
      "The Academy Peaks," Dwight Hamilton, No. 517, January 1962,
      pp. 3-4, 1 Illustration, Front cover illustration.

MT. ACHONEE, 12,649'   Front Range, Indian Peaks   Monarch Lake 1958
   Trail and Timberline
      "Some 1940 Outing Observations,"* Roy R. Murchison, No. 261,
      September 1940, p. 143.

      "Our Indian Peaks,"* Karl E. Boehm, No. 497, May 1960, pp. 73-
      74.

MT. ADAMS, 12,121'   Front Range, Rocky Mountain National Park
                 Isolation Peak 1958
   Trail and Timberline
      "Mountain Climbing and Statistics in Rocky Mountain National
      Park,"* John C. Whitnah and Robert C. Peterson, No. 343,
      July 1947, pp. 116-117.

MT. ADAMS, 13,931'   Sangre de Cristo Range   Horn Peak 1959
   Trail and Timberline
      "The Sangre de Cristo Range,"* Eva and Bill Rathbun, No. 460,
      April 1957, pp. 55-60, 64, 1 Map.

      "New Maps of the Sangre de Cristo Range,"* John L. J. Hart,
      No. 519, March 1962, pp. 32-33.

      "Sangre de Cristo Saga,"* Lester A. Michel, with Wilbur F.
      Arnold, No. 525, September 1962, pp. 139-142, 150, (Continued
      from August 1962 T&T).

      "A Guide to Colorado's Almost-Fourteens,"* William A. Graves,
      No. 683, November 1975, pp. 225-227.

MT. AETNA, 13,771'   Sawatch Range   Garfield 15M 1940
   Trail and Timberline
      Illustration, "Mt. Etna from Monarch Pass," Monarch Air Lines,
      No. 369, September 1949, p. 129.

      Back cover illustration, "Mount Etna from Monarch Pass,"
      Charlie Wunder, No. 436, April 1955.

      Illustration, "On Top of Mount Etna," No. 442, October 1955,
      p. 168.

"AIGUILLE NUMBER ONE", 12,900'[#]   San Juan Mountains, Sneffels Range
                                    (Unnamed) Mount Sneffels 1967
    American Alpine Journal
        "Southwestern Colorado Climbing Notes - 1933,"* Dwight G.
        Lavender, Vol. 2, 1934, p. 256.
        First ascent note, T. M. Griffiths, L. V. Giesecke, B. M.
        Souder, and Dwight G. Lavender.

    The Mountaineering Journal (British)
        "Correspondence,"* Dwight Lavender, Vol. 2, No. 1, December,
        January, February 1933-34, pp. 47-51.
        First ascent note, Dwight Lavender, T. Melvin Griffiths, Lewis
        V. Giesecke, and Byron Souder.

    Trail and Timberline
        "The 1933 Climbing Season in Colorado,"* Carleton C. Long,
        No. 184, February 1934, pp. 20-23.
        First ascent note.

AJAX PEAK, 12,785'   San Juan Mountains   Telluride 1955
    Trail and Timberline
        "The San Juan Ho!"* Dwight Lavender, No. 142, August 1930,
        pp. 5-6.

MT. ALBION, 12,609'   Front Range, Indian Peaks   Ward 1957
    Trail and Timberline
        "Our Indian Peaks,"* Karl E. Boehm, No. 497, May 1960, pp. 73-
        74.

MT. ALICE, 13,310'   Front Range, Rocky Mountain National Park
                      Isolation Peak 1958
    American Alpine Journal
        "Mount Alice, East Wall," Robert D. Culp, Vol. 18, 1973,
        p. 432.
        New route note of the east wall, Jack Turner and Robert D.
        Culp.

    Appalachia
        "Alpina: United States," John A. Woodworth, Vol. 39,
        June 1973, p. 147.
        First ascent (new route) note of the east wall, Bob Culp and
        Jack Turner.

    Climbing
        "'Mt. Alice East Wall', Rocky Mountain National Park, Colo.,"
        No. 16, November-December 1972, p. 34.
        First ascent (new route) note of the east wall, Bob Culp and
        Jack Turner.

        "Basecamp: Colorado,"* No. 39, November-December 1976, pp. 3-5,
        1 Illustration.
        New route note on the east face, Harry Kent and Mike Neri.

[#]Elevation figure from the American Alpine Journal.

Off Belay
    "Two New Technical Climbs in Rocky Mountain National Park,"*
Walt Fricke, No. 5, October 1972, p. 40, 1 Illustration.
New route note of the east wall, Bob Culp and Jack Turner.

Summit
    "Exploring New Routes in Rocky Mountain National Park,"*
Philip C. Ritterbush, Vol. 5, No. 2, February 1959, pp. 10-13,
20-21, 1 Illustration, 1 Map.
First direct ascent noted of the east face, Charles Ehlert,
James Walker, David Fedson, and Clinton Brooks.

Trail and Timberline
    "The Wilds of Wild Basin,"* No. 16, October 1919, pp. 2-3.

    "The Wild Basin Outing,"* Elinor Eppich Kingery, No. 298,
October 1943, pp. 123-126.

    "Mountain Climbing and Statistics in Rocky Mountain National
Park,"* John C. Whitnah and Robert C. Peterson, No. 343,
July 1947, pp. 116-117.

    "Boulder Rock Climbers: Faces of the Sixties,"* Bob Culp,
No. 623, November 1970, pp. 238-244.
First ascent noted of the east wall by the central ramp, Bob
Culp and Larry Dalke.

ANDREWS PEAK, 12,565'   Front Range, Rocky Mountain National Park
                    Isolation Peak 1958
  Appalachia
    "The Peaks of Rocky Mountain National Park,"* Roger W. Toll,
Vol. 17, June 1929, pp. 252-260.

ANIMAS MOUNTAIN, 13,786' Needle Mountains   Snowdon Peak 1964
  American Alpine Journal
    "Colorado Climbing Notes, 1934,"* Carleton C. Long, Vol. 2,
1935, p. 416.
First ascent note, John Nelson, Everett Long, and Carleton C.
Long.

    "A.A.C. and C.M.C. Joint Outing, Needle Mountains, Colorado,
July 19 - August 9, 1953,"* Henry L. McClintock, Vol. 9, 1954,
pp. 169-171.
New route note.

  Chicago Mountaineering Club Newsletter
    "Needles Outing of the American Alpine Club,"* Dave Bidwell,
Vol. 7, No. 5, November 1953, pp. 10-12.

  The Mountaineering Journal (British)
    "Outstanding Climbing Centres in the South-Western Colorado
Rockies,"* Dwight G. Lavender, Vol. 1, No. 4, June, July,
August 1933, pp. 238-248, 2 Illustrations.

Trail and Timberline
    "The 1934 Climbing Season in Colorado,"* Carleton C. Long,
No. 196, February 1935, pp. 15-18.
First ascent note, John Nelson, Everett Long, and Carleton C.
Long.

    "Noname Prospects,"* Mel Griffiths, No. 340, April 1947,
pp. 56-59, 1 Illustration.

    "Climbers Guide to Noname,"* No. 342, June 1947, pp. 97-98,
1 Map.

    "Climber's Guide from Noname Creek,"* Henry Buchtel, No. 345,
September 1947, pp. 143-144.

    "Revised Climbers' Guide from Noname Creek,"* William E.
Davis, No. 502, October 1960, pp. 149-154, 1 Map.

MT. ANTERO, 14,269'   Sawatch Range   Poncha Springs 15M 1956
    Appalachia
        "All the 14,000's,"* Carl Melzer, Vol. 22, December 1939,
pp. 466-479.

Chicago Mountaineering Club Newsletter
    "Sneaking Up on Colorado Peaks by Way of Texas,"* Groves
Kilbourn, Vol. 17, No. 1, February 1964, pp. 4-5.

Trail and Timberline
    "Climbing Notes,"* No. 143, September 1930, p. 6.
Ascent note, Erl Ellis, Joe Holland, and John L. J. Hart.

    "Denver Activities,"* No. 154, August 1931, p. 126.
Ascent note, first by CMC.

    "Junior Outing,"* Anonymous, No. 227, October 1937, p. 107.

    "14,000 Feet,"* Russell Briggs, No. 246, June 1939, p. 77.

    "A Conglomerate Review of the C.M.C. Summer Outing,
August 15-23, 1942 - Collegiate Range,"* Nancy Plowman, Eliot
Moses, Harold Brewer, Mary Wagner, No. 287, November 1942,
pp. 141-143, 1 Map p. 140.

    "Backpacking the Sawatch Range,"* Bud Boylard, No. 378,
June 1950, pp. 83-85, 90-91, 1 Illustration.

    "Mt. Antero on Skis," Don Peel, No. 483, March 1959, p. 41.

ANTERO PEAK, 13,266'   Sawatch Range   Bonanza 15M 1959
    Trail and Timberline
        "The Mountain Ranges of Colorado,"* Kenneth Segerstrom,
No. 215, September 1936, pp. 109-115, 1 Map.

APACHE PEAK, 13,441'   Front Range, Indian Peaks   Monarch Lake 1958
American Alpine Journal
      "Technical Climbing in the Mountains of Colorado and Wyoming,"*
      Albert Russell Ellingwood, Vol. 1, 1930, pp. 140-147.

   Chicago Mountaineering Club Newsletter
      "Club Outing in the Araphoes,"* Bobby Palser, Vol. 4, No. 5,
      November 1950, pp. 11-12.

   Harvard Mountaineering
      "Climbing Notes, 1964: Colorado, Front Range,"* Dave Roberts,
      No. 17, May 1965, pp. 60-61.
      Winter ascent note, Dave Roberts and Burt Redmayne.

   Trail and Timberline
      "Some First Ascent Possibilities in Colorado,"* Kenneth
      Segerstrom, No. 165, July 1932, pp. 103-104.

      "Some 1940 Outing Observations,"* Roy R. Murchison, No. 261,
      September 1940, p. 143.

      "The Long Lake Region,"* A. Gayle Waldrop, No. 281, May 1942,
      pp. 69-70, 1 Illustration.

      "I Survived A Glissade," Baker Armstrong, No. 472, April 1958,
      pp. 49-50.

      "Our Indian Peaks,"* Karl E. Boehm, No. 497, May 1960, pp. 73-
      74.

"APACHE THUMB",   Front Range, Indian Peaks
   American Alpine Journal
      "Apache Thumb," Stanley Shepard, Vol. 14, 1964, p. 196.
      First ascent note of the west pillar, Bob Sandefur and Stanley
      Shepard.

ARGENTINE PEAK, 13,738'   Front Range   Montezuma 1958
   Trail and Timberline
      "Summit Lake to Adolph's (Winter Park),"* Edward F. Taylor,
      No. 304, April 1944, pp. 39-40, 45, 1 Illustration.

ARIKAREE PEAK, 13,150'   Front Range, Indian Peaks   Monarch Lake 1958
   Summit
      "Arapaho Glacier Country,"* Weldon F. Heald, Vol. 9, No. 10,
      November 1963, pp. 20-23.
      See the following corrections to the above article:
      "Letters," John M. Clark, Vol. 9, No. 11, December 1963, p. 31.
      "Letters," David Parkhurst, Vol. 10, No. 1, January-
      February 1964, p. 36.

   Trail and Timberline
      "A Circle Trip in the Arikarees,"* Ronald L. Ives, No. 256,
      April 1940, pp. 56-57.

"Our Indian Peaks,"* Karl E. Boehm, No. 497, May 1960, pp. 73-74.

ARIKAREE PEAKS, Front Range, Indian Peaks   Monarch Lake 1958
    Trail and Timberline
        "A New Country," No. 70, July 1924, p. 5, 1 Illustration,
        1 Illustration p. 3, 1 Illustration p. 4.

MT. ARKANSAS, 13,795'   Mosquito Range   Climax 1970
    Appalachia
        Illustration,* "Fremont Pass - Peaks Left to Right: Clinton,
        MacNamee, Democrat, Buckskin, and Arkansas," L. Larmore,
        Vol. 26, June 1946, Following p. 32.

ARKANSAS MOUNTAIN, 11,853'   Elk Range   Snowmass Mtn. 1960
See MEADOW MOUNTAIN

ARROW PEAK, 13,803'   Needle Mountains   Storm King Peak 1964
    American Alpine Journal
        "Southwestern Colorado Climbing Notes - 1932,"* Dwight G.
        Lavender, Vol. 2, 1933, p. 128.
        First ascent note, Carleton Long and John Nelson. See T&T,
        No. 672, December 1974, pp. 284-288 for correct first ascent
        by William S. Cooper and John Hubbard.

        "Club Activities: Harvard Mountaineering Club,"* David S.
        Roberts, Vol. 14, 1964, pp. 243-244.
        First winter ascent note.

    Chicago Mountaineering Club Newsletter
        "Grenadiers 1962,"* John C. Ohrenschall, Vol. 17, No. 2,
        April 1963, pp. 1-4.
        First recorded ascent noted of the east face, John C.
        Ohrenschall and Doug Ward.

    Climbing
        Inside front cover illustration,* "Glacier-Polished Quartzite
        Slabs, Wham Ridge of Vestal Peak and Arrow Peak," Steve
        Miller, No. 15, September-October 1972.

    Harvard Mountaineering
        "Climbing Notes, 1963: Colorado, Needle Mountains,"* Dave
        Roberts, No. 17, May 1965, pp. 55-56.
        (First) winter ascent note, Larry Muir and Burt Redmayne.

    The Mountaineering Journal (British)
        Illustration,* "View North from Heisspitz," Carleton C. Long,
        Vol. 1, No. 4, June, July, August 1933, p. 241.

    Sierra Club Bulletin
        "Notes and Correspondence: The Colorado Mountain Club,"* David
        Rosendale, Vol. 18, No. 1, February 1933, pp. 123-124.
        Ascent note, party of two.

Summit
   "Climbing in the Grenadiers,"* Larry Kline, Vol. 17, No. 1,
   January-February 1971, pp. 22-25, 1 Illustration.

Trail and Timberline
   "Arrow Peak: Its First Ascent," Carleton C. Long, No. 169,
   November 1932, pp. 155-157, 2 Illustrations.
   First ascent noted, Carleton Long and John Nelson. See T&T,
   No. 672, December 1974, pp. 284-288 for correct first ascent
   by William S. Cooper and John Hubbard.

   Illustration,* "Arrow Peak (Left) and Vestal Peak (Right) from
   an Unnamed Peak 13,500 Feet High About One Mile North of
   Leviathan Peak," Percy Hagerman, No. 178, August 1933, p. 110.

   "Needle Mountaimania,"* Dave Lavender, No. 265, January 1941,
   pp. 3-4, 14-15, 1 Illustration, Front cover sketch map.

   "The Colorado Mountain Club Announces the Twenty-Eighth Annual
   Summer Outing,"* Henry Buchtel, Lewis Giesecke, Kenneth
   Segerstrom, No. 265, January 1941, pp. 9-14, 2 Illustrations,
   1 Map, Front cover sketch map.

   "Grenadier Reminiscences,"* Carleton C. Long, No. 266,
   February 1941, pp. 29-31.
   First ascent noted, Carleton C. Long and John Nelson. See T&T,
   No. 672, December 1974, pp. 284-288 for correct first ascent
   by William S. Cooper and John Hubbard.

   Front cover illustration,* "Arrow and Vestal from Peak No. 6,"
   Percy Hagerman, No. 274, October 1941.

   "The Grenadiers, 1962,"* John C. Ohrenschall, No. 534,
   June 1963, pp. 107-109.
   First recorded ascent noted of the east face, John C.
   Ohrenschall and Doug Ward.

   "The Grenadiers in Winter,"* David S. Roberts, No. 547,
   July 1964, pp. 111-117.
   First winter ascent noted, Burt Redmayne and Larry Muir.

   "Letters to the Editor: NW Face of Arrow Peak," Martin A.
   Etter, No. 610, October 1969, pp. 186-187.
   Probable first ascent note via Arrowhead Pinnacle, Sam Casey
   and Martin Etter.

   "Colorado Mountain Club History: William S. Cooper - Explorer
   of the Needles and Grenadiers,"* William M. Bueler, No. 672,
   December 1974, pp. 284-288.
   First ascent noted, William S. Cooper and John Hubbard.

ARROWHEAD, 12,387'   Front Range, Rocky Mountain National Park
                     McHenrys Peak 1957
   American Alpine Journal
   "Various Notes: Chicago Mountaineering Club,"* John F.
   Fralick, Vol. 8, 1952, p. 356.
   New route note.

"Club Activities: Yale Mountaineering Club,"* Charles Ehlert,
Vol. 11, 1958, p. 137.
Ascent note of buttress on south side.

"Arrowhead Peak, South Face," Lawrence Hamilton, Vol. 20,
1976, pp. 460-461.
New route note, "Artemis", Tom Gries and Lawrence Hamilton.
New route note, "Warhead", John Byrd, Tom Gries, and Lawrence
Hamilton.

Chicago Mountaineering Club Newsletter
"Arrowhead," Merritt Kastens, Jack Fralick, Bill Primak,
Vol. 5, No. 5, November 1951, pp. 14-15, 1 Map p. 6.

Summit
"Exploring New Routes in Rocky Mountain National Park,"*
Philip C. Ritterbush, Vol. 5, No. 2, February 1959, pp. 10-13,
20-21, 1 Map.
Ascent noted of the south face and probable first traverse of
Arrowhead ridge to McHenrys Peak, Prentiss Sawyer, Charles
Sawyer, Charles Ehlert, and Philip Ritterbush.

Trail and Timberline
"Seven Spires: A Story of Some Climbs in Rocky Mountain
National Park,"* Kent Keller, No. 651, March 1973, pp. 70-74.

MT. AUDUBON, 13,223'   Front Range, Indian Peaks   Ward 1957
Alpine Journal
"The Rockies of Colorado,"* Evelio Echevarría C., Vol. 71,
May 1966, pp. 26-36, 1 Map, Bibliography.

American Alpine Journal
"Activities of Members,"* Vol. 1, 1930, p. 208.
Winter ascent note, John L. J. Hart.

"American Rockies - Notes, 1929,"* J. L. J. Hart, Vol. 1,
1930, p. 243.
Ski ascent note, Erl Ellis and John L. J. Hart.

Summit
"Arapaho Glacier Country,"* Weldon F. Heald, Vol. 9, No. 10,
November 1963, pp. 20-23.
See the following corrections to the above article:
"Letters," John M. Clark, Vol. 9, No. 11, December 1963, p. 31.
"Letters," David Parkhurst, Vol. 10, No. 1, January-
February 1964, p. 36.

Trail and Timberline
"The 1918 Outing,"* Nos. 6 and 7, September, October 1918,
pp. 1-4.

"Our Mountains in Winter,"* No. 138, April 1930, p. 12.
Winter ascent noted.

"Climbing Notes,"* No. 144, October 1930, p. 9.
Partial ski ascent note, Erl Ellis and John L. J. Hart.

"Winter Ascent of Audubon," John D. McLucas, No. 151,
May 1931, p. 68.

"The Long Lake Region,"* A. Gayle Waldrop, No. 281, May 1942,
pp. 69-70.

"Our Indian Peaks,"* Karl E. Boehm, No. 497, May 1960, pp. 73-74.

"Adventure, Culture and Prunes,"* Susan Gibbs, No. 555,
March 1965, pp. 58-59.

AUGUSTA MOUNTAIN, 12,559'   Ruby Range   Oh-Be-Joyful 1961
    Trail and Timberline
        "Some Took the High Road,"* Stan Shepard, No. 455,
November 1956, pp. 165-167.

AZTEC MOUNTAIN, 13,310'   Needle Mountains   Columbine Pass 1973
    Appalachia
        "Excursions: Colorado Trip,"* E. Folger Taylor and Walter D.
Howe, Vol. 23, December 1940, pp. 257-259, 1 Illustration
following p. 262.
North face ascent noted.

        "The Old and New West in the Needle Mountains,"* Duncan A.
MacInnes, Vol. 23, June 1941, pp. 374-379.

    Trail and Timberline
        "Where We Went and What We Climbed,"* No. 25, October 1920,
pp. 8-11.

        "Aztec Mountain," No. 107, September 1927, p. 5.

BAKER MOUNTAIN, 12,397'   Never Summer Range, Rocky Mountain National Park
                            Mount Richthofen 1957
    Trail and Timberline
        Illustration, "Mount Baker - Near Site of 1921 Outing," No. 32,
        May 1921, p. 5.

        "The Trips of the Outing,"* No. 37, October 1921, pp. 2-4.

        "Mount Baker," Esther Holt, No. 494, February 1960, p. 22.

MT. BANCROFT, 13,250'   Front Range   Empire 1958
    Trail and Timberline
        "Up Mamma, Pappa, and Baby Peaks,"* Esther Holt, No. 386,
        February 1951, pp. 18-19, 1 Illustration.

        "Mt. Bancroft - Buhl Style," Gregg Blomberg, No. 570,
        June 1966, pp. 104-105, 1 Illustration.

BANNER PEAK, 8,480'   Front Range   Pine 1965
    Trail and Timberline
        "The Conquest of Banner," Robert E. More, No. 381,
        September 1950, pp. 131-133, 2 Illustrations.

        "The Second Conquest of Banner," William E. Davis, No. 513,
        September 1961, pp. 162-165.

BARD PEAK, 13,641'   Front Range   Grays Peak 1958
    Trail and Timberline
        "Parnassus and Bard Peaks,"* Esther L. Holt, No. 499,
        July 1960, pp. 102-103, 1 Illustration.

BEAR MOUNTAIN, 8,461'   Front Range   Eldorado Springs 1965
    Trail and Timberline
        "Guerilla Tactics Useful for Doggy Climbs: The Gentle Art of
        Freddy Peaking,"* Bob Michael, No. 689, May 1976, pp. 112-115.

MT. BELFORD, 14,197'   Sawatch Range   Mt. Harvard 15M 1955
    Trail and Timberline
        "The High Peaks of the La Plata Mining Region,"* John L. J.
        Hart, No. 159, January 1932, pp. 3-4, 14, 1 Map.

        "Some Trails of the La Plata Mining Region,"* Bruce and
        Elisabeth MacCannon, No. 159, January 1932, pp. 5-6,
        1 Illustration.

        "Editorial Notes," David Rosendale, No. 161, March 1932, p. 36.
        Elevation note.

        "Surveying the La Plata Mining Region,"* Ronald L. Ives,
        No. 192, October 1934, p. 139, 1 Map.
        "A Correction," No. 196, February 1935, p. 22.
        Map correction.

        "Innocent Bystander,"* No. 259, July 1940, p. 110.
        Elevation note.

"A Conglomerate Review of the C.M.C. Summer Outing, August 15-23, 1942 - Collegiate Range,"* Nancy Plowman, Eliot Moses, Harold Brewer, Mary Wagner, No. 287, November 1942, pp. 141-143, 1 Map p. 140, Front cover illustration.

"Colorado's Mountains are Higher than You Think,"* Arthur J. McNair, No. 323, November 1945, pp. 139-142.

"Junior Jottings,"* No. 371, November 1949, pp. 172-173.

"First Official Measurement of Many 14,000 Foot Peaks,"* John L. J. Hart, No. 446, February 1956, pp. 29-30.

Front cover illustration, "Party Approaching Mount Belford," Fred Barton, No. 468, December 1957.

Illustration, "Sunrise on Mount Belford," Leonard C. Ellis, No. 595, July 1968, p. 169.

MT. BELLVIEW, 12,519'   Elk Range   Snowmass Mtn. 1960
    Trail and Timberline
        "1873 Tells 1949,"* Louisa Ward Arps, No. 365, May 1949, pp. 68-70, 1 Illustration following p. 70.

MT. BETHEL, 12,705'   Front Range   Loveland Pass 1958
    Trail and Timberline
        "U.S. Names Peak in Honor of Ellsworth Bethel," No. 106, July 1927, p. 3.

        "Group Activities: Denver Notes,"* Evelyn Runnette, No. 236, July 1938, p. 82.
        Ascent note.

MT. BIERSTADT, 14,060'   Front Range   Mt. Evans 1957
    Alpine Journal
        "The Rockies of Colorado,"* Evelio Echevarría C., Vol. 71, May 1966, pp. 26-36, 1 Map, Bibliography.

    American Alpine Journal
        "Colorado Climbing Notes, 1934,"* Carleton C. Long, Vol. 2, 1935, p. 415.
        Probable first complete ski ascent note (along with Quandary Peak) of 14,000 foot peak, Donald McBride and party.

    Appalachia
        "All the 14,000's,"* Carl Mclzer, Vol. 22, December 1939, pp. 466-479.

    Trail and Timberline
        "Editorial Notes,"* David Rosendale, No. 193, November 1934, p. 151.
        Ski ascent note, Donald McBride.

        "The High Trails of Winter,"* Reynolds Morse, No. 194, December 1934, pp. 163-165, 1 Illustration.

"The 1934 Climbing Season in Colorado,"* Carleton C. Long,
No. 196, February 1935, pp. 15-18.
First complete ski ascent note (along with Quandary Peak) of
14,000 foot peak, Donald McBride and party.

Illustration, "On the Summit of Mt. Bierstadt," Bob Johnston,
No. 233, April 1938, p. 41.

"The Tale,"* No. 310, October 1944, pp. 117-121.

"Evans and Bierstadt,"* Bill Arnold, No. 398, February 1952,
pp. 25-26.

"The Rigors and Joys of Winter Climbing,"* Stan Stephan,
No. 643, July 1972, pp. 143-145.

Front cover illustration,* "Mt. Bierstadt to Mt. Evans,"
Spencer Swanger, No. 668, August 1974.

Front cover illustration,* "Ridge Between Mt. Bierstadt and
Mt. Evans," Spencer Swanger, No. 678, June 1975.

BIG AGNES MOUNTAIN, 12,059'   North Park Range   Mount Zirkel 1955
    Trail and Timberline
        "The Mountain Ranges of Colorado,"* Kenneth Segerstrom,
    No. 215, September 1936, pp. 109-115, 1 Map.

        "Exploring the Mount Zirkel - Dome Peak Wild Area,"* Margaret
    B. Chase, No. 464, August 1957, pp. 111-113, 1 Illustration,
    1 Map following p. 116.

        "Highlights of the Outing,"* Janet M. Johnson, No. 514,
    October 1961, pp. 171-173, 1 Illustration, 1 Illustration
    p. 176.

"BIG BEAR MOUNTAIN", 13,498'   San Miguel Range
                                (Unnamed) Dolores Peak 1953
    Trail and Timberline
        "The 1931 Outing Country,"* Dwight G. Lavender, No. 151,
    May 1931, pp. 63-66.

MT. BIG CHIEF, 11,224'   Pikes Peak Region   Mount Big Chief 1961
    Climbing
        "'Mash and Mangle', Mount Big Chief, Colorado," No. 6, March-
    April 1971, p. 21.
    First ascent note, Keith Angus and Kevin Murray.

        "Mount Big Chief Premiere," Kevin Murray, No. 10, November-
    December 1971, p. 15.

    Trail and Timberline
        "That Climb Up Big Chief," Mary L. Shirer, No. 288,
    December 1942, pp. 157-158.

"THE BISCUIT", 12,368'[#]   San Juan Mountains, Sneffels Range
                      (Unnamed) Mount Sneffels 1967
    American Alpine Journal
        "Southwestern Colorado Climbing Notes - 1933,"* Dwight G.
        Lavender, Vol. 2, 1934, p. 256.
        First ascent note, T. M. Griffiths, L. V. Giesecke, B. M.
        Souder, and Dwight G. Lavender.

    The Mountaineering Journal (British)
        "Correspondence,"* Dwight Lavender, Vol. 2, No. 1, December,
        January, February 1933-34, pp. 47-51.
        First ascent note, Dwight Lavender, T. Melvin Griffiths, Lewis
        V. Giesecke, and Byron Souder.
        Second ascent note.

    Trail and Timberline
        "The 1933 Climbing Season in Colorado,"* Carleton C. Long,
        No. 184, February 1934, pp. 20-23.
        First ascent note.

"THE BISHOP",   Front Range   (Unnamed) Pine 1965
    American Alpine Journal
        Illustration, "Chimney on the Bishop Rock, Canyon of the South
        Platte," A. R. Ellingwood, Vol. 1, 1930, Following p. 144.

    Climbing
        "Nostalgia/Part II Mundus Est Mons,"* Harvey T. Carter, No. 6,
        March-April 1971, pp. 3-5.
        First ascent noted.

    Trail and Timberline
        "The Bishop: A Rock Climb in Platte Canyon," Stephen H. Hart,
        No. 143, September 1930, pp. 5-6, 1 Illustration, Front cover
        illustration.
        (First) ascent noted, Albert Ellingwood, Agnes Vaille, and
        Stephen H. Hart.

        "First Ascent Criteria,"* Carleton C. Long and Dwight G.
        Lavender, No. 174, April 1933, pp. 48, 52-53.

        "Inside Stuff," Roy R. Murchison, No. 425, May 1954, pp. 73, 78.

BISON PEAK, 12,431' Tarryall Range   McCurdy Mountain 1956
    Trail and Timberline
        "The Mountain Ranges of Colorado,"* Kenneth Segerstrom,
        No. 215, September 1936, pp. 109-115, 1 Map.

        "The Second Back-Pack Trip," Mrs. Arthur W. Kidder, No. 271,
        July 1941, p. 108.

        "A Wilderness in the Tarryalls: Lost Creek," Hugh E. Kingery,
        No. 570, June 1966, pp. 96-99, 1 Illustration, 2 Maps.

[#]Elevation figure from the American Alpine Journal.

BLACK FACE, 12,147'   San Miguel Range   Mount Wilson 1953
    Trail and Timberline
        "San Miguel Mountains,"* Dwight Lavender, No. 137, March 1930,
        p. 3.

"BLAINE PEAK", 12,910'   San Juan Mountains, Sneffels Range
                         (Unnamed) Mount Sneffels 1967
    American Alpine Journal
        "Southwestern Colorado Climbing Notes - 1933,"* Dwight G.
        Lavender, Vol. 2, 1934, p. 256.
        East face ascent note, T. M. Griffiths, L. V. Giesecke, B. M.
        Souder, and Dwight G. Lavender.

    Trail and Timberline
        "Winter Mountaineering in the San Juan,"* G. K. Williams and
        T. M. Griffiths, No. 185, March 1934, pp. 31-33.

        "1934 Summer Outing Climbs,"* Everett C. Long, No. 192,
        October 1934, pp. 131-133.

        "The 1934 Climbing Season in Colorado,"* Carleton C. Long,
        No. 196, February 1935, pp. 15-18.
        Winter ascent note, San Juan Mountaineers.

BLANCA PEAK, 14,345'   Sangre de Cristo Range   Blanca Peak 1967
    Alpine Journal
        "The Rockies of Colorado,"* Evelio Echevarría C., Vol. 71,
        May 1966, pp. 26-36, 1 Map, Bibliography.

    American Alpine Journal
        "Technical Climbing in the Mountains of Colorado and Wyoming,"*
        Albert Russell Ellingwood, Vol. 1, 1930, pp. 140-147.

        "The Rocky Mountains of the United States,"* Howard Palmer,
        Vol. 1, 1931, pp. 360-367.

        "Colorado Climbing Notes, 1937,"* Carl Blaurock, Vol. 3, 1938,
        p. 218.
        Second ascent note of the northeast ridge and face, Mary Cronin
        and Carl Blaurock.

        "Club Activities: Colorado College Mountain Club,"* Jim
        McChristal and Steve Specht, Vol. 16, 1968, pp. 236-237.
        Attempt note, north face.

        "Club Activities: Colorado College Mountain Club,"* James
        McChristal, Vol. 16, 1969, p. 475.
        Attempt note, east ridge.

        "Club Activities: Colorado College Mountain Club,"* Jim
        McChristal, Vol. 19, 1974, pp. 229-230.
        First winter ascent note of the north face, Curt Haire and Russ
        Hotchkiss.

"Club Activities: Colorado College Mountain Club,"* Jim
McChristal, Vol. 20, 1975, p. 229.
North face route attempt note, Al Erickson and Jim McChristal.

Appalachia
"A Partial Ascent of Sierra Blanca," Samuel H. Scudder, Vol. 1,
February 1878, pp. 258-266, 1 Map (Plate X) following p. 304.

"Exploration,"* F. O. Carpenter, Vol. 5, December 1888, p. 234.
Expedition note, F. H. Chapin.

"A Trip to Sierra Blanca," F. H. Chapin, Vol. 5, December 1888,
pp. 239-242.

"Through San Luis Park to Sierra Blanca,"* Charles E. Fay,
Vol. 5, May 1889, pp. 261-283, 2 Illustrations.

"An Ascent of Sierra Blanca," Charles G. Van Brunt, Vol. 6,
December 1890, pp. 163-177.

"All the 14,000's,"* Carl Melzer, Vol. 22, December 1939,
pp. 466-479.

Climbing
"Nostalgia/Part II Mundus Est Mons,"* Harvey T. Carter, No. 6,
March-April 1971, pp. 3-5.
First ascent noted of the north face.

"Sierra Blanca Northface," James R. McCrea, No. 8, July-
August 1971, pp. 5, 20-21, 1 Illustration.

"Basecamp: Colorado,"* No. 16, November-December 1972, p. 19.
Accident note.

"Winter on the North Face of Blanca Peak," Martin Teale,
No. 38, September-October 1976, pp. 26-28, 3 Illustrations.

Summit
"Blanca: The North Face in Winter," James McChristal, Vol. 19,
No. 3, April 1973, pp. 8-9, 1 Illustration.

Trail and Timberline
"Climbing in the Sangre de Cristo,"* Albert R. Ellingwood,
No. 81, June 1925, pp. 1-5.

"Blanca Peak," Elinor Eppich, No. 84, September 1925, pp. 6-7,
2 Illustrations p. 3.

"The Mountain Ranges of Colorado,"* Kenneth Segerstrom,
No. 215, September 1936, pp. 109-115, 1 Map.

"Climbing Notes,"* No. 217, November 1936, p. 133.
New elevation note.

"Group Activities: Denver Notes,"* Evelyn Runnette, No. 226,
September 1937, p. 94.
(Second) ascent note of the northeast ridge and north face,
Carl Blaurock and Mary Cronin.

"Those Glorious Sangre de Cristos,"* Cedric Kaub, Russell Briggs, Evelyn Runnette, No. 236, July 1938, pp. 78-79.

"Huerfano Playgrounds,"* Thomas J. Everly, No. 248, August 1939, pp. 103-104, 1 Illustration, Front cover illustration.

"Junior Diary, July 1-4,"* No. 248, August 1939, pp. 111-112.

"Trails,"* Leola Crump, No. 286, October 1942, p. 129.

Front cover illustration,* "Old Baldy and Blanca," Harry Standley, No. 297, September 1943.

"Historic Blanca," E. H. Perkins, No. 311, November 1944, pp. 129-131.

"Junior Fourth of July Outing," Pat Greenwell, No. 321, September 1945, p. 116.

"An Exagbination into Sundry Doings of the C.C.C.M.C.: First Semester,"* Stanley Boucher, No. 351, March 1948, pp. 43-44.
"Correction," No. 352, April 1948, p. 51.
Note on title correction.

"Sangre, Rain, No Tears,"* Dorothy Teague Swartz, No. 355, July 1948, p. 107.

"Backpacking the Sawatch Range,"* Bud Boylard, No. 378, June 1950, pp. 83-85, 90-91.
Ascent noted of Blanca Peak.

"Little Bear and Blanca,"* Bill Bueler, No. 380, August 1950, pp. 121-122, 1 Illustration.

"Denver Junior Summer Outing,"* Jim Ross, No. 459, March 1957, pp. 39-40.

"The Sangre de Cristo Range,"* Eva and Bill Rathbun, No. 460, April 1957, pp. 55-60, 64, 1 Map.

"Blanca - Lake Como Route," Gale Holcomb, No. 607, July 1969, p. 139.

"Blanca in Winter: Success is Survival," Dan Friedman, No. 626, February 1971, pp. 38-40, 1 Illustration.

"Climbing in the Blanca Massif,"* Roger Fuehrer, No. 637, January 1972, pp. 3-5, 1 Illustration, 1 Map.

"Route to Blanca, Ellingwood and Hamilton from the Huerfano Basin,"* Rich Riefenberg, No. 637, January 1972, p. 6.

"Avalanche on Sierra Blanca," George I. Bell, No. 646, October 1972, pp. 213-214, 1 Illustration.

"Private Property: No Trespassing!"* Sally Richards, Nos. 679-680, July-August 1975, pp. 148-150.

"No Trespassing! Blanca Access and Climbing Route," No. 683, November 1975, p. 223.

"They're There Because ...,"* James McChristal, No. 687, March 1976, pp. 63-67.
Reprinted from The Colorado College Bulletin, May, 1975, pp. 43-45.
First ascent noted of Ormes' Buttress of the north face, Robert Ormes (and Harold Wilm).
First direct ascent noted of the north face, Stanley Boucher, John Alexander, Dan King, and Dave Johnson.
First winter ascent noted of the north face, Curt Haire and Russ Hotchkiss.

BLODGETT PEAK, 9,423'   Rampart Range   Cascade 1961
   Summit
      "Pikes Peak Region,"* Major James E. Banks, U.S.A.F., Vol. 10, No. 7, September 1964, pp. 14-15, 1 Illustration.

   Trail and Timberline
      "Outdoors at the Air Force Academy,"* Jim Banks, No. 548, August 1964, pp. 127-130, 1 Illustration, 1 Map.

"BLUE NEEDLE", 13,500'#   San Juan Mountains, Sneffels Range
                         (Unnamed) Mount Sneffels 1967
   American Alpine Journal
      "Colorado Climbing Notes, 1934,"* Carleton C. Long, Vol. 2, 1935, p. 416.
      First ascent note, John (Jack) Seerley and Robert Thallon.

   The Mountaineering Journal (British)
      "Outstanding Climbing Centres in the South-Western Colorado Rockies,"* Dwight G. Lavender, Vol. 1, No. 4, June, July, August 1933, pp. 238-248.

   Trail and Timberline
      Illustration,* "South from 'The Hand'. Aiguilles Monolith and Blue Needle to the Left. Block Tops of Gilpin to the Right," D. G. Lavender, No. 169, November 1932, p. 158.

      "1934 Summer Outing Climbs,"* Everett C. Long, No. 192, October 1934, pp. 131-133.
      First ascent note, John Seerley and Robert Thallon.

      Illustration,* "South from 'The Hand'. Aiguilles Monolith and Blue Needle to the Left. Block Tops of Gilpin to the Right," Dwight G. Lavender, No. 400, April 1952, p. 80.

_____
#Elevation figure from The San Juan Mountaineers' Climber's Guide to Southwestern Colorado.

BRECKINRIDGE PEAK, 12,889'   Front Range   Empire 1958
    Trail and Timberline
       "Presenting Breckinridge Peak," Frances Higgins, No. 95,
      August 1926, pp. 3-5.

BROKEN HAND PEAK, 13,573'   Sangre de Cristo Range   Crestone Peak 1967
    Trail and Timberline
       "New Names in Sangres,"* No. 621, September 1970, p. 206.

MT. BROSS, 14,172'   Mosquito Range   Alma 1970
    Appalachia
       "All the 14,000's,"* Carl Melzer, Vol. 22, December 1939,
      pp. 466-479.

    Trail and Timberline
       "Recent Trips: Lincoln and Bross,"* Nos. 6 and 7, September,
      October 1918, p. 4.

       "Better Route to the Mt. Lincoln Group,"* Ronald L. Ives,
      No. 223, May 1937, p. 57.

       "Reaching the High Spots,"* George J. Kubricht, No. 325,
      January 1946, pp. 3-4.

       "Mosquito Range Ramble,"* Joseph W. Miller, No. 396,
      December 1951, pp. 164-165.

       "Mt. Bross - My First Fourteener," Judy Childers, No. 618,
      June 1970, p. 123.

BUCK MOUNTAIN, 11,396'   North Park Range   Mount Zirkel 1955
    Trail and Timberline
       "Exploring the Mount Zirkel - Dome Peak Wild Area,"* Margaret
      B. Chase, No. 464, August 1957, pp. 111-113, 1 Map following
      p. 116.

MT. BUCKSKIN, 13,865'   Mosquito Range   Climax 1970
    Appalachia
       Illustration,* "Fremont Pass - Peaks Left to Right: Clinton,
      MacNamee, Democrat, Buckskin, and Arkansas," L. Larmore,
      Vol. 26, June 1946, Following p. 32.

BUSHNELL PEAK, 13,105'   Sangre de Cristo Range   Howard 15M 1959
    Trail and Timberline
       "New Maps of the Sangre de Cristo Range,"* John L. J. Hart,
      No. 519, March 1962, pp. 32-33.

       "Sangre de Cristo Saga,"* Lester A. Michel, with Wilbur F.
      Arnold, No. 524, August 1962, pp. 123-126, 133.

BYERS PEAK, 12,804'   Front Range, Vasquez Mountains   Byers Peak 1957
    Trail and Timberline
       "New Regions,"* No. 140, June 1930, p. 16.

Illustration,* "Vasquez Peak and Byers Peak from the Oberland in April," Erl Ellis, No. 151, May 1931, p. 70.

"The Mountain Ranges of Colorado,"* Kenneth Segerstrom, No. 215, September 1936, pp. 109-115, 1 Map.

"PEAK C", 13,200'   Gore Range   (Unnamed) Vail East 1970
    Trail and Timberline
        "Notes on the 1932 Climbing Season,"* Carleton C. Long,
        No. 171, January 1933, pp. 9-11.
        First ascent note, Carl Ericson (Erickson) and Edmund Cooper.

        "Climbs in the Gore Range,"* Kenneth Segerstrom, No. 197,
        March 1935, pp. 32-35, 37-38, 1 Map, Front cover illustration.
        First ascent noted, Carl Erickson and Edmund Cooper.
        "The Gore Map - A Correction," No. 198, April 1935, p. 47,

        Illustration, "West from Peak 'C'," E. W. Cooper, No. 296,
        August 1943, p. 101.

        "Alphabet Soup,"* Alene W. Conover, No. 357, September 1948,
        pp. 129-130.

        "From 'B' to 'H' in Seven Days,"* Louise Roloff, No. 357,
        September 1948, pp. 131, 138.

        Illustration, "Bill Davis Points Out Peak C to Aspiring
        Juniors," No. 484, April 1959, p. 51.

        "Junior Summer Outing, 1962,"* Dave Abbott and Chip Bishop,
        No. 532, April 1963, pp. 69-71.

        "Names on the Gores,"* William Bird Mounsey, No. 568,
        April 1966, pp. 63-65, 1 Map.

        "The Gorgeous Gore,"* Beth LaLonde, No. 574, October 1966,
        pp. 167-168, Front cover illustration.

CALIFORNIA PEAK, 13,849'   Sangre de Cristo Range   Blanca Peak 1967
    Trail and Timberline
        "The Upper Huerfano - Reflections,"* Nancy Booth, No. 624,
        December 1970, pp. 254-255.

        "Lower Peaks in the Massif,"* Jim Schofield, No. 638,
        February 1972, pp. 43-46.

MT. CAMERON, 14,238'   Mosquito Range   Alma 1970
    Appalachia
        "All the 14,000's,"* Carl Melzer, Vol. 22, December 1939,
        pp. 466-479.

    Trail and Timberline
        "Better Route to the Mt. Lincoln Group,"* Ronald L. Ives,
        No. 223, May 1937, p. 57.

        "New Altitudes for Some Colorado Peaks,"* Allen W. Greene,
        No. 435, March 1955, pp. 57-58.

CAMERON CONE, 10,707'   Pikes Peak Region   Manitou Springs 1961
    Trail and Timberline
        "Guerilla Tactics Useful for Doggy Climbs: The Gentle Art of
        Freddy Peaking,"* Bob Michael, No. 689, May 1976, pp. 112-115.

CAMERON PEAK, 12,127'   Rawah Range   Clark Peak 1962
   <u>Trail and Timberline</u>
      "The Poudre Canyon Road and the Mountain Club,"* George
   McCormick, No. 99, December 1926, pp. 2-3, 1 Map.

      "The Upper Cache La Poudre,"* No. 122, December 1928, pp. 7-8.

"CAP ROCK SPIRE",   Tarryall Range
   <u>American Alpine Journal</u>
      "Club Activities: Colorado College Mountain Club,"* John W.
   Kuglin, Vol. 13, 1962, pp. 291-292.
   First ascent note.

CAPITOL PEAK, 14,130'   Elk Range   Capitol Peak 1960
   <u>American Alpine Journal</u>
      "Technical Climbing in the Mountains of Colorado and Wyoming,"*
   Albert Russell Ellingwood, Vol. 1, 1930, pp. 140-147.

      "Colorado Climbing Notes, 1936,"* Kenneth Segerstrom, Vol. 3,
   1937, p. 109.
   West face attempt note.

      "Colorado Climbing Notes, 1937,"* Carl Blaurock, Vol. 3, 1938,
   p. 218.
   First ascent note of the west face, Elwyn Arps, Harold Popham,
   and Carl Blaurock.

      "Naming America's Mountains - The Colorado Rockies,"* Francis
   P. Farquhar, Vol. 12, 1961, pp. 319-346.

      "Capitol Peak, Elk Range," George I. Bell, Vol. 14, 1964,
   pp. 194-195.
   Ascent note of route on northwest face and north-northwest
   ridge, David Michael, Michael Cohen, and George I. Bell.

   <u>Appalachia</u>
      "The Call of Colorado,"* Edward W. Harnden, Vol. 16,
   June 1925, pp. 158-164.

      "Rock Climbing,"* K. A. H., Vol. 21, December 1937, p. 530.
   First ascent note of the west face, Elwyn Arps, Carl Blaurock,
   and Harold Popham.

      "All the 14,000's,"* Carl Melzer, Vol. 22, December 1939,
   pp. 466-479.

      "Accidents: On Capitol Peak, Colorado," J. Charles Fox,
   Vol. 31, December 1957, p. 569.

   <u>Chicago Mountaineering Club Newsletter</u>
      "Colorado's Elk Mountains,"* Weldon F. Heald, Vol. 13, No. 6,
   October 1959, pp. 1-5, Front cover map.

   <u>Climbing</u>
      "Basecamp: Ice Climbing,"* No. 7, May-June 1971, p. 3.
   Attempt note, Fritz Stammberger and party, and Chris Landry
   and party.

Front cover illustration, "Summer Party of Climbers
Approaching Capitol Peak from the North," David Hiser, No. 8,
July-August 1971.

"'North Face', Capitol Peak (14,140')," No. 12, March-
April 1972, p. 31, 1 Illustration.
First winter ascent note of the north face, Fritz Stammberger
and Gordon Whitmer.

"Basecamp: Colorado," No. 15, September-October 1972, p. 12.
Accident note.

Illustration, "Waiting to Start the Knife Edge Ridge, Capitol
Peak, Colorado," David Hiser, No. 19, May-June 1973, p. 11.

Illustration, "Lew Dawson Leading Last Pitch of North Face of
Capitol Peak (14,137') Near Aspen, Colorado January, 1974,"
Michael Kennedy, No. 24, March-April 1974, p. 35.

"Capitol Peak: An Aspen Winter Ascent," Michael Kennedy,
No. 27, September-October 1974, pp. 20-23, 6 Illustrations.
Second winter ascent noted via a new route of the northwest
face, Lou Dawson and Michael Kennedy. See T&T, No. 579,
March 1967, p. 34 and Climbing, No. 12, March-April 1972,
p. 31 for two previous winter ascents.

"Basecamp: Colorado,"* No. 31, July-August 1975, p. 37.
Solo winter ascent note of the knife-edge ridge, Lou Dawson.

"Basecamp: Colorado,"* No. 38, September-October 1976, pp. 3-5,
1 Illustration.
North face direct ascent note, Mike Kennedy and Chris Landry.

The Mountaineering Journal (British)
"American Notes: Climbing in the Snowmass Region of the Elk
Mountains of Colorado,"* Hubert M. Walters, Vol. 2, No. 2,
March, April, May 1934, p. 98, 1 Illustration.
Traverse note.
Ascent note, cleaver ridge from Pierre Lakes Basin.

Summit
"A Trip Up Colorado's Capitol Peak," Lester Michel, Vol. 5,
No. 5, June 1959, pp. 24-28, 1 Illustration, 1 Map.
Reprinted from Trail and Timberline.

"Colorado's High Rising Elks,"* Weldon F. Heald, Vol. 8,
No. 11, November 1962, pp. 20-23.

Trail and Timberline
"More High Ones,"* No. 52, January 1923, pp. 12-13.

Illustration,* "Snowmass and Capitol Peaks from Hagerman
Peak," Wm. H. Crisp, No. 114, April 1928, p. 5.

"The King of Climbs," No. 120, October 1928, pp. 13-14,
2 Illustrations.

"Climbing Capitol Peak (Elevation 14,000 Feet)," Carl
Blaurock, No. 126, April 1929, pp. 7-8, 2 Illustrations.

"Capitol Peak," Bestor Robinson, No. 180, October 1933,
pp. 135-136, 147, 1 Illustration, 1 Illustration p. 140.
Traverse noted, Don McBride, Bob Lewis, and Bestor Robinson.
Ascent noted of the cleaver ridge, Louis Hough, Glen
Strassburg, and Bestor Robinson.

"The 1933 Climbing Season in Colorado,"* Carleton C. Long,
No. 184, February 1934, pp. 20-23.
New route notes of the south ridge, cleaver ridge, and
variation on the regular route.

"Climbing Notes,"* K. S., No. 214, August 1936, p. 95.
Reconnaissance note of the west face, Walter Scott, Carl
Blaurock, Evelyn Runnette, and Dudley T. Smith.

"Climbing Notes,"* K. S., No. 215, September 1936, p. 116.
West face note.

"Capitol Peak, The West Face: A First Ascent," Carl Blaurock
as Told to W. L. L. S., No. 225, July 1937, pp. 79, 84,
2 Illustrations, Front cover illustration.
First ascent noted of the west face, Carl Blaurock, Elwyn
Arps, and Harold Popham.

"Clark Peak?"* Percy Hagerman, No. 228, November 1937, pp. 120,
126.
First ascent noted of Capitol Peak, Percy Hagerman and Harold
Clark.

"Group Activities: Denver Group,"* No. 237, August 1938, p. 93.
Second ascent note of the west (N.W.?) face, Krieg, Melvin
Griffiths, and Dudley Smith.

"Junior Outing,"* Rex A. Young, No. 239, Novemebr 1938,
pp. 115-116.

"A Junior Climb of Capitol Peak," Rit Burrows and Werner
Schnackenberg, No. 255, March 1940, pp. 39-40, 1 Illustration.

Illustration, "North Face of Capitol Peak," Harry Standley,
No. 257, May 1940, p. 69.

"Correspondence," Bob Ormes, No. 273, September 1941, p. 128.
Approach note.

"We Climb Capitol," Charles A. and Marion R. Rymer, No. 317,
May 1945, pp. 55-59, 1 Illustration.

"Capitol Peak Climbed by Crossing Snowmass," Don Aylesworth,
No. 322, October 1945, pp. 127-128.

"1873 Tells 1949,"* Louisa Ward Arps, No. 365, May 1949,
pp. 68-70, 1 Illustration following p. 70.

"My Most Interesting Climb: Capitol Peak," Don Peel, No. 366,
June 1949, pp. 82-83, 87, 2 Illustrations, 1 Map p. 85.

"1949 Snowmass Outing was A Great Success,"* Karl T. Neuberger,
No. 370, October 1949, pp. 143, 152.

"It Could Happen Only Once," No. 370, October 1949, p. 147.

"Teen-agers Find Outing to be Huge Success," Sal Hitch and
Jeanne Hauselman, No. 370, October 1949, p. 151.

"Hi-Peak Ascents of 1949 Summer Outing,"* Bob Steele, No. 371,
November 1949, pp. 164-165.

Illustration, "Capitol Peak and Pierre Basin," H. L. Standley,
No. 388, April 1951, p. 46.

"Confessions of A Solo Climber or How I Recanted My Heresy,"*
Wilbur F. Arnold, No. 389, May 1951, pp. 51-55.

Illustration, "Capitol Peak (West Side)," Carl Blaurock,
No. 391, July 1951, p. 90.

"The Snowmass-Capitol Ridge,"* Karl Gustafson, No. 404,
August 1952, pp. 119-121, Front cover illustration.

"A Rugged Ten-Day Outing,"* Neil Wernette, No. 426, June 1954,
pp. 83-84.

"The J.C.M.C. Capitol Trip," Betsy Herrick, No. 441,
September 1955, p. 153.

"The Recovery Party," Gus F. Hallum, No. 467, November 1957,
p. 172.

"Capitol Peak - With Luck," Lester Michel, No. 482,
February 1959, pp. 19-24, Front cover illustration.

"Capitol Peak," Barbara Nagel, No. 484, April 1959, pp. 49-50,
1 Illustration p. 52.

"F is for Fiasco," Dave Buckman, No. 555, March 1965, pp. 52-53.

"Climbing News," No. 579, March 1967, p. 34.
Probable first winter ascent note, Matt Wells, Karl Arndt,
Skip Hamilton, and Bill Roos.

Illustration, "East Ridge/Capitol Peak," Glen Denny, No. 583,
July 1967, p. 138.

Illustration, "Steve Ruckhaus on Knife Edge Ridge," Fred
Ruckhaus, No. 676, April 1975, p. 74.

CASCO PEAK, 13,908'   Sawatch Range   Mount Elbert 1967
   Trail and Timberline
      "A Guide to Colorado's Almost-Fourteens,"* William A. Graves,
      No. 683, November 1975, pp. 225-227.

CASTLE PEAK, 14,265'   Elk Range   Hayden Peak 1960
   Alpine Journal
      "The Rockies of Colorado,"* Evelio Echevarría C., Vol. 71,
      May 1966, pp. 26-36, 1 Map, Bibliography.

   American Alpine Journal
      "The Rocky Mountains of the United States,"* Howard Palmer,
      Vol. 1, 1931, pp. 360-367.

      "Various Notes: Colorado Mountain Club,"* Evelyn Runnette,
      Vol. 7, September 1949, pp. 347-348.
      Ski ascent note.

      "Naming America's Mountains - The Colorado Rockies,"* Francis
      P. Farquhar, Vol. 12, 1961, pp. 319-346.

   Appalachia
      "All the 14,000's,"* Carl Melzer, Vol. 22, December 1939,
      pp. 466-479.

   Chicago Mountaineering Club Newsletter
      "Colorado's Elk Mountains,"* Weldon F. Heald, Vol. 13, No. 6,
      October 1959, pp. 1-5, Front cover map.

   Climbing
      "Castle Peak, Colo. (14,256')," No. 13, May-June 1972, p. 36.
      First winter ascent note, Mike Flynn and Leslie Thorpe via
      northwest saddle route.

   Summit
      "Colorado's High Rising Elks,"* Weldon F. Heald, Vol. 8,
      No. 11, November 1962, pp. 20-23.

   Trail and Timberline
      "High Lights on the Ten Annual Outings: The Aspen Outing
      (1917)," Grace M. Harvey, No. 43, April 1922, pp. 31-32.

      "The Mountain Ranges of Colorado,"* Kenneth Segerstrom,
      No. 215, September 1936, pp. 109-115, 1 Map.

      "Clark Peak?"* Percy Hagerman, No. 228, November 1937, pp. 120,
      126.
      East face ascent noted of Castle Peak, Harold Clark.

      Front cover illustration, "Castle Peak from the Summit of Star
      Peak," Otto Schneibs, No. 247, July 1939.

      "Ski Ascent,"* Whitney Borland, No. 277, January 1942,
      pp. 181-183.

"Castle Peak and Surrounding Country," Franklin Ebaugh, Jr., No. 292, April 1943, pp. 51-52.

"1873 Tells 1949,"* Louisa Ward Arps, No. 365, May 1949, pp. 68-70, 1 Illustration following p. 70.

"The 1949 Winter Outing," No. 367, July 1949, pp. 98-99.

"Junior Jottings," No. 377, May 1950, p. 75.

"A Junior Trip to Castle Peak," Rowland Tabor, Cindy Miller, Jeanne Hauselmann, Sally Hitch, Izzy Blanchard, and Jugh Kingery, No. 378, June 1950, pp. 92-93.

"On Skis in the Elks,"* Bob Beverly, No. 446, February 1956, pp. 23-26, 1 Map.

Illustration, "Tom Noble on Castle Peak," No. 459, March 1957, p. 43.

"The Old-Timers' Corner - Castle in the Sky," Wm. L. Myatt, No. 475, July 1958, pp. 94-95, 1 Illustration.

"Pearl Pass, Castle, and Taylor,"* Paul Stewart, No. 478, October 1958, p. 143.

"Letters to the Editors," Edna S. Spencer, No. 513, September 1961, pp. 161, 165.
Letter noting the Aetherius Society believing Castle Peak to be a holy mountain.

Front cover illustration, "Ski Mountaineering Near Castle Peak," Gwen Beiler, No. 541, January 1964.

"Report on Climb of Castle Peak," Hugo Schmidt, No. 629, May 1971, pp. 112-113, 1 Map.

THE CASTLES, 12,000'   West Elk Range   West Elk Peak 1965
    Trail and Timberline
      "Some Took the High Road,"* Stan Shepard, No. 455, November 1956, pp. 165-167.

CATHEDRAL PEAK, 13,943'   Elk Range   Hayden Peak 1960
    Chicago Mountaineering Club Newsletter
      "Colorado's Elk Mountains,"* Weldon F. Heald, Vol. 13, No. 6, October 1959, pp. 1-5, Front cover map.

    Trail and Timberline
      "Innocent Bystander,"* No. 259, July 1940, p. 110.
      Elevation note.

      "1873 Tells 1949,"* Louisa Ward Arps, No. 365, May 1949, pp. 68-70.

"New Maps of the Elk Mountains," John L. J. Hart, No. 524, August 1962, p. 131.

"A Guide to Colorado's Almost-Fourteens,"* William A. Graves, No. 683, November 1975, pp. 225-227.

CATHEDRAL SPIRES, 8,560'   Front Range   Pine 1965
Trail and Timberline
    "Recent Trips: Cathedral Spires," No. 8, November 1918, p. 2.

    "An Exagbination into Sundry Doings of the C.C.C.M.C.: First Semester,"* Stanley Boucher, No. 351, March 1948, pp. 43-44.
    Fourth ascent noted of "Ormes' Chimney", first by a woman, Mary Epler.
    "Correction," No. 352, April 1948, p. 51.
    Note on title correction.

    "Along the Trail ... First Ascents,"* H. J. S., No. 463, July 1957, p. 105.
    First ascent note of southeast Cathedral Spire, "Cynical Pinnacle".

    "Guerilla Tactics Useful for Doggy Climbs: The Gentle Art of Freddy Peaking,"* Bob Michael, No. 689, May 1976, pp. 112-115.

"CATHEDRAL SPIRES", Front Range, Rocky Mountain National Park
                    (Unnamed) McHenrys Peak 1957
See also names of individual spires, "PETIT GREPON", "THE SABER",
                    THE SHARKSTOOTH
    American Alpine Journal
    "Colorado Climbing Notes, 1936,"* Kenneth Segerstrom, Vol. 3, 1937, p. 109.
    First ascent and east-west traverse note of spire, Carl Erickson, Robert C. Lewis, and Kenneth Segerstrom.

    Trail and Timberline
    "Some First Ascent Possibilities in Colorado,"* Kenneth Segerstrom, No. 165, July 1932, pp. 103-104.

    "Climbing Notes,"* K. S., No. 214, August 1936, p. 95.
    First ascent note of minor summit, Carl Erickson, Robert C. Lewis, Jr., Richard B. Morris, and Kenneth Segerstrom.

CHAIR MOUNTAIN, 12,721'   Elk Range   Chair Mountain 1963
Trail and Timberline
    "Climbing Notes,"* No. 217, November 1936, p. 133.
    Ascent note from 1893, E. M. Douglas.

    "1873 Tells 1949,"* Louisa Ward Arps, No. 365, May 1949, pp. 68-70.

CHALK MOUNTAIN, 12,017'   Gore Range   Climax 1970
Trail and Timberline
    "Notes on the Gore Range, Summer, 1942,"* Carl Melzer, No. 284, August 1942, pp. 103-106.

MT. CHAPIN, 12,454'   Mummy Range, Rocky Mountain National Park
                       Trail Ridge 1957

Appalachia
    "The Peaks of Rocky Mountain National Park,"* Roger W. Toll,
    Vol. 17, June 1929, pp. 252-260.

    "An Autumn Climb," Richard Fleck, Vol. 34, June 1963, pp. 489-
    492, 2 Illustrations.

Chicago Mountaineering Club Newsletter
    "A Look into the Mummy Range," Lothar Kolbig, Vol. 5, No. 5,
    November 1951, pp. 11-12.

Trail and Timberline
    "Mountain Climbing and Statistics in Rocky Mountain National
    Park,"* John C. Whitnah and Robert C. Peterson, No. 343,
    July 1947, pp. 116-117.

    "Circle Trips in RMNP,"* William C. Ramaley, No. 630,
    June 1971, pp. 125-128.

    "Thunder in the Rockies,"* Richard F. Fleck, No. 638,
    February 1972, pp. 39-42, 1 Illustration.

CHEYENNE MOUNTAIN, 9,565'   Pikes Peak Region   Mount Big Chief 1961

Climbing
    "'Itsallyours', Old Stage Rock, NE, Cheyenne Mt., Colo.,"
    No. 5, January 1971, p. 22.
    First ascent note, Harvey T. Carter and Robert Grow.

Trail and Timberline
    Illustration, "The Cloud Filled Valley. Cheyenne Mountain in
    Distance," H. L. Standley, No. 133, November 1929, p. 12.

    "We Circle Cheyenne," Alvin B. Christensen, No. 259,
    July 1940, pp. 111-112.

    "An Exagbination into Sundry Doings of the C.C.C.M.C.: First
    Semester,"* Stanley Boucher, No. 351, March 1948, pp. 43-44.
    "Correction," No. 352, April 1948, p. 51.
    Note on title correction.

CHIEFS HEAD PEAK, 13,579'   Front Range, Rocky Mountain National Park
                             Isolation Peak 1958

American Alpine Journal
    "Technical Climbing in the Mountains of Colorado and Wyoming,"*
    Albert Russell Ellingwood, Vol. 1, 1930, pp. 140-147.

    "Northwest Face of Chief's Head," Robert Culp, Vol. 13, 1962,
    p. 229.
    First ascent note of the northwest face, Layton Kor and Robert
    Culp.

"Chief's Head, Northeast Face, Glacier Gorge, Rocky Mountain
National Park," Layton Kor, Vol. 14, 1965, p. 433.
First ascent note of the northeast face, Bob Bradley and
Layton Kor.

"Climbs in Rocky Mountain National Park, 1975,"* Michael
Covington, Vol. 20, 1976, pp. 457, 459.
Second ascent and first all-free ascent note of the northwest
face, Bill Westbay and Dan McClure.

Appalachia
"The Peaks of Rocky Mountain National Park,"* Roger W. Toll,
Vol. 17, June 1929, pp. 252-260.

Chicago Mountaineering Club Newsletter
"Chief's Head and Spear Head,"* Jerry Wolkoff, Vol. 5, No. 5,
November 1951, pp. 17-18, 1 Map p. 6.

"Traverse of Chief's Head and Pagoda,"* Jack Fralick, Vol. 5,
No. 5, November 1951, pp. 18-19, 1 Map p. 6.

"Our Western Alps,"* Don Simpson, Vol. 12, No. 6,
November 1958, pp. 19-20.

Climbing
"View from Within: Colorado Rocky Mountain National Park,"*
No. 28, Winter 1974-75, p. 36.
Attempt note of the northwest face.

Mountain
"Info: Rocky Mountains,"* Mike Covington, No. 46, November/
December 1975, p. 15.
Second ascent and first all free ascent note of the north-west
face, Dan McClure and Billy Westbay.

Trail and Timberline
"The Wilds of Wild Basin,"* No. 16, October 1919, pp. 2-3.

"Some First Ascent Possibilities in Colorado,"* Kenneth
Segerstrom, No. 165, July 1932, pp. 103-104.

"Climbing Notes,"* K. S., No. 215, September 1936, p. 115.
Note on unclimbed north face.

"Chief's Head - Pagoda,"* Roy R. Murchison, No. 249,
September 1939, pp. 121-122, 1 Illustration.

"Mountain Climbing and Statistics in Rocky Mountain National
Park,"* John C. Whitnah and Robert C. Peterson, No. 343,
July 1947, pp. 116-117.

"Boulder Rock Climbers: Faces of the Sixties,"* Bob Culp,
No. 623, November 1970, pp. 238-244.
First ascent noted of the northwest face, Layton Kor and Bob
Culp.

CHIMNEY ROCK ("PEAK"), 11,781'   San Juan Mountains
                                   Courthouse Mountain 1963

American Alpine Journal
    "Colorado Climbing Notes, 1934,"* Carleton C. Long, Vol. 2,
    1935, p. 417.
    (First) ascent note, T. Melvin Griffiths and Robert Ormes, via
    south face chimney and crack.

    "Colorado Climbing Notes, 1935,"* Carleton C. Long, Vol. 2,
    1936, p. 546.
    Second ascent note, T. Melvin Griffiths, Joe Buswell, and
    Floyd Griffiths.

The Mountaineering Journal (British)
    "Outstanding Climbing Centres in the South-Western Colorado
    Rockies,"* Dwight G. Lavender, Vol. 1, No. 4, June, July,
    August 1933, pp. 238-248.

Trail and Timberline
    "The 1934 Climbing Season in Colorado,"* Carleton C. Long,
    No. 196, February 1935, pp. 15-18, 1 Illustration.
    First ascent note, Melvin Griffiths and Robert Ormes.

    "The Valley of the C's,"* Hugh E. Kingery, No. 508,
    April 1961, pp. 72-73, 1 Illustration.

    Illustration, "Peaks in the Upper Cimarron Area: Chimney
    Rock," No. 557, May 1965, p. 94.

    "An Outing is Born,"* Allen W. Greene, No. 564, December 1965,
    pp. 245-249, 1 Illustration p. 254.

    Illustration,* "From Coxcomb Peak, Courthouse Mountain and
    Chimney Peak, Grand Mesa in the Far Background," Hugh E.
    Kingery, No. 569, May 1966, p. 82.

CHIMNEY ROCK, 7,800'   Colorado-Wyoming Border   Sand Creek Pass 1967
American Alpine Journal
    "Colorado Climbing Notes, 1937,"* Carl Blaurock, Vol. 3, 1938,
    p. 218.
    First ascent note, Jack Stickles, via west side.
    Second ascent note, Robert Ormes and Roy Murchison, via south
    side.

Appalachia
    "Rock Climbing,"* K. A. H., Vol. 21, December 1937, p. 530.
    First ascent note, Jack Stickles.
    Second ascent note, Robert Ormes and Roy R. Murchison.

Trail and Timberline
    "Chimney Rock on the Screen," Major Roy G. Coffin, No. 99,
    December 1926, pp. 5-6, 1 Illustration, 1 Illustration p. 7.

"Chimney Rock," Ruth Coffman, No. 226, September 1937, p. 91,
1 Illustration.
First ascent noted, Jack Stickles, via west side.
Second ascent noted, Robert M. Ormes and Roy R. Murchison.

"Chimney Rock Near Wyoming Line Climbed Again," James G.
Hodgson, No. 376, April 1950, pp. 51-52, 1 Illustration.

MT. CHIQUITA, 13,069'   Mummy Range, Rocky Mountain National Park
                        Trail Ridge 1957
  Appalachia
    "The Peaks of Rocky Mountain National Park,"* Roger W. Toll,
    Vol. 17, June 1929, pp. 252-260.

CIMARRON RIVER PEAKS, San Juan Mountains   Courthouse Mountain 1963
                                            Wetterhorn Peak 1963
  Trail and Timberline
    Front cover illustration, "Cimarron River Peaks - Uncompahgre
    Wilderness," Don McNabb, No. 630, June 1971.

CINNAMON MOUNTAIN, 12,293'   Ruby Range   Oh-Be-Joyful 1961
  Trail and Timberline
    "1873 Tells 1949,"* Louisa Ward Arps, No. 365, May 1949,
    pp. 68-70.

    "Some Took the High Road,"* Stan Shepard, No. 455,
    November 1956, pp. 165-167.

CIRQUE MOUNTAIN, 13,686'   San Juan Mountains, Sneffels Range
                           Mount Sneffels 1967
  American Alpine Journal
    "Climbing in the Mount Sneffels Region, Colorado,"* Dwight G.
    Lavender and T. Melvin Griffiths, Vol. 2, 1933, pp. 97-102,
    1 Map.
    First ascent noted, Gordon Williams, Melvin Griffiths, and
    Dwight Lavender.

    "Southwestern Colorado Climbing Notes - 1932,"* Dwight G.
    Lavender, Vol. 2, 1933, p. 127.
    First ascent note, Gordon Williams, T. M. Griffiths, and
    Dwight G. Lavender.

    "Southwestern Colorado Climbing Notes - 1933,"* Dwight G.
    Lavender, Vol. 2, 1934, p. 256.
    Second ascent note, San Juan Mountaineers Geological Survey.

  The Mountaineering Journal (British)
    Illustration,* "East from Mt. Sneffels," D. G. Lavender,
    Vol. 1, No. 4, June, July, August 1933, p. 245.

    "Correspondence,"* Dwight Lavender, Vol. 2, No. 1, December,
    January, February 1933-34, pp. 47-51.
    Second ascent note, San Juan Mountaineers.

Trail and Timberline
"Editorial Notes,"* David Rosendale, No. 166, August 1932,
p. 120.
First ascent note, Dwight Lavender, Melvin Griffiths, and
Gordon Williams.

"The 1933 Climbing Season in Colorado,"* Carleton C. Long,
No. 184, January 1934, pp. 20-23.
Second ascent note, San Juan Mountaineers Survey.

"A Novice's View of the San Juans,"* David Slawson, No. 538,
October 1963, pp. 171-172.

Front cover illustration,* "Cirque Peak, Teakettle and Potosi
from Cirque Shoulder," Sam Alfend, No. 539, November 1963.

MT. CIRRUS, 12,797'   Never Summer Range, Rocky Mountain National Park
Mount Richthofen 1957
Trail and Timberline
"The Never Summers Revisited,"* Esther Holt, No. 437,
May 1955, pp. 87-88, 98.

CLARK PEAK, 12,951'   Rawah Range   Clark Peak 1962
Trail and Timberline
"The Poudre Canyon Road and the Mountain Club,"* George
McCormick, No. 99, December 1926, pp. 2-3, 1 Map.

"The Upper Cache La Poudre,"* No. 122, December 1928, pp. 7-8.

Front cover illustration, "Clark's Peak in Winter," No. 136,
February 1930.

"The Mountain Ranges of Colorado,"* Kenneth Segerstrom,
No. 215, September 1936, pp. 109-115, 1 Map.

CLARK PEAK, 13,560'   Elk Range   Capitol Peak 1960
Trail and Timberline
"Clark Peak?"* Percy Hagerman, No. 228, November 1937, pp. 120,
126.

THE CLEAVER, 12,200'   Front Range, Rocky Mountain National Park
Isolation Peak 1958
Trail and Timberline
"Seven Spires: A Story of Some Climbs in Rocky Mountain
National Park,"* Kent Keller, No. 651, March 1973, pp. 70-74,
1 Illustration.
Possible first ascent noted, Brooke Lyman, Diana Milne, James
Douglas, and Kent Keller.

CLINTON PEAK, 13,857'   Mosquito Range   Climax 1970
Appalachia
Illustration,* "Fremont Pass - Peaks Left to Right: Clinton,
MacNamee, Democrat, Buckskin, and Arkansas," L. Larmore,
Vol. 26, June 1946, Following p. 32.

COFFIN TOP MOUNTAIN, 8,049'   Front Range   Lyons 1968
    Trail and Timberline
        "Foothill Climbs Near Longmont,"* Dave Taylor, No. 649,
        January 1973, pp. 3-5, 1 Illustration.

"COLONY" BALDY PEAK, 13,705'   Sangre de Cristo Range   Crestone Peak 1967
    Trail and Timberline
        "New Names in Sangres,"* No. 621, September 1970, p. 206.

MT. COLUMBIA, 14,071'   Sawatch Range   Mt. Harvard 15M 1955
    American Alpine Journal
        "Naming America's Mountains - The Colorado Rockies,"* Francis
        P. Farquhar, Vol. 12, 1961, pp. 319-346.

        "Club Activities: Simian Climbing Club,"* Peter Zvengrowski,
        Vol. 16, 1969, pp. 479-480.
        Ascent note via south ridge.

    Appalachia
        "All the 14,000's,"* Carl Melzer, Vol. 22, December 1939,
        pp. 466-479.

    Trail and Timberline
        "More High Ones,"* No. 52, January 1923, pp. 12-13.

        "A Note on Certain Elevations,"* Albert R. Ellingwood, No. 93,
        June 1926, pp. 4, 6.

        "The High Peaks of the La Plata Mining Region,"* John L. J.
        Hart, No. 159, January 1932, pp. 3-4, 14, 1 Map.

        "A Conglomerate Review of the C.M.C. Summer Outing,
        August 15-23, 1942 - Collegiate Range,"* Nancy Plowman, Eliot
        Moses, Harold Brewer, Mary Wagner, No. 287, November 1942,
        pp. 141-143, 1 Map p. 140.

        "Colorado's Mountains are Higher than You Think,"* Arthur J.
        McNair, No. 323, November 1945, pp. 139-142.

        "Junior Fall Trips,"* Cynthia Cummings, No. 326,
        February 1946, p. 27.

        "Rocky Mountain Rambles,"* D. Williams, No. 381,
        September 1950, pp. 140-141.
        Reprinted from Colorado Springs Independent, Thursday,
        August 3, 1950.

        "Columbia Peak - First, Last and Always A Fourteen," Linda Jo
        Callaway, No. 471, March 1958, pp. 38-39.

        "A Climb of Harvard and Columbia,"* Russ Palmer, No. 486,
        June 1959, pp. 77-78, 80.

        "A New Harvard and Columbia Route,"* Ed H. Hilliard, No. 545,
        May 1964, pp. 90-91.

COMANCHE PEAK, 13,277'   Sangre de Cristo Range   Horn Peak 1959
    Trail and Timberline
        "The Sangre de Cristo Range,"* Eva and Bill Rathbun, No. 460,
    April 1957, pp. 55-60, 64, 1 Map.

        "New Maps of the Sangre de Cristo Range,"* John L. J. Hart,
    No. 519, March 1962, pp. 32-33.

        "Sangre de Cristo Saga,"* Lester A. Michel, with Wilbur F.
    Arnold, No. 525, September 1962, pp. 139-142, 150, (Continued
    from August 1962 T&T).

COON HILL, 12,757'   Williams Fork Mountains   Loveland Pass 1958
    Trail and Timberline
        "The Mountain Ranges of Colorado,"* Kenneth Segerstrom,
    No. 215, September 1936, pp. 109-115, 1 Map.

COPELAND MOUNTAIN, 13,176'   Front Range, Rocky Mountain National Park
                             Isolation Peak 1958
    Appalachia
        "The Peaks of Rocky Mountain National Park,"* Roger W. Toll,
    Vol. 17, June 1929, pp. 252-260.

    Trail and Timberline
        "The Wilds of Wild Basin,"* No. 16, October 1919, pp. 2-3.

        "High Lights on the Ten Annual Outings: Fifth Annual Outing -
    Wild Basin," Grace M. Harvey, No. 43, April 1922, pp. 30-31.

        "Editorial Notes," David Rosendale, No. 202, August 1935,
    p. 96.
    Ski ascent note, James Maguire and Paul Hauk.

        Front cover illustration, "Lion Lake with Mt. Copeland in
    Background," W. R. Bailey, No. 298, October 1943.

        "Mountain Climbing and Statistics in Rocky Mountain National
    Park,"* John C. Whitnah and Robert C. Peterson, No. 343,
    July 1947, pp. 116-117.

COTTONWOOD PEAK, 13,588'   Sangre de Cristo Range
                          Valley View Hot Springs 1967
    Trail and Timberline
        "Sangre de Cristo Saga,"* Lester A. Michel, with Wilbur F.
    Arnold, No. 524, August 1962, pp. 123-126, 133.

COURTHOUSE MOUNTAIN, 12,152'   San Juan Mountains   Courthouse Mountain 1963
    Trail and Timberline
        "American Flats,"* Whitney Borland, No. 272, August 1941,
    pp. 115-117, 122-123, 1 Illustration.

        "The Valley of the C's,"* Hugh E. Kingery, No. 508,
    April 1961, pp. 72-73.

"An Outing is Born,"* Allen W. Greene, No. 564, December 1965,
pp. 245-249, 1 Illustration.

Illustration,* "From Coxcomb Peak, Courthouse Mountain and
Chimney Peak, Grand Mesa in the Far Background," Hugh E.
Kingery, No. 569, May 1966, p. 82.

COXCOMB PEAK, 13,656'   San Juan Mountains   Wetterhorn Peak 1963
Appalachia
    "Club Excursions: Colorado Excursion, 1951,"* Jean K. Kent,
    Vol. 28, December 1951, pp. 584-589.

The Mountaineering Journal (British)
    "Outstanding Climbing Centres in the South-Western Colorado
    Rockies,"* Dwight G. Lavender, Vol. 1, No. 4, June, July,
    August 1933, pp. 238-248.

Trail and Timberline
    Illustration,* "Wetterhorn, Matterhorn and Coxcomb Peaks, All
    to be Climbed During the 1929 Summer Outing," U.S. Forest
    Service, No. 127, May 1929, p. 7.

    "Coxcomb," Elwyn Arps, No. 132, October 1929, pp. 7-8.
    (First) ascent noted, Henry Buchtel, Elwyn Arps, and party.

    "Climbing Notes,"* Dwight Lavender, No. 156, October 1931,
    p. 165.
    Second ascent note, T. M. Griffiths and companion.

    "American Flats,"* Whitney Borland, No. 272, August 1941,
    pp. 115-117, 122-123, 1 Illustration.

    "The Valley of the C's,"* Hugh E. Kingery, No. 508,
    April 1961, pp. 72-73.

    Illustration, "Peaks in the Upper Cimarron Area: Coxcomb
    Peak," No. 557, May 1965, p. 94.

    "An Outing is Born,"* Allen W. Greene, No. 564, December 1965,
    pp. 245-249, 1 Illustration.

    "Coxcomb," Dave Waddington, No. 564, December 1965, pp. 252-
    253, 2 Illustrations.
    Climbing routes noted.

    "Coxcomb: North Face," No. 564, December 1965, p. 254.
    (First) ascent noted of the north face, M. Etter, R. Guadagno,
    M. Stults, and R. Yeatts.

    "Letters to the Editor: North Face of Coxcomb Peak from
    Cimarron Creek," Martin A. Etter, No. 610, October 1969,
    p. 186.
    Possible first ascent note, Mike Stults, Dick Guadagno, and
    Martin Etter.

MT. CRAIG, 12,007'   Front Range, Rocky Mountain National Park
                     Isolation Peak 1958

Appalachia
    "The Peaks of Rocky Mountain National Park,"* Roger W. Toll,
    Vol. 17, June 1929, pp. 252-260.

Trail and Timberline
    "High Lights on the Ten Annual Outings: Third Annual Outing -
    Commonly Known as 'The 1914 Outing'," Grace M. Harvey, No. 43,
    April 1922, pp. 25-29, 1 Illustration.

    "Mountain Climbing and Statistics in Rocky Mountain National
    Park,"* John C. Whitnah and Robert C. Peterson, No. 343,
    July 1947, pp. 116-117.

CRESTONE NEEDLE, 14,197'   Sangre de Cristo Range   Crestone Peak 1967
American Alpine Journal
    "Technical Climbing in the Mountains of Colorado and Wyoming,"*
    Albert Russell Ellingwood, Vol. 1, 1930, pp. 140-147,
    1 Illustration.
    First ascent noted of the needle and the east arete.

    "Colorado Climbing Notes, 1937,"* Carl Blaurock, Vol. 3, 1938,
    p. 218.
    Second ascent note of the east arete, Robert Ormes and Jack
    Seerley.

    "The Crestones, Colorado,"* R. M. Ormes, Vol. 7, 1950, pp. 507-
    509, 1 Illustration following p. 510.
    New route noted, Whitney route, Roger Whitney and Hassler
    Whitney.

    "Club Activities: Harvard Mountaineering Club,"* Edward C.
    Carman, Vol. 13, 1963, pp. 536-537.
    Winter ascent note, Dave Roberts, Don Jensen, and Bert
    Redmayne.

    "Club Activities: Colorado College Mountain Club,"* Jim
    McChristal, Vol. 20, 1975, p. 229.
    Ascent note of the east face, Ken Michaels and Lester Michaels.

Appalachia
    "All the 14,000's,"* Carl Melzer, Vol. 22, December 1939,
    pp. 466-479.

    "Club Excursions: Colorado, 1946,"* Emma Rutherford, Vol. 26,
    December 1946, pp. 261-264, 2 Illustrations.

Climbing
    "Ellingwood Ridge," Don Doucette, No. 2, July 1970, pp. 10-11,
    3 Illustrations.

    "Nostalgia/Part II Mundus Est Mons,"* Harvey T. Carter, No. 6,
    March-April 1971, pp. 3-5.
    First ascent noted of the needle and the east arete.

Harvard Mountaineering
"Christmas at 14,000 Feet,"* David S. Roberts, No. 16,
May 1963, pp. 37-38.

Summit
"Crestone Needle," Michael W. Borghoff, Vol. 6, No. 8,
August 1960, pp. 22-23.
Ascent of Whitney route and first ascent noted of the Black
Gendarme on north ridge, Michael W. Borghoff and Harvey Carter.

Trail and Timberline
"More High Ones,"* No. 52, January 1923, pp. 12-13.

"Climbing in the Sangre de Cristo,"* Albert R. Ellingwood,
No. 81, June 1925, pp. 1-5, 1 Illustration.
First ascent noted, Albert Ellingwood and Eleanor Davis.

"Crestone Needle and Crestone Peak,"* Elwyn Arps, No. 84,
September 1925, pp. 5-6.

"The Eastern Arete of the Crestone Needle," Albert R.
Ellingwood, No. 86, November 1925, pp. 6-9, 2 Illustrations.
First ascent noted, Albert Ellingwood, Eleanor Davis, Marion
Warner, and Stephen Hart.

"A Note on Certain Elevations,"* Albert R. Ellingwood, No. 93,
June 1926, pp. 4, 6.

Illustration,* "Crestone Needles - Sangre de Cristo Range,"
Carl Blaurock, No. 114, April 1928, p. 6.

"The Junior Outing," Bob Luke, No. 168, October 1932, pp. 148-
149, 1 Illustration.

"The Ellingwood Ledges," Bob Ormes, No. 226, September 1937,
p. 92, Front cover illustration.
Second ascent noted of east arete, Bob Ormes and Jack Seerley.

Front cover illustration, "Crestone Needle, Site of the 1938
Outing," Carl Blaurock, No. 235, June 1938.

"Those Glorious Sangre de Cristos,"* Cedric Kaub, Russell
Briggs, Evelyn Runnette, No. 236, July 1938, pp. 78-79.

"Outing - Not: The Outing. But: Our Outing,"* E. R., No. 238,
September-October 1938, pp. 99-101.

"The Juniors and the Crestones,"* Rex Young, No. 251,
November 1939, pp. 156-157, 1 Illustration.

"Unofficial Summer Outing,"* Bobbie Buchtel, No. 359,
November 1948, pp. 161-162.

"Schoolhouse Steps,"* Wilbur Arnold, No. 379, July 1950,
pp. 109-110.

"A New Route in the Crestones," Wilbur F. Arnold, No. 422, February 1954, pp. 15-16, 1 Illustration, Front cover illustration.
New route noted, Arnold-Michel, Wilbur F. Arnold and Lester Michel.

"A Poor Man's Summer Outing or Four Days of Footwork in the Crestones,"* Lester A. Michel, No. 422, February 1954, pp. 17-19.

"The Ellingwood Ledges," Wilbur F. Arnold, No. 439, July 1955, pp. 131-132.

"Denver Junior Summer Outing,"* Jim Ross, No. 459, March 1957, pp. 39-40, 1 Illustration p. 42, Front cover illustration.

"The Sangre de Cristo Range,"* Eva and Bill Rathbun, No. 460, April 1957, pp. 55-60, 64, 1 Map.

"A New Route Up the Crestones," Cecil M. Ouellette, No. 464, August 1957, pp. 114-116.

"Crestone Outing,"* Wilbur Arnold, No. 521, May 1962, pp. 73-74.

"Sangre de Cristo Saga,"* Lester A. Michel, with Wilbur F. Arnold, No. 525, September 1962, pp. 139-142, 150, (Continued from August 1962 T&T).

"Fun at the Crestones,"* J. O. Rose, No. 526, October 1962, pp. 159-160, 166, Front and back cover illustrations.

"Thoughts from A Litter," David H. Tripp, No. 526, October 1962, pp. 161, 164, Front and back cover illustrations.

"Rocks and Sam," Sam Alfend, No. 529, January 1963, pp. 7-8, 1 Illustration.

Illustration, "Crestone Needle from South Colony Lake," H. L. Standley, No. 602, February 1969, p. 23.

Front cover illustration,* "North Milwaukee and Crestone Needle," Sam Alfend, No. 611, November 1969.

"A Winter Ascent of the Crestone Needle," Spencer Swanger, No. 625, January 1971, pp. 4-6, Front cover illustration.

Illustration,* "Crestone Needle and Crestone Peak," Carl Blaurock, No. 630, June 1971, p. 121.

"The Rigors and Joys of Winter Climbing,"* Stan Stephan, No. 643, July 1972, pp. 143-145.

"The Needle to Peak Traverse in Winter,"* Charles Campbell, No. 651, March 1973, pp. 84-86, 2 Illustrations.

Front cover illustration, "On Crestone Needle," Spencer Swanger, No. 655, July 1973.

"Western Slope Group Threads the Eye of the Needle,"* Art Tauchen, No. 665, May 1974, pp. 118-120, 2 Illustrations.

"The Crestone Needle," Thomas M. Jenkins, No. 682, October 1975, pp. 206-209, 1 Illustration.

"They're There Because ...,"* James McChristal, No. 687, March 1976, pp. 63-67.
Reprinted from The Colorado College Bulletin, May, 1975, pp. 43-45.
First ascent noted of the Ellingwood Arete, Albert Ellingwood and party.

"Citadel of Beauty - Crestone Needle," Thomas M. Jenkins, No. 690, June 1976, pp. 138-140, 1 Illustration.

CRESTONE PEAK, 14,294'   Sangre de Cristo Range   Crestone Peak 1967
American Alpine Journal
"Technical Climbing in the Mountains of Colorado and Wyoming,"* Albert Russell Ellingwood, Vol. 1, 1930, pp. 140-147, 1 Illustration.

"The Rocky Mountains of the United States,"* Howard Palmer, Vol. 1, 1931, pp. 360-367.

"The Crestones, Colorado,"* R. M. Ormes, Vol. 7, 1950, pp. 507-509, 1 Illustration following p. 510.
New route noted, India route, Roger Whitney, Hassler Whitney, and Bob Ormes.

Appalachia
"All the 14,000's,"* Carl Melzer, Vol. 22, December 1939, pp. 466-479.

"Club Excursions: Colorado, 1946,"* Emma Rutherford, Vol. 26, December 1946, pp. 261-264, 2 Illustrations.

Trail and Timberline
"More High Ones,"* No. 52, January 1923, pp. 12-13.

"Climbing in the Sangre de Cristo,"* Albert R. Ellingwood, No. 81, June 1925, pp. 1-5, 1 Illustration.
First ascent noted, Albert Ellingwood, Eleanor Davis, Bee Rogers, and Jo Deutschbein.

"Crestone Needle and Crestone Peak,"* Elwyn Arps, No. 84, September 1925, pp. 5-6.

"A Note on Certain Elevations,"* Albert R. Ellingwood, No. 93, June 1926, pp. 4, 6.

Illustration,* "Crestone Needles - Sangre de Cristo Range," Carl Blaurock, No. 114, April 1928, p. 6.

"Those Glorious Sangre de Cristos,"* Cedric Kaub, Russell Briggs, Evelyn Runnette, No. 236, July 1938, pp. 78-79.

"Outing - Not: The Outing. But: Our Outing,"* E. R., No. 238, September-October 1938, pp. 99-101.

"The North Face of Crestone Peak," Alene Wharton Conover, No. 238, September-October 1938, pp. 102-103.

"The Juniors and the Crestones,"* Rex Young, No. 251, November 1939, pp. 156-157, 1 Illustration.

"Unofficial Summer Outing,"* Bobbie Buchtel, No. 359, November 1948, pp. 161-162.

"Schoolhouse Steps,"* Wilbur Arnold, No. 379, July 1950, pp. 109-110.

"A Poor Man's Summer Outing or Four Days of Footwork in the Crestones,"* Lester A. Michel, No. 422, February 1954, pp. 17-19.

"Denver Junior Summer Outing,"* Jim Ross, No. 459, March 1957, pp. 39-40, Front cover illustration.

"The Sangre de Cristo Range,"* Eva and Bill Rathbun, No. 460, April 1957, pp. 55-60, 64, 1 Map.

"Crestone Outing,"* Wilbur Arnold, No. 521, May 1962, pp. 73-74.

"Sangre de Cristo Saga,"* Lester A. Michel, with Wilbur F. Arnold, No. 525, September 1962, pp. 139-142, 150, (Continued from August 1962 T&T).

"Fun at the Crestones,"* J. O. Rose, No. 526, October 1962, pp. 159-160, 166.

"An East-Side Route on Crestone Peak," Wilbur Arnold, No. 591, March 1968, p. 74.

Illustration,* "Crestone Needle and Crestone Peak," Carl Blaurock, No. 630, June 1971, p. 121.

"The Needle to Peak Traverse in Winter,"* Charles Campbell, No. 651, March 1973, pp. 84-86.

"Western Slope Group Threads the Eye of the Needle,"* Art Tauchen, No. 665, May 1974, pp. 118-120, 2 Illustrations.

CRESTONE PEAKS, Sangre de Cristo Range   Crestone Peak 1967
    Trail and Timberline
        "Rescue in the Crestones," Steve Goodman, No. 611,
        November 1969, pp. 211-212.

CRYSTAL PEAK, 12,632'   Elk Range   Snowmass Mtn. 1960
    Trail and Timberline
        "Hikes and Climbs from Crystal,"* John Beyer, No. 598,
        October 1968, pp. 224-229, 1 Map.

CRYSTAL PEAK, 13,852'   Tenmile Range   Breckenridge 1970
    Trail and Timberline
        "Ten Mile Range Traverse,"* Carl Melzer, No. 326,
        February 1946, pp. 19-23.

CULEBRA PEAK, 14,047'   Culebra Range   Culebra Peak 1967
    Appalachia
        "All the 14,000's,"* Carl Melzer, Vol. 22, December 1939,
        pp. 466-479.

    Trail and Timberline
        "Group Activities: Denver Group,"* Evelyn Runnette and R. B.
        Morris, No. 214, August 1936, p. 100.
        Ascent note.

        "The Mountain Ranges of Colorado,"* Kenneth Segerstrom,
        No. 215, September 1936, pp. 109-115, 1 Map.

        "A Climb Up Culebra," Irma Frazy Zanoni, No. 248, August 1939,
        p. 105.

        "The Mount Culebra Climb," Lois E. Bates, No. 275,
        November 1941, p. 154, Front cover illustration.

        "Trails,"* Leola Crump, No. 286, October 1942, p. 129.

        "Boulder Group Doings,"* Marie Hulse, No. 379, July 1950,
        p. 106.
        Ascent note.

        "Route on Culebra," Jim Banks, No. 557, May 1965, p. 92.

        "For Climbing Culebra," No. 632, August 1971, p. 179.

        "Private Property: No Trespassing!"* Sally Richards, Nos. 679-
        680, July-August 1975, pp. 149-150.

        "No Trespassing! Culebra Access and Culebra Climbing Route,"
        No. 683, November 1975, p. 224.

MT. CUMULUS, 12,725'   Never Summer Range, Rocky Mountain National Park
                    Mount Richthofen 1957
    Trail and Timberline
        "Never Summer Backpack,"* Esther Holt, No. 397, January 1952,
        pp. 9-11.

CURECANTI NEEDLE, 7,856'   Black Canyon of the Gunnison
Curecanti Needle 1956

American Alpine Journal
"Southwestern Colorado Climbing Notes - 1932,"* Dwight G.
Lavender, Vol. 2, 1933, p. 127.
(First) ascent note of the southeast face, Tony Ronzio,
George Pond, Gordon Williams, Wm. Macomber, Don Bingham, and
Frank Ronzio.

Climbing
"'Time Test', Curranti (sic) Needle, Westridge, Black Canyon,
Colorado," No. 4, November 1970, p. 23.
First ascent note, Harvey T. Carter, Ray Northcutt, and Don
Sell.

"Nostalgia/Part II Mundus Est Mons,"* Harvey T. Carter, No. 6,
March-April 1971, pp. 3-5.
First ascent noted of the west edge.

Trail and Timberline
"Notes on the 1932 Climbing Season,"* Carleton C. Long,
No. 171, January 1933, pp. 9-10.
First ascent note of the south face, Gordon Williams, Tony
Ronzio, George Pond, Bill Macomber, and Don Bingham.

"PEAK D", 13,047'   Gore Range   (Unnamed) Vail East 1970
   American Alpine Journal
      "Colorado Climbing Notes, 1935,"* Carleton C. Long, Vol. 2,
      1936, p. 545.
      First ascent note, Fred Nagel, Bob Thallon, Gene Schaetzel,
      and Bob Blair.

   Trail and Timberline
      "The Gore Range Outing,"* Everett Long, No. 204, October 1935,
      pp. 111-113.
      First ascent noted, Fred Nagel, Bob Thallon, Gene Schaetzel,
      and Bob Blair.

      "Alphabet Soup,"* Alene W. Conover, No. 357, September 1948,
      pp. 129-130.

      "From 'B' to 'H' in Seven Days,"* Louise Roloff, No. 357,
      September 1948, pp. 131, 138.

"DALLAS HUMP", 13,640'   San Juan Mountains, Sneffels Range
                          (Unnamed) Telluride 1955
   American Alpine Journal
      "Colorado Climbing Notes, 1934,"* Carleton C. Long, Vol. 2,
      1935, p. 416.
      First ascent note, Everett Long and Don McBride.

   Trail and Timberline
      Illustration,* "Blue Lakes from the Summit of Mt. Sneffels:
      Peaks on the Skyline are, from Left to Right, Dallas Peak,
      Dallas Hump, West Dallas, and Peak T-O," H. L. McClintock,
      No. 184, February 1934, p. 19.

      "1934 Summer Outing Climbs,"* Everett C. Long, No. 192,
      October 1934, pp. 131-133.
      First ascent noted, Donald McBride and Everett Long.

DALLAS PEAK, 13,809'   San Juan Mountains, Sneffels Range   Telluride 1955
   American Alpine Journal
      "Colorado Climbing Notes, 1934,"* Carleton C. Long, Vol. 2,
      1935, p. 416.
      First ascent note, Everett Long and Don McBride.

   The Mountaineering Journal (British)
      "Outstanding Climbing Centres in the South-Western Colorado
      Rockies,"* Dwight G. Lavender, Vol. 1, No. 4, June, July,
      August 1933, pp. 238-248.

   Trail and Timberline
      Illustration,* "Block Tops of Gilpin to Left. Dallas Peak to
      Right. Wilsons in Distance," D. G. Lavender, No. 169,
      November 1932, p. 161.

      Illustration, "Dallas Peak," T. Melvin Griffiths, No. 171,
      January 1933, p. 7.

Illustration,* "Aiguilles Northwest of Mt. Sneffels,
Photographed from Blaine Peak," D. G. Lavender, No. 171,
January 1933, p. 10.

Illustration,* "Blue Lakes from the Summit of Mt. Sneffels:
Peaks on the Skyline are, from Left to Right, Dallas Peak,
Dallas Hump, West Dallas, and Peak T-0," H. L. McClintock,
No. 184, February 1934, p. 19.

Front cover illustration,* "Looking Up Blue Lakes Fork of
Dallas Creek Towards Dallas Peak (Center) and Wolcott Peak
(Right)," S.J.M., No. 185, March 1934.

"1934 Summer Outing Climbs,"* Everett C. Long, No. 192,
October 1934, pp. 131-133.
First ascent noted, Donald McBride and Everett Long.

"The 1934 Climbing Season in Colorado,"* Carleton C. Long,
No. 196, February 1935, pp. 15-18.
First ascent note, Everett Long and Donald McBride.

Illustration,* "Gilpin to Left. Dallas Peak to Right. Wilsons
in Distance," Dwight G. Lavender, No. 400, April 1952, p. 79.

Front cover illustration,* "Gilpin, Dallas and Mt. Sneffels
from Yankee Boy Basin," Alice B. Rawson, No. 407,
November 1952.

"Climbing Dallas Peak: Fascination and A Near Escape," Spencer
Swanger, No. 693, September 1976, pp. 170-174, 2 Illustrations.

"Letters to the Editor," Everett C. Long, Spencer Swanger,
No. 696, December 1976, pp. 234-235.
Letters noting first ascent, Everett Long and Don McBride.

MT. DALY, 13,280'   Elk Range   Capitol Peak 1960
   Trail and Timberline
      "1873 Tells 1949,"* Louisa Ward Arps, No. 365, May 1949,
      pp. 68-70, 1 Illustration following p. 70.

DEER MOUNTAIN, 9,937'   Front Range, Rocky Mountain National Park
                         Estes Park 1961
   Appalachia
      "Exploration,"* F. O. Carpenter, Vol. 5, December 1888, p. 234.
      Ascent note, F. H. Chapin.

      "The Peaks of Rocky Mountain National Park,"* Roger W. Toll,
      Vol. 17, June 1929, pp. 252-260.

MT. DEMOCRAT, 14,148'   Mosquito Range   Climax 1970
   Appalachia
      "All the 14,000's,"* Carl Melzer, Vol. 22, December 1939,
      pp. 466-479.

Illustration,* "Fremont Pass - Peaks Left to Right: Clinton, MacNamee, Democrat, Buckskin, and Arkansas," L. Larmore, Vol. 26, June 1946, Following p. 32.

Trail and Timberline
"The High Trails of Winter,"* Reynolds Morse, No. 194, December 1934, pp. 163-165.

"Better Route to the Mt. Lincoln Group,"* Ronald L. Ives, No. 223, May 1937, p. 57.

"Reaching the High Spots,"* George J. Kubricht, No. 325, January 1946, pp. 3-4.

"An Exagbination into Sundry Doings of the C.C.C.M.C.: First Semester,"* Stanley Boucher, No. 351, March 1948, pp. 43-44.
"Correction," No. 352, April 1948, p. 51.
Note on title correction.

"Mosquito Range Ramble,"* Joseph W. Miller, No. 396, December 1951, pp. 164-165.

"Boulder Notes,"* Margaret M. Bivans, No. 437, May 1955, p. 96.
Winter ascent note.

Illustration, "Juniors on Mount Democrat," No. 471, March 1958, p. 33.

Front cover illustration, "Mt. Democrat," Jack Olson, Nos. 679-680, July-August 1975.

DEVILS HEAD, 9,748'   Rampart Range   Devils Head 1954
See also "THE TAJ MAHAL"
   Summit
         "The Devil's Head is not for the Timid!" Cecil M. Ouellette, Vol. 3, No. 7, July 1957, pp. 16-19, 3 Illustrations, 1 Map.
First ascent noted of the Taj Mahal, Dick Woodford and Cecil Ouellette.

   Trail and Timberline
         "Devil's Head," Jeanette Mayer, No. 263, November 1940, pp. 168-169.

         "Guerilla Tactics Useful for Doggy Climbs: The Gentle Art of Freddy Peaking,"* Bob Michael, No. 689, May 1976, pp. 112-115.

DEVILS THUMB, 12,000'   Front Range   East Portal 1958
   American Alpine Journal
         "Colorado Climbing Notes, 1934,"* Carleton C. Long, Vol. 2, 1935, p. 416.
First ascent note, Everett Long, Caye Corr Breitenstein, and Carleton C. Long.

"Colorado Climbing Notes, 1936,"* Kenneth Segerstrom, Vol. 3,
1937, p. 109.
Fourth ascent note, Robert C. Lewis and Kenneth Segerstrom.

Trail and Timberline
"The 1934 Climbing Season in Colorado,"* Carleton C. Long,
No. 196, February 1935, pp. 15-18.
First ascent note, Everett Long, Caye Corr, and Carleton C.
Long.

"Climbing Notes,"* K. S., No. 214, August 1936, pp. 92, 95.
Fourth ascent note, Robert C. Lewis, Jr. and Kenneth
Segerstrom.

"One of the Devil's Thumbs," Elnora Martinelli, No. 451,
July 1956, p. 109.

MT. DICKINSON, 11,831'   Mummy Range, Rocky Mountain National Park
                    Estes Park 1961
Trail and Timberline
"High Country Names," Louisa Ward Arps and Elinor Eppich
Kingery, No. 568, April 1966, pp. 73-74, 1 Illustration.

DOLLY VARDEN MOUNTAIN, 12,932'   San Juan Mountains   Handies Peak 1955
Trail and Timberline
"The 1934 Climbing Season in Colorado,"* Carleton C. Long,
No. 196, February 1935, pp. 15-18.
Winter ascent note, Gordon Williams and Melvin Griffiths.

DOLORES PEAK, 13,261'   San Miguel Range   Dolores Peak 1953
Trail and Timberline
"San Miguel Mountains,"* Dwight Lavender, No. 137, March 1930,
p. 3.

Front cover illustration,* "Dunn Peak and Dolores Peak Above
Navajo Lake," Raoul Bates, No. 586, October 1967.

THE DOME, 11,739'   North Park Range   Mount Ethel 1955
Trail and Timberline
"North Park and Mt. Zirkle,"* No. 202, August 1935, p. 95.

"DOOZY POINT",   Sangre de Cristo Range
Trail and Timberline
"Sangre de Cristo Saga,"* Lester A. Michel, with Wilbur F.
Arnold, No. 525, September 1962, pp. 139-142, 150, (Continued
from August 1962 T&T).

"DOPPLEHORN",   Front Range, Indian Peaks
                    (Unnamed) Monarch Lake 1958
Trail and Timberline
"Notes on the 1932 Climbing Season,"* Carleton C. Long,
No. 171, January 1933, p. 11.
First ascent note, Carl Ericson (Erickson), Edmund Cooper,
and companion.

DORA MOUNTAIN, 12,119'   Gore Range   Mt. Powell 15M 1933
   Trail and Timberline
     "Climbs in the Gore Range,"* Kenneth Segerstrom, No. 197,
    March 1935, pp. 32-35, 37-38, 1 Map.
    "The Gore Map - A Correction," No. 198, April 1935, p. 47.

    "Notes on the Gore Range, Summer, 1942,"* Carl Melzer,
    No. 284, August 1942, pp. 103-106.

DUNN PEAK, 13,290'   San Miguel Range   Dolores Peak 1953
   Trail and Timberline
     "The 1931 Outing Country,"* Dwight G. Lavender, No. 151,
    May 1931, pp. 63-66.

    "The Lesser Climbs,"* Mark Bostwick, No. 586, October 1967,
    pp. 181-182, 1 Map, Front cover illustration.

DUNSINANE MOUNTAIN, 12,742'   San Juan Mountains   Courthouse Mountain 1963
   Trail and Timberline
     "An Outing is Born,"* Allen W. Greene, No. 564, December 1965,
    pp. 245-249, 1 Illustration p. 257.

    "'Dunsinane'," No. 564, December 1965, p. 254, 1 Illustration
    p. 257.

"DWIGHT MORROW PEAK", 12,130'(?)   Front Range, Indian Peaks
                                 (Unnamed) Monarch Lake 1958
   Trail and Timberline
     "A New Peak in the Hell Hole," Ronald L. Ives, No. 178,
    August 1933, p. 113, 1 Illustration.
    Probable first ascent noted, Ronald L. Ives.

    "Some 1940 Outing Observations,"* Roy R. Murchison, No. 261,
    September 1940, p. 143.

"PEAK E", 13,230'   Gore Range   (Unnamed) Vail East 1970
                                   (Unnamed) Minturn 15M 1934, 13,188'
   American Alpine Journal
      "Colorado Climbing Notes, 1935,"* Carleton C. Long, Vol. 2,
      1936, p. 545.
      First ascent note, Fred Nagel, Bob Thallon, Gene Schaetzel,
      and Bob Blair.

   Trail and Timberline
      "The Gore Range Outing,"* Everett Long, No. 204, October 1935,
      pp. 111-113.
      First ascent noted, Fred Nagel, Bob Thallon, Gene Schaetzel,
      and Bob Blair.

      "Alphabet Soup,"* Alene W. Conover, No. 357, September 1948,
      pp. 129-130.

      "From 'B' to 'H' in Seven Days,"* Louise Roloff, No. 357,
      September 1948, pp. 131, 138.

"EAGLE PEAK", 9,368'   Rampart Range   (Unnamed) Cascade 1961
   Summit
      "Pikes Peak Region,"* Major James E. Banks, U.S.A.F., Vol. 10,
      No. 7, September 1964, pp. 14-15, 1 Illustration.

   Trail and Timberline
      "Outdoors at the Air Force Academy,"* Jim Banks, No. 548,
      August 1964, pp. 127-130, 1 Illustration, 1 Map.

EAGLE PEAK, 13,221'   Sangre de Cristo Range   Electric Peak 15M 1959
   Trail and Timberline
      "New Maps of the Sangre de Cristo Range,"* John L. J. Hart,
      No. 519, March 1962, pp. 32-33.

EAGLES BEAK, 12,200'   Front Range, Rocky Mountain National Park
                        Isolation Peak 1958
   Trail and Timberline
      "Seven Spires: A Story of Some Climbs in Rocky Mountain
      National Park,"* Kent Keller, No. 651, March 1973, pp. 70-74.

EAGLES NEST MOUNTAIN, 13,397'   Gore Range   Mt. Powell 15M 1933
   Trail and Timberline
      "Some First Ascent Possibilities in Colorado,"* Kenneth
      Segerstrom, No. 165, July 1932, pp. 103-104.

      "The 1933 Climbing Season in Colorado,"* Carleton C. Long,
      No. 184, February 1934, pp. 20-23.
      Ascent note, Weaver and Segerstrom.

      "Climbs in the Gore Range,"* Kenneth Segerstrom, No. 197,
      March 1935, pp. 32-35, 37-38, 1 Map.
      "The Gore Map - A Correction," No. 198, April 1935, p. 47.

      "Notes on the Gore Range, Summer, 1942,"* Carl Melzer,
      No. 284, August 1942, pp. 103-106, Front cover illustration.

"A Weekend in the Gore Range: August 21-22, 1943,"* Curt E.
Krieser, No. 315, March 1945, pp. 31-32, 1 Illustration.

"Summer Outings - Then and Now,"* No. 354, June 1948, pp. 88-
89, 1 Illustration.

Illustration,* "Panorama from Little Powell - (Powell and
Eagle's Nest to the Right)," No. 356, August 1948, p. 115.

"From 'B' to 'H' in Seven Days,"* Louise Roloff, No. 357,
September 1948, pp. 131, 138.

"Names on the Gores,"* William Bird Mounsey, No. 568,
April 1966, pp. 63-65, 1 Map.

EAST GLACIER KNOB, 10,225'   Front Range, Rocky Mountain National Park
                              McHenrys Peak 1957
    Trail and Timberline
        "Undiscovered Jewels of Rocky Mountain National Park,"* R. D.
    Martin, No. 618, June 1970, pp. 132-134.

"EAST PARTNER PEAK" ("PEAK V"), 13,057'   Gore Range
See also "PEAK V"   (Unnamed) Vail East 1970
    Trail and Timberline
        "Backpacking in the Gore Range,"* Shirli Voigt, No. 667,
    July 1974, pp. 177-180, 1 Map.

EAST SPANISH PEAK, 12,683'   Spanish Peaks   Spanish Peaks 1971
See also SPANISH PEAKS
    Trail and Timberline
        "The Legend of Wahatoyeh,"* Janet Chatin, No. 142,
    August 1930, pp. 8-9, 1 Illustration.

        "The Spanish Peaks,"* Leola Crump, No. 248, August 1939,
    pp. 106-107, 1 Illustration.

        "The Mystic Huajatolla,"* Frances P. Evans, No. 271,
    July 1941, pp. 107-108.

        "An Early Climb of East Spanish Peak," Louis B. Sporleder, Sr.,
    No. 344, August 1947, pp. 131-132, Front cover illustration.

        "The Mystic Huajatolla,"* Frances P. Evans, No. 476,
    August 1958, p. 103.
    Reprinted in condensed form from July 1941 T&T.

        "Wahatoyah,"* Irma Zanoni, No. 476, August 1958, p. 104.

"EAST THORN", 13,333'   Gore Range   (Unnamed) Willow Lakes 1970
See "PEAK 13,330'"   (Unnamed) Dillon 15M 1929, 13,330'

EAST TRINITY PEAK, 13,745'   Needle Mountains   Storm King Peak 1964
See also TRINITY PEAKS
    American Alpine Journal
        "Club Activities: Harvard Mountaineering Club,"* David S.
    Roberts, Vol. 14, 1964, pp. 243-244.
    First winter ascent note.

Appalachia
   Illustration,* "Grenadier Range, Colorado: Peaks Above Balsam
   Lake; East Trinity on Left, Storm King in Right Distance,"
   A. B. Fielding, Vol. 23, December 1941, Following p. 536.

Chicago Mountaineering Club Newsletter
   "The Trinity Peaks and Vestal Peak,"* Frank Babb, Vol. 24,
   No. 1, March 1970, pp. 13-14.

Harvard Mountaineering
   "Climbing Notes, 1963: Colorado, Needle Mountains,"* Dave
   Roberts, No. 17, May 1965, pp. 55-56.
   (First) winter ascent note, Don Jensen and Dave Roberts.

Trail and Timberline
   "The Colorado Mountain Club Announces the Twenty-Eighth Annual
   Summer Outing,"* Henry Buchtel, Lewis Giesecke, Kenneth
   Segerstrom, No. 265, January 1941, pp. 9-14, 1 Map, Front
   cover sketch map.

   "The Grenadiers in Winter,"* David S. Roberts, No. 547,
   July 1964, pp. 111-117.
   First winter ascent noted, Dave Roberts and Don Jensen.

"ECHO POINT", 7,600'   Black Canyon of the Gunnison National Monument
                     (Unnamed) Grizzly Ridge 1957
   American Alpine Journal
   "Southwestern Colorado Climbing Notes - 1932,"* Dwight G.
   Lavender, Vol. 2, 1933, p. 127.
   First ascent note, T. M. Griffiths, Charles Kane, Gordon
   Williams, and Wm. Macomber.

EDITH MOUNTAIN, 12,620'   San Juan Mountains   Handies Peak 1955
   Appalachia
   "Club Excursions: Colorado Excursion, 1951,"* Jean K. Kent,
   Vol. 28, December 1951, pp. 584-589.

MT. EDWARDS, 13,850'   Front Range   Grays Peak 1958
   Trail and Timberline
   "The Tale,"* No. 310, October 1944, pp. 117-121.

   "The Four Fourteen Foible,"* William L. Myatt, No. 545,
   May 1964, pp. 87-88.

EL DIENTE PEAK, 14,159'   San Miguel Range   Dolores Peak 1953
   Alpine Journal
   "New Expeditions in 1890: Rocky Mountains, Colorado, U.S.A.,"
   Vol. 15, November 1890, p. 316.
   First ascent note, Percy W. Thomas and N. G. Douglass.
   Thomas mistakenly identified El Diente Peak as Mt. Wilson.
   See T&T, No. 155, September 1931, p. 143 for explanation.

"Mountaineering in Southern Colorado,"* Percy W. Thomas,
Vol. 15, August 1891, pp. 480-490.
First ascent noted, Percy W. Thomas and N. G. Douglass.
Thomas mistakenly identified El Diente Peak as Mt. Wilson.
See T&T, No. 155, September 1931, p. 143 for explanation.

"Alpine Notes: Rocky Mountain Sickness,"* Percy W. Thomas,
Vol. 17, May 1894, pp. 140-141.
Thomas mistakenly identified El Diente Peak as Mt. Wilson.
See T&T, No. 155, September 1931, p. 143 for explanation.

American Alpine Journal
"Various Notes,"* Vol. 1, 1931, p. 422.
Ascent note, Dwight Lavender, Forrest Greenfield, and Chester
Prince (Price).

Appalachia
"Colorado Climbs, 1931,"* Winthrop Means, Vol. 18,
December 1931, pp. 357-364.

"All the 14,000's,"* Carl Melzer, Vol. 22, December 1939,
pp. 466-479.

Mazama
"Ramble Number 21,"* A. H. Marshall, Vol. 21, No. 12,
December 1939, pp. 55-61.

The Mountaineering Journal (British)
"Outstanding Climbing Centres in the South-Western Colorado
Rockies,"* Dwight G. Lavender, Vol. 1, No. 4, June, July,
August 1933, pp. 238-248, 1 Illustration.
First ascent noted, Percy Thomas (and N. G. Douglass).

Sierra Club Bulletin
"Notes and Correspondence: The Colorado Mountain Club,"* David
Rosendale, Vol. 17, No. 1, February 1932, pp. 109-110.
Ascent note during C.M.C. outing.

Trail and Timberline
"San Miguel Mountains,"* Dwight Lavender, No. 137, March 1930,
p. 3.

"Climbing in the San Miguels,"* Dwight Lavender, No. 143,
September 1930, pp. 3-4, 2 Illustrations.
First ascent noted, Dwight Lavender, Forrest Greenfield, and
Chester Price. See T&T, No. 155, September 1931, p. 143 for
correct first ascent by Percy Thomas and N. G. Douglass.

"The 1931 Outing Country,"* Dwight G. Lavender, No. 151,
May 1931, pp. 63-66.

"First Ascent of El Diente 1890," D. G. Lavender, No. 155,
September 1931, p. 143.
First ascent noted, Percy W. Thomas and N. G. Douglass.

"Note," No. 156, October 1931, p. 157.
Ascent note by first woman, Mary A. Cronin.

"Climbing Notes,"* Dwight Lavender, No. 156, October 1931,
p. 165.
Third recorded ascent note, T. M. Griffiths, Charles Kane, and
Gordon Williams.

"First Ascent Criteria,"* Carleton C. Long and Dwight G.
Lavender, No. 174, April 1933, pp. 48, 52-53.
First and second ascents noted.

"S.J.M. Geological Survey," Dwight G. Lavender, No. 179,
September 1933, pp. 125-126.

"'The Tooth' and Its Companion,"* Hugh W. Hetherington,
No. 283, July 1942, pp. 91-93, Front cover illustration.
Second ascent noted of the south face, Jack Graham and Allan
Griffith.

Front cover illustration, "El Diente, from Summit of Mt.
Wilson," Molly Sethman Grund, No. 369, September 1949.

"San Miguels 1949,"* W. F. Arnold, No. 382, October 1950,
pp. 147-148.

"Report on the 1952 San Juan Outing,"* Robert Ellingwood,
No. 407, November 1952, pp. 159-161, 1 Illustration p. 167.

"A Rugged Ten-Day Outing,"* Neil Wernette, No. 426, June 1954,
pp. 83-84.

"New Altitudes for Some Colorado Peaks,"* Allen W. Greene,
No. 435, March 1958, pp. 57-58.

"Fifty-Two in '52,"* Dwight Hamilton, No. 482, February 1959,
pp. 25-26.

"The San Juan Fly Camps,"* Wilma Epp, No. 538, October 1963,
pp. 175-177, 1 Illustration.

"The High Ones: A San Miguel Adventure,"* Raoul Bates and Bob
Stuemky, No. 586, October 1967, pp. 179-180.

Front cover illustration,* "CMC Group on Wilson-El Diente
Ridge," Sam Alfend, No. 632, August 1971.

Illustration,* "Mark Stanton, Mike Ruckhaus, Dave Harmon and
Robbie Dubin on Wilson-El Diente Ridge," Glenn Ruckhaus,
No. 676, April 1975, p. 71.

"EL PUNTO", 13,280'   San Juan Mountains   (Unnamed) Uncompahgre Peak 1963
   Trail and Timberline
      "Two New Peaks,"* Dwight Lavender, No. 132, October 1929,
      p. 6.
      (First) ascent noted, Dwight Lavender and Forrest Greenfield.

MT. ELBERT, 14,433'   Sawatch Range   Mount Elbert 1967
    Alpine Journal
        "The Rockies of Colorado,"* Evelio Echevarría C., Vol. 71,
        May 1966, pp. 26-36, 1 Map, Bibliography.

    American Alpine Journal
        "The Rocky Mountains of the United States,"* Howard Palmer,
        Vol. 1, 1931, pp. 360-367.

        "Climbing the State High Points of the U.S.,"* Lawrence I.
        Grinnell, Vol. 5, 1944, pp. 212-221, 1 Illustration, 1 Map,
        1 Chart.

        "Naming America's Mountains - The Colorado Rockies,"* Francis
        P. Farquhar, Vol. 12, 1961, pp. 319-346.

    Appalachia
        "The Call of Colorado,"* Edward W. Harnden, Vol. 16,
        June 1925, pp. 158-164.

        "High Points of the Forty-Eight States,"* Perceval Sayward,
        Vol. 20, December 1934, pp. 206-212.

        "Forty-Eight State Summits,"* A. H. Marshall, Vol. 21,
        December 1936, pp. 167-182.

        "All the 14,000's,"* Carl Melzer, Vol. 22, December 1939,
        pp. 466-479.

        "Climbs and Trips by Members: Climbing by Members,"* Vol. 23,
        December 1941, p. 534.
        Ascent note, Edmund Bassett.

        "Excursions: August Camp, 1956,"* David Wilson, Vol. 31,
        December 1956, pp. 259-261.

        "Excursions: Mountaineering and Hiking Trip to the Colorado
        Rockies,"* Wilbur W. Squire, Vol. 37, December 1968, p. 326.

        "Alpina: Mt. Elbert," John A. Woodworth, Vol. 38,
        December 1971, p. 183.
        Winter ascent note, David Keer, Jim Babcock, Dick Arnold, and
        Jim Ward.

    Chicago Mountaineering Club Newsletter
        "Ski-Mountaineering in Colorado," Don Johnson, Vol. 5, No. 3,
        June 1951, pp. 6-8.

        "Sneaking Up on Colorado Peaks by Way of Texas,"* Groves
        Kilbourn, Vol. 17, No. 1, February 1964, pp. 4-5.

    Climbing
        "Basecamp: Winter Climbs,"* No. 8, July-August 1971, p. 14.
        Winter ascent note, David Keer, Jim Babcock, Dick Arnold, and
        Jim Ward.

Iowa Mountaineers Journal
"Pikes Peak Crags Outing,"* Harvey and Annie T. Carter, Vol. 5,
No. 5, 1965, pp. 54-59.
Ascent noted of Mt. Elbert.

Mazama
"Hitting the High Spots,"* A. H. Marshall, Vol. 12, No. 12,
December 1930, pp. 44-56, 1 Illustration.

The Mountaineer
"A Mountaineer in Colorado,"* Edward W. Harnden, Vol. 15,
December 15, 1922, pp. 47-53.

Sierra Club Bulletin
"Mountaineering Notes: Tour of the Six Highest Peaks in the
United States,"* edited by Francis P. Farquhar, Vol. 12,
No. 3, 1926, p. 307.
Ascent note on climbing the first six peaks in altitude in the
U.S., Captain John Henry Cuntz.

Summit
"Changing Weather on Mt. Elbert," Stewart Aitchison, Vol. 15,
No. 8, October 1969, pp. 8-11, 4 Illustrations.

Trail and Timberline
"Recent Trips: Mt. Elbert," No. 15, August 1919, pp. 4-5.

"Trailing the Colorado Mountain Club on the High Peaks,"*
Lloyd Shaw, No. 17, January 1920, pp. 5-6.

"The Mountain Ranges of Colorado,"* Kenneth Segerstrom,
No. 215, September 1936, pp. 109-115, 1 Map.

"A Conglomerate Review of the C.M.C. Summer Outing,
August 15-23, 1942 - Collegiate Range,"* Nancy Plowman, Eliot
Moses, Harold Brewer, Mary Wagner, No. 287, November 1942,
pp. 141-143, 1 Map p. 140.

"Contrasting Ski Climbs of Mt. Elbert," John V. Ambler,
No. 290, February 1943, p. 19.

"Fourth of July Outing - Junior Style,"* Dorothy Sethman,
No. 308, August 1944, p. 95.

"Mt. Elbert Ski Trip," Fletcher W. Birney, Jr., No. 317,
May 1945, p. 65.

"Reaching the High Spots,"* George J. Kubricht, No. 325,
January 1946, pp. 3-4.

"A Vote of Thanks to the Juniors,"* John and Mary Hitch,
No. 356, August 1948, pp. 115-116.

"My Most Exciting Climb," Bill Bueler, No. 358, October 1948,
pp. 145-146.

"Backpacking the Sawatch Range,"* Bud Boylard, No. 378,
June 1950, pp. 83-85, 90-91.

"Elbert in May," Esther Holt, No. 379, July 1950, pp. 105-106.

"Junior Jottings," No. 379, July 1950, p. 108.

"Centennial Special - Climb of Mt. Elbert," No. 487,
July 1959, p. 90.

"Running A Junior Trip for Fun and Fiasco," Dave Fitzgerald,
No. 567, March 1966, pp. 53-54.

ELECTRIC PEAK, 13,292'   Needle Mountains   Storm King Peak 1964
    Chicago Mountaineering Club Newsletter
        "Grenadiers 1962,"* John C. Ohrenschall, Vol. 17, No. 2,
        April 1963, pp. 1-4.
        First ascent noted, John C. Ohrenschall and Doug Ward, via
        east face.

        "Electric Peak," John Smith, Vol. 24, No. 1, March 1970, p. 5.

    Trail and Timberline
        "The Grenadiers, 1962,"* John C. Ohrenschall, No. 534,
        June 1963, pp. 107-109.
        First ascent noted, John C. Ohrenschall and Doug Ward, via
        east face.

ELECTRIC PEAK, 13,621'   Sangre de Cristo Range   Electric Peak 15M 1959
    Trail and Timberline
        "New Maps of the Sangre de Cristo Range,"* John L. J. Hart,
        No. 519, March 1962, pp. 32-33.

        "Sangre de Cristo Saga,"* Lester A. Michel, with Wilbur F.
        Arnold, No. 524, August 1962, pp. 123-126, 133.

"THE ELEPHANT", 12,865'   Gore Range   (Unnamed) Vail East 1970
                                          (Unnamed) Minturn 15M 1934, 12,782'
    American Alpine Journal
        "Colorado Climbing Notes, 1935,"* Carleton C. Long, Vol. 2,
        1936, p. 545.
        First ascent note, Stanley Midgely, Don McBride, Clifton
        Snively, and Everett Long.

    Chicago Mountaineering Club Newsletter
        "Ascents by Club Members,"* Stanley Midgely, Vol. 1, No. 3,
        September to December 1945, pp. 10-11.
        First ascent note, Stanley Midgely (and party).

    Trail and Timberline
        "The Gore Range Outing,"* Everett Long, No. 204, October 1935,
        pp. 111-113.
        First ascent noted, Stanley Midgely, Don McBride, Clifton
        Snively, and Everett Long.

ELK MOUNTAIN, 12,693'   Gore Range   Copper Mountain 1970
   Trail and Timberline
      "Notes on the Gore Range, Summer, 1942,"* Carl Melzer,
      No. 284, August 1942, pp. 103-106.

ELK TOOTH ("OGALALLA HORN"), 12,848'   Front Range, Indian Peaks
                                        Isolation Peak 1958
   Trail and Timberline
      "Our Indian Peaks,"* Karl E. Boehm, No. 497, May 1960, pp. 73-
      74.

"ELLINGWOOD PEAK", 14,042'   Sangre de Cristo Range
                             (Unnamed) Blanca Peak 1967
   Trail and Timberline
      "New Names," No. 608, August 1969, p. 148.

      "New 14 Mapped," H. E. K., No. 613, January 1970, p. 17.

      "Climbing in the Blanca Massif,"* Roger Fuehrer, No. 637,
      January 1972, pp. 3-5, 1 Map.

      "Route to Blanca, Ellingwood and Hamilton from the Huerfano
      Basin,"* Rich Riefenberg, No. 637, January 1972, p. 6.

      "The Rigors and Joys of Winter Climbing,"* Stan Stephan,
      No. 643, July 1972, pp. 143-145, 1 Illustration.

EMERALD PEAK, 13,904'   Sawatch Range   Mt. Harvard 15M 1955
   Trail and Timberline
      "The High Peaks of the La Plata Mining Region,"* John L. J.
      Hart, No. 159, January 1932, pp. 3-4, 14, 1 Illustration,
      1 Map.

      "Some Trails of the La Plata Mining Region,"* Bruce and
      Elisabeth MacCannon, No. 159, January 1932, pp. 5-6.

      "A Guide to Colorado's Almost-Fourteens,"* William A. Graves,
      No. 683, November 1975, pp. 225-227.

MT. EMMONS, 12,392'   Ruby Range   Oh-Be-Joyful 1961
   Trail and Timberline
      "Some Took the High Road,"* Stan Shepard, No. 455,
      November 1956, pp. 165-167.

ENGINEER MOUNTAIN, 13,218'   San Juan Mountains   Handies Peak 1955
   Trail and Timberline
      "The 1934 Climbing Season in Colorado,"* Carleton C. Long,
      No. 196, February 1935, pp. 15-18.
      Winter ascent note, Gordon Williams and Melvin Griffiths.

MT. EOLUS, 14,083'   Needle Mountains   Columbine Pass 1973
   American Alpine Journal
      "Technical Climbing in the Mountains of Colorado and Wyoming,"*
      Albert Russell Ellingwood, Vol. 1, 1930, pp. 140-147.

"Colorado Climbing Notes, 1937,"* Carl Blaurock, Vol. 3, 1938,
p. 218.
Traverse note of ridge from Jupiter Mountain to Mt. Eolus,
Jack Seerley.

Appalachia
"Colorado Climbs, 1931,"* Winthrop Means, Vol. 18,
December 1931, pp. 357-364.

"All the 14,000's,"* Carl Melzer, Vol. 22, December 1939,
pp. 466-479.

"Excursions: Colorado Trip,"* E. Folger Taylor and Walter D.
Howe, Vol. 23, December 1940, pp. 257-259, 1 Illustration
following p. 262.

"The Old and New West in the Needle Mountains,"* Duncan A.
MacInnes, Vol. 23, June 1941, pp. 374-379.

Chicago Mountaineering Club Newsletter
"1959 'Big Hike' in the Needles Mountain Area of Colorado,"*
Charles I. Pierce, Vol. 14, No. 1, February 1960, pp. 3-6.

Climbing
"Mt. Eolus, (14,086 Ft.), Needle Range, San Juan Mts.,
Colorado," No. 7, May-June 1971, p. 20.
First winter ascent note, Rick Nolting, Barry Nash, Floyd
Frank, and Steve Lewis.

The Mountaineering Journal (British)
Illustration,* "View Southwards from Point Pun in the
Grenadiers," Carleton C. Long, Vol. 1, No. 4, June, July,
August 1933, p. 242.

Summit
"Lightning on Eolus," Spencer Swanger, Vol. 16, No. 10,
December 1970, pp. 18-22, 2 Illustrations.
Reprinted from Trail and Timberline.

"Mt. Eolus," Hugh E. Kingery, Vol. 16, No. 10, December 1970,
p. 23, 1 Illustration.

Trail and Timberline
"Where We Went and What We Climbed,"* No. 25, October 1920,
pp. 8-11.

"Mt. Eolus and Mt. 'North Eolus',"* Grace M. Harvey, No. 107,
September 1927, p. 8.

"Four in One Day,"* Dr. Corwin S. Clarke, No. 107,
September 1927, p. 18.

Illustration,* "Mt. Eolus (Left), Turret Peak (Center), and
Pigeon Peak (Right)," Percy Hagerman, No. 178, August 1933,
p. 110.

"Needle Mountain Notes,"* David Lavender, No. 225, July 1937, pp. 80-81.

"The Colorado Mountain Club Announces the Twenty-Eighth Annual Summer Outing,"* Henry Buchtel, Lewis Giesecke, Kenneth Segerstrom, No. 265, January 1941, pp. 9-14, 1 Illustration.

"Reaching the High Spots,"* George J. Kubricht, No. 325, January 1946, pp. 3-4.

"Noname Prospects,"* Mel Griffiths, No. 340, April 1947, pp. 56-59.

"Climbers Guide to Noname,"* No. 342, June 1947, pp. 97-98, 1 Map.

"Climber's Guide from Noname Creek,"* Henry Buchtel, No. 345, September 1947, pp. 143-144.

"Confessions of A Solo Climber or How I Recanted My Heresy,"* Wilbur F. Arnold, No. 389, May 1951, pp. 51-55.

"New York Basin Ascents,"* Henry L. McClintock, No. 393, September 1951, pp. 113-114, 1 Illustration.
First ascent noted of the west face, Joe Merhar, Chris Schoredos, Frank McClintock, and Henry McClintock.

"We Started at the Top,"* Virginia Copeland, No. 395, November 1951, pp. 145-147.

"A Rugged Ten-Day Outing,"* Neil Wernette, No. 426, June 1954, pp. 83-84.

"San Juan Idyll,"* Joseph W. Miller, No. 430, October 1954, pp. 131-133, 139, Front cover illustration.

"Denver Junior Summer Outing,"* Louise Jackson, No. 443, November 1955, pp. 190-191.

"The Needles, June 1957,"* Gene White, No. 471, March 1958, pp. 31-35.

"Fifty-Two in '52,"* Dwight Hamilton, No. 482, February 1959, pp. 25-26.

"Climber's Paradise,"* Lester Michel, No. 496, April 1960, pp. 60-62.

"Revised Climbers' Guide from Noname Creek,"* William E. Davis, No. 502, October 1960, pp. 149-154, 1 Map.

"Chicago Basin Expedition,"* Al Ossinger, No. 559, July 1965, pp. 131-133.

"Lightning on Eolus," Spencer Swanger, No. 619, July 1970, pp. 144-145, 147, 1 Illustration.

"First Winter Ascent of Mount Eolus," Barry Nash, No. 631, July 1971, pp. 146-150, 2 Illustrations, Front cover illustration.
First winter ascent noted, Barry Nash, Rick Nolting, Steve Lewis, and Floyd Frank.

Illustration, "Mt. Eolus," Bob Wiegel, No. 649, January 1973, p. 14.

"Chicago Basin Grand Slam,"* Carl C. Hinrichs, No. 659, November 1973, pp. 291-294.

"Denver Junior Summer Outing," John Scott, No. 664, April 1974, pp. 88-91.

Illustration, "Roped Climbing: A CMC Party Ascends Mt. Eolus in 1920," No. 669, September 1974, p. 215.

"MT. ESTABROOK" (SAYRES), 13,738'   Sawatch Range
                                     (Unnamed) Mount Elbert 1967
    Trail and Timberline
        "The High Peaks of the La Plata Mining Region,"* John L. J. Hart, No. 159, January 1932, pp. 3-4, 14, 1 Illustration, 1 Map.

        "Some Trails of the La Plata Mining Region,"* Bruce and Elisabeth MacCannon, No. 159, January 1932, pp. 5-6.

MT. ETHEL, 11,924'   North Park Range   Mount Ethel 1955
    Trail and Timberline
        "North Park and Mt. Zirkle,"* No. 202, August 1935, p. 95.

        "Exploring the Mount Zirkel - Dome Peak Wild Area,"* Margaret R. Chase, No. 464, August 1957, pp. 111-113, 1 Map following p. 116.

EUREKA MOUNTAIN, 13,489'   Sangre de Cristo Range   Electric Peak 15M 1959
    Trail and Timberline
        "The Sangre de Cristo Range,"* Eva and Bill Rathbun, No. 460, April 1957, pp. 55-60, 64, 1 Map.

        "New Maps of the Sangre de Cristo Range,"* John L. J. Hart, No. 519, March 1962, pp. 32-33.

        "Sangre de Cristo Saga,"* Lester A. Michel, with Wilbur F. Arnold, No. 525, September 1962, pp. 139-142, 150, (Continued from August 1962 T&T).

MT. EVANS, 14,264'   Front Range   Mt. Evans 1957
    Alpine Journal
        "The Rockies of Colorado,"* Evelio Echevarria C., Vol. 71, May 1966, pp. 26-36, 1 Map, Bibliography.

Appalachia
"All the 14,000's,"* Carl Melzer, Vol. 22, December 1939,
pp. 466-479.

Iowa Mountaineers Journal
"Colorado's Rockies,"* Ruth Norman, Vol. 1, No. 10,
February 1945, pp. 53-57.

Trail and Timberline
"Recent Trips: Mt. Evans," No. 16, October 1919, p. 5.

"A New Year's Trip Up Mt. Evans," Carl A. Blaurock, No. 17,
January 1920, pp. 29-30, 1 Illustration.

"High Lights on the Ten Annual Outings: First Annual Outing -
Bear Creek Basin, Near Mount Evans," Grace M. Harvey, No. 43,
April 1922, p. 24.

"The Mount Evans Area," E. S. Kiethley, Supervisor, Pike
National Forest, No. 127, May 1929, pp. 3-6, 11,
1 Illustration, 1 Map.

"Does Denver Want the Mount Evans Recreation Area?" W. H.
Crisp, No. 171, January 1933, pp. 3-4, 1 Map.

"Editorial Notes," David Rosendale, No. 171, January 1933,
p. 12.
Partial ski ascent note.

"The Tale,"* No. 310, October 1944, pp. 117-121.

"Evans and Bierstadt,"* Bill Arnold, No. 398, February 1952,
pp. 25-26.

"The Long Way to Evans," Esther Holt, No. 475, July 1958,
pp. 91-93, 1 Illustration.

"The Rigors and Joys of Winter Climbing,"* Stan Stephan,
No. 643, July 1972, pp. 143-145.

Front cover illustration,* "Mt. Bierstadt to Mt. Evans,"
Spencer Swanger, No. 668, August 1974.

Front cover illustration,* "Ridge Between Mt. Bierstadt and
Mt. Evans," Spencer Swanger, No. 678, June 1975.

"They're There Because ...,"* James McChristal, No. 687,
March 1976, pp. 63-67.
Reprinted from The Colorado College Bulletin, May, 1975,
pp. 43-45.
First ascent noted of the north face, Albert Ellingwood.

"PEAK F", 13,200'   Gore Range   (Unnamed) Vail East 1970
   American Alpine Journal
     "Colorado Climbing Notes, 1935,"* Carleton C. Long, Vol. 2,
     1936, p. 545.
     First ascent note, Stanley Midgely, Clifton Snively, Maxwell
     Mery, and Pete Alexander.

   Chicago Mountaineering Club Newsletter
     "Ascents by Club Members,"* Stanley Midgely, Vol. 1, No. 3,
     September to December 1945, pp. 10-11.
     First ascent note, Stanley Midgely (and party).

   Trail and Timberline
     "The Gore Range Outing,"* Everett Long, No. 204, October 1935,
     pp. 111-113.
     First ascent noted, Stanley Midgely, Clifton Snively, Maxwell
     Mery, and Pete Alexander.

     "Alphabet Soup,"* Alene W. Conover, No. 357, September 1948,
     pp. 129-130.

     "From 'B' to 'H' in Seven Days,"* Louise Roloff, No. 357,
     September 1948, pp. 131, 138.

FAIRCHILD MOUNTAIN, 13,502'   Mummy Range, Rocky Mountain National Park
                       Trail Ridge 1957
   American Alpine Journal
     "Fairchild Mountain, Haunch Bauncho (sic) Buttress, East Face,"
     David P. Johnson, Vol. 14, 1965, p. 433.
     First ascent note, Peter H. Robinson and David P. Johnson.

   Trail and Timberline
     "Circle Trips in RMNP,"* William C. Ramaley, No. 630,
     June 1971, pp. 125-128.

"THE FATES", 11,000'#   Tarryall Range   (Unnamed) McCurdy Mountain 1956
   Trail and Timberline
     "The Sinks - A New Area for Mountaineers,"* Don Howe and Dick
     Slusser, No. 512, August 1961, pp. 142-144, 1 Map.

THE FLATIRONS, 8,144'+   Front Range   Eldorado Springs 1965
   Chicago Mountaineering Club Newsletter
     "Flatiron Climb," Merritt Kastens, Vol. 5, No. 1,
     January 1951, pp. 8-9.

   Summit
     "Tragedy in the Flatirons," Vol. 14, No. 6, July-August 1968,
     p. 31.

#Elevation figure from Trail and Timberline.

+Elevation of Green Mountain.

Trail and Timberline
"Scaling the Flatirons," Rudolph Johnson, No. 54, March 1923,
p. 4.

Illustration, "Flatirons in Winter," Harry M. Vars, No. 79,
April 1925, p. 8.

"Group Activities: Denver Group,"* No. 178, August 1933,
p. 116, Front cover illustration.
Note on rock climbing.

"Boulder Rock Climbs,"* John D. McCrumm and Carleton C. Long,
No. 187, May 1934, pp. 55-67, 1 Illustration, 1 Map.

"Mass Climbing: A C.M.C. Trip Report," Carleton C. Long,
No. 199, May 1935, pp. 58-59.
Ascents noted on three different routes on the third flatiron.

"Group Activities: Denver Group,"* No. 205, November 1935,
p. 133.
Ascent note of the north arete of the first flatiron, Charles
Hardin and David Rosendale.

"Joint Trip of the Denver and Boulder Groups to the Flatirons,"
Glen Wakeham, No. 235, June 1938, p. 67.

Front cover illustration, "Boulder Flatirons," Charles F. Snow,
No. 313, January 1945.

"Accident on the Third Flatiron - 14 July, 1946," No. 333,
September 1946, p. 148.

"Climbing on the Fourth Flatiron," Fred Crowle and Nelson
Crowle, No. 637, January 1972, pp. 14-16, 5 Illustrations.

FLATTOP MOUNTAIN, 12,324'   Front Range, Rocky Mountain National Park
                               McHenrys Peak 1957
Chicago Mountaineering Club Newsletter
"Flattop, Hallett, Otis, and Taylor Peaks,"* Barbara Heiberg,
Vol. 5, No. 5, November 1951, pp. 9-10, 1 Map p. 6.

Climbing
"View from Within: Colorado Rocky Mountain National Park,"*
No. 28, Winter 1974-75, p. 36.
Free ascent note of "The Mosquito Wall", Larry Hamilton, John
Byrd, and Gary Hall.

Iowa Mountaineers Journal
"Colorado's Rockies,"* Ruth Norman, Vol. 1, No. 10,
February 1945, pp. 53-57.

Trail and Timberline
"Across Flat Top in 1892," Charles H. Hanington, No. 153,
July 1931, pp. 103-104.

"Back-Packing Over Flat Top," Iva M. Oakes, No. 304,
April 1944, pp. 43-44.

FLETCHER MOUNTAIN, 13,951'   Tenmile Range   Copper Mountain 1970
   Trail and Timberline
      Illustration,* "Ten Mile Range Between Mt. Fletcher and
Pacific Peak," Curt E. Krieser, No. 326, February 1946, p. 19.

   "A Guide to Colorado's Almost-Fourteens,"* William A. Graves,
No. 683, November 1975, pp. 225-227.

   "Original Mountain of the Holy Cross," William M. Bueler,
No. 696, December 1976, pp. 236-237, 1 Illustration.

MT. FLORA, 13,132'   Front Range   Empire 1958
   Trail and Timberline
      Front cover illustration, "Mt. Flora," Richard Morris,
Nos. 209-210, March-April 1936.

   "Climbing Notes,"* No. 217, November 1936, p. 139.
Note on ski ascents.

   Illustration, "Wind Accelerates the Sublimation of Snow on the
Lee of Mt. Flora," No. 336, December 1946, p. 197.

"THE FOURTH APOSTLE", 13,175'   Sawatch Range
                          (Unnamed) Mt. Harvard 15M 1955
   Trail and Timberline
      "The Fourth Apostle," Louise L. Roloff, No. 468,
December 1957, pp. 188-189.

FRENCH MOUNTAIN, 13,920'   Sawatch Range   Mount Massive 1967
   Trail and Timberline
      "A Guide to Colorado's Almost-Fourteens,"* William A. Graves,
No. 683, November 1975, pp. 225-227.

FULLER PEAK, 13,761'   San Juan Mountains   Ophir 1955
   Trail and Timberline
      "1932 Summer Outing,"* Jack Kendrick, No. 162, April 1932,
pp. 47, 57-58.

   "Exploring Ice Lake Basin,"* Allen W. Greene, No. 474,
June 1958, pp. 75-76, 87.

   "Silverton - Mountain Mecca,"* Art Porter, No. 620,
August 1970, pp. 169, 171-172, 1 Illustration.

"PEAK G", 13,240'   Gore Range   (Unnamed) Vail East 1970
                                   (Unnamed) Minturn 15M 1934, 13,274'
    American Alpine Journal
        "Colorado Climbing Notes, 1935,"* Carleton C. Long, Vol. 2,
        1936, p. 545.
        First ascent note, Stanley Midgely, Clifton Snively, Maxwell
        Mery, and Pete Alexander.

    Chicago Mountaineering Club Newsletter
        "Ascents by Club Members,"* Stanley Midgely, Vol. 1, No. 3,
        September to December 1945, pp. 10-11.
        First ascent note, Stanley Midgely and Colorado Mountain Club
        party.

    Trail and Timberline
        "The Gore Range Outing,"* Everett Long, No. 204, October 1935,
        pp. 111-113.
        First ascent noted, Stanley Midgely, Clifton Snively, Maxwell
        Mery, and Pete Alexander.

        "From 'B' to 'H' in Seven Days,"* Louise Roloff, No. 357,
        September 1948, pp. 131, 138.

        "A Day in the Mountains,"* Kurt Beam, No. 532, April 1963,
        pp. 67-68, 71, 1 Illustration.

        "Names on the Gores,"* William Bird Mounsey, No. 568,
        April 1966, pp. 63-65, 1 Map.

GALENA MOUNTAIN, 12,580'   Elk Range   Snowmass Mtn. 1960
    Trail and Timberline
        "Hikes and Climbs from Crystal,"* John Beyer, No. 598,
        October 1968, pp. 224-229, 1 Map.

GALENA PEAK, 12,483'   Sangre de Cristo Range   Howard 15M 1959
    Trail and Timberline
        "Sangre de Cristo Saga,"* Lester A. Michel, with Wilbur F.
        Arnold, No. 524, August 1962, pp. 123-126, 133.

MT. GARFIELD, 13,074'   Needle Mountains   Snowdon Peak 1964
    Trail and Timberline
        "Some First Ascent Possibilities in Colorado,"* Kenneth
        Segerstrom, No. 165, July 1932, pp. 103-104.

GARFIELD PEAK, 13,760'   Sawatch Range   Independence Pass 1960
    Trail and Timberline
        "A Traverse of the Garfield Cirque," Ronald L. Ives, No. 191,
        September 1934, pp. 123-124, 1 Illustration, Front cover
        illustration.

"GARRET PEAK",
    Climbing
        "Basecamp: Winter Climbing,"* No. 6, March-April 1971, p. 3.
        First winter ascent note, Jim Koontz, Bill Sands, and Kern
        Krapohl.

MT. GEORGE, 12,876'   Front Range, Indian Peaks   Monarch Lake 1958
     Trail and Timberline
          "The Long Lake Region,"* A. Gayle Waldrop, No. 281, May 1942,
          pp. 69-70.

          "Our Indian Peaks,"* Karl E. Boehm, No. 497, May 1960, pp. 73-
          74.

GIBBS PEAK, 13,575'   Sangre de Cristo Range   Electric Peak 15M 1959
     Trail and Timberline
          "Climbing in the Sangre de Cristo,"* Albert R. Ellingwood,
          No. 81, June 1925, pp. 1-5.

          "The Sangre de Cristo Range,"* Eva and Bill Rathbun, No. 460,
          April 1957, pp. 55-60, 64, 1 Map.

          "New Maps of the Sangre de Cristo Range,"* John L. J. Hart,
          No. 519, March 1962, pp. 32-33.

"GILPIN BLOCK TOPS", 13,543'   San Juan Mountains, Sneffels Range
See also "T1", "T2", "T3", "T4" (Unnamed) Telluride 1955
     The Mountaineering Journal (British)
          "Outstanding Climbing Centres in the South-Western Colorado
          Rockies,"* Dwight G. Lavender, Vol. 1, No. 4, June, July,
          August 1933, pp. 238-248.

     Trail and Timberline
          Illustration,* "South from 'The Hand'. Aiguilles Monolith and
          Blue Needle to the Left. Block Tops of Gilpin to the Right,"
          D. G. Lavender, No. 169, November 1932, p. 158.

          Illustration,* "Block Tops of Gilpin to Left. Dallas Peak to
          Right. Wilsons in Distance," D. G. Lavender, No. 169,
          November 1932, p. 161.

          Illustration,* "Gilpin to Left. Dallas Peak to Right. Wilsons
          in Distance," Dwight G. Lavender, No. 400, April 1952, p. 79.

          Illustration,* "South from 'The Hand'. Aiguilles Monolith and
          Blue Needle to the Left. Block Tops of Gilpin to the Right,"
          Dwight G. Lavender, No. 400, April 1952, p. 80.

GILPIN PEAK, 13,694'   San Juan Mountains, Sneffels Range   Telluride 1955
     American Alpine Journal
          "Southwestern Colorado Climbing Notes - 1933,"* Dwight G.
          Lavender, Vol. 2, 1934, p. 256.
          First ascent note, T. M. Griffiths and L. V. Giesecke.

     The Mountaineering Journal (British)
          "Correspondence,"* Dwight Lavender, Vol. 2, No. 1, December,
          January, February 1933-34, pp. 47-51.
          First ascent note, Lewis V. Giesecke and T. Melvin Griffiths.

Trail and Timberline
"The 1933 Climbing Season in Colorado,"* Carleton C. Long,
No. 184, February 1934, pp. 20-23.
First ascent note, San Juan Mountaineers.

Front cover illustration,* "Gilpin, Dallas and Mt. Sneffels
from Yankee Boy Basin," Alice B. Rawson, No. 407,
November 1952.

GLACIER POINT, 13,704'   Needle Mountains   Storm King Peak 1964
American Alpine Journal
Illustration,* "Noname Basin Camp: North Thumb and Glacier
Point Behind It," H. L. McClintock, Vol. 9, 1954, Following
p. 126.

The Mountaineering Journal (British)
Illustration,* "View Southwards from Point Pun in the
Grenadiers," Carleton C. Long, Vol. 1, No. 4, June, July,
August 1933, p. 242.

Trail and Timberline
"San Juan Testimony,"* H. L. McClintock, No. 224, June 1937,
p. 68, 1 Illustration p. 67, 1 Illustration p. 69.

"Noname Prospects,"* Mel Griffiths, No. 340, April 1947,
pp. 56-59.

"Climbers Guide to Noname,"* No. 342, June 1947, pp. 97-98,
1 Map.

"Revised Climbers' Guide from Noname Creek,"* William E.
Davis, No. 502, October 1960, pp. 149-154, 1 Map.

GLADSTONE PEAK, 13,913'   San Miguel Range   Mount Wilson 1953
American Alpine Journal
"Technical Climbing in the Mountains of Colorado and Wyoming,"*
Albert Russell Ellingwood, Vol. 1, 1930, pp. 140-147.

The Mountaineering Journal (British)
"Outstanding Climbing Centres in the South-Western Colorado
Rockies,"* Dwight G. Lavender, Vol. 1, No. 4, June, July,
August 1933, pp. 238-248.

Trail and Timberline
"The 1931 Outing Country,"* Dwight G. Lavender, No. 151,
May 1931, pp. 63-66.

"Outing Impressions,"* Evelyn Runnette, No. 156, October 1931,
pp. 152-157, 1 Illustration.

"Climbing Notes,"* Dwight Lavender, No. 156, October 1931,
p. 165.
Second ascent note, twenty-four members of the Colorado
Mountain and Appalachian Mountain Clubs.

Front cover illustration,* "El Diente, Mount Wilson,
Gladstone Peak and the Lizard Head, from Black Face," Douglas
Anger, No. 283, July 1942.

Illustration,* "Mount Wilson and Gladstone Peak from Somewhere
by Lizard Head," Douglas Anger, No. 283, July 1942, p. 92.

"The Lesser Climbs,"* Mark Bostwick, No. 586, October 1967,
pp. 181-182, 1 Map.

"A Guide to Colorado's Almost-Fourteens,"* William A. Graves,
No. 683, November 1975, pp. 225-227.

GOLD DUST PEAK, 13,365'   Sawatch Range   Mount Jackson 1970
    Trail and Timberline
        "Gold Dust and Ghost Town: Gold Dust - Straight Up," Hollis
        Thayer, No. 510, June 1961, p. 111, 1 Illustration.

GOLDEN HORN, 13,760'   San Juan Mountains   Ophir 1955
    Trail and Timberline
        "1932 Summer Outing,"* Jack Kendrick, No. 162, April 1932,
        pp. 47, 57-58.

        "Notes on the 1932 Climbing Season,"* Carleton C. Long,
        No. 171, January 1933, p. 11.
        Possible first ascent note, students from the Michigan School
        of Mines, Robert Jones, Jerome S. Baer, K. Spencer, and Chas.
        Speer, via south face.

        "Exploring Ice Lake Basin,"* Allen W. Greene, No. 474,
        June 1958, pp. 75-76, 87.

GORE RANGE, Gore Range   (Main Maps) Mt. Powell 15M 1933,
                                Vail East 1970, Willow Lakes 1970
    Trail and Timberline
        Illustration, "New Peaks in the Gore Range," Everett Long,
        No. 201, July 1935, p. 83.

GOTHIC MOUNTAIN, 12,625'   Elk Range   Oh-Be-Joyful 1961
    Trail and Timberline
        "1873 Tells 1949,"* Louisa Ward Arps, No. 365, May 1949,
        pp. 68-70.

        "Pittsburgh on the Slate,"* Louisa Ward Arps, No. 450,
        June 1956, pp. 87-90.

        "Some Took the High Road,"* Stan Shepard, No. 455,
        November 1956, pp. 165-167.

"GRADE O-O PINNACLE", 9,000'[#]   Tarryall Range
                                (Unnamed) McCurdy Mountain 1956
    Trail and Timberline
        "The Sinks - A New Area for Mountaineers,"* Don Howe and Dick
        Slusser, No. 512, August 1961, pp. 142-144, 1 Map.

[#]Elevation figure from Trail and Timberline.

GRANITE MOUNTAIN, 12,848'   Sawatch Range   Mt. Harvard 15M 1955
    Trail and Timberline
        Illustration, "Our Camp, Granite Mountain in the Background,"
        No. 468, December 1957, p. 184.

GRAY NEEDLE, 13,430'   Needle Mountains   Storm King Peak 1964
    American Alpine Journal
        "A.A.C. and C.M.C. Joint Outing, Needle Mountains, Colorado,
        July 19 - August 9, 1953,"* Henry L. McClintock, Vol. 9, 1954,
        p. 170.
        First ascent note.

    Appalachia
        "Organizations: The American Alpine Club," Vol. 29,
        December 1953, p. 605.
        First ascent note.

    Chicago Mountaineering Club Newsletter
        "Needles Outing of the American Alpine Club,"* Dave Bidwell,
        Vol. 7, No. 5, November 1953, pp. 10-12.

    Trail and Timberline
        "Noname Prospects,"* Mel Griffiths, No. 340, April 1947,
        pp. 56-59.

        "Climbers Guide to Noname,"* No. 342, June 1947, pp. 97-98,
        1 Map.

GRAY WOLF MOUNTAIN, 13,602'   Front Range   Mt. Evans 1957
    Trail and Timberline
        "A Ski Ascent of Gray Wolf Mountain," Eliot B. Moses, No. 312,
        December 1944, pp. 141-142, 147.

GRAYS PEAK, 14,270'   Front Range   Grays Peak 1958
    Alpine Journal
        "Mountaineering in Central Africa, with An Attempt on Mt.
        Kenya,"* Dr. J. W. Gregory, Vol. 17, May 1894, pp. 89-104.
        Ascent noted of Grays Peak, p. 101.

        "The Rockies of Colorado,"* Evelio Echevarría C., Vol. 71,
        May 1966, pp. 26-36, 1 Map, Bibliography.

    American Alpine Journal
        "Colorado Climbing Notes, 1934,"* Carleton C. Long, Vol. 2,
        1935, p. 415.
        New Year's Day ascent note.

    Appalachia
        "All the 14,000's,"* Carl Melzer, Vol. 22, December 1939,
        pp. 466-479.

    Trail and Timberline
        Illustration,* "Grays (14,341 Ft.) and Torreys (14,336 Ft.)
        Peaks from Near Clear Creek Camp," Geo. H. Harvey, Jr.,
        No. 48, September 1922, p. 9.

"Mountain Registers,"* Carl Blaurock, No. 52, January 1923,
p. 6.

Illustration,* "Grays and Torreys Peaks - Climb from Camp
July 4th," Geo. H. Harvey, Jr., No. 56, May 1923, p. 16.

"The 1934 Climbing Season in Colorado,"* Carleton C. Long,
No. 196, February 1935, pp. 15-18.
Probable first recorded New Year's Day ascent note, Jim Foley
and friend.

"The Mountain Ranges of Colorado,"* Kenneth Segerstrom,
No. 215, September 1936, pp. 109-115, 1 Map.

"The Gray and Torrey Reunion Fable,"* Erl H. Ellis, No. 301,
January 1944, pp. 6-7.
Reprinted from The Colorado Magazine.

"Junior Jottings,"* Dorothy Sethman, No. 308, August 1944,
p. 94.

"The Tale,"* No. 310, October 1944, pp. 117-121.

"An Accident on Grays Peak," John H. Morrison Jr., No. 354,
June 1948, p. 91.

"Ascent of Gray's Peak," No. 435, March 1955, pp. 55-56, 58.
Condensed from an article in Scribner's, Vol. 4, No. 5,
September 1872.

"The Colorado Mountaineer: CMC Winter Mountaineering School,"*
Gregg Blomberg, No. 542, February 1964, pp. 28-29.

"The Four Fourteen Foible,"* William L. Myatt, No. 545,
May 1964, pp. 87-88.

GREENHORN MOUNTAIN, 12,347'   Wet Mountains   San Isabel 1969
    Trail and Timberline
    "The Mountain Ranges of Colorado,"* Kenneth Segerstrom,
    No. 215, September 1936, pp. 109-115, 1 Map.

    "Trails,"* Leola Crump, No. 286, October 1942, p. 129.

    "A Parallelism," Caroline Sporleder Young, No. 314,
    February 1945, pp. 15, 17.

GRENADIER RANGE, Needle Mountains   Snowdon Peak 1964, Storm King Peak 1964
    Summit
    Front cover illustration, "Looking Across Molas Lake to the
    Grenadier Range in Southwestern Colorado," Vol. 7, No. 6,
    June 1961.

GREYROCK MOUNTAIN, 7,613'   Rawah Range   Poudre Park 1962
    Trail and Timberline
    "Good Old Grayrock (sic)," E. B. Crone, No. 425, May 1954,
    p. 74.

"Guerilla Tactics Useful for Doggy Climbs: The Gentle Art of Freddy Peaking,"* Bob Michael, No. 689, May 1976, pp. 112-115.

GRIZZLY PEAK, 13,427'   Front Range   Grays Peak 1958
    Trail and Timberline
    "Summit Lake to Adolph's (Winter Park),"* Edward F. Taylor, No. 304, April 1944, pp. 39-40, 45, 1 Illustration.

    "The Tale,"* No. 310, October 1944, pp. 117-121.

    "The Rigors and Joys of Winter Climbing,"* Stan Stephan, No. 643, July 1972, pp. 143-145.

GRIZZLY PEAK, 13,680'   Needle Mountains   Columbine Pass 1973
    Trail and Timberline
    "Where We Went and What We Climbed,"* No. 25, October 1920, pp. 8-11, 1 Illustration.

    Illustration,* "Mts. Grizzly (13,695, Left) and McCauley (13,551, Right) Seen from Summit of Jupiter," George H. Harvey, Jr., No. 104, May 1927, p. 5.

    Illustration,* "Mts. Grizzly and McCauley Seen from Summit of Jupiter," No. 107, September 1927, p. 21.

    Illustration,* "Grizzly and McCauley Peaks from Top of Jupiter," George Harvey, No. 223, May 1937, p. 55.

GRIZZLY PEAK, 13,738'   San Juan Mountains   Ophir 1955
    Trail and Timberline
    "The Mountain Ranges of Colorado,"* Kenneth Segerstrom, No. 215, September 1936, pp. 109-115, 1 Map.

GRIZZLY PEAK, 13,988'   Sawatch Range   Independence Pass 1960
    Climbing
    "Basecamp: Aspen,"* No. 10, November-December 1971, p. 4. Accident note.

    Trail and Timberline
    "New Survey Figures,"* Kenneth Segerstrom, No. 171, January 1933, p. 12.

    Illustration, "Where the Sawatch Range and Elk Mountains Meet: View Southwest from Grizzly Peak," H. L. Standley, No. 215, September 1936, p. 115.

    "Colorado's Mountains are Higher than You Think,"* Arthur J. McNair, No. 323, November 1945, pp. 139-142, 1 Illustration.

    "A Guide to Colorado's Almost-Fourteens,"* William A. Graves, No. 683, November 1975, pp. 225-227.

GROUNDHOG MOUNTAIN, 12,165'   San Miguel Range   Groundhog Mountain 1964
    Trail and Timberline
    "San Miguel Mountains,"* Dwight Lavender, No. 137, March 1930, p. 3.

THE GUARDIAN, 13,617'   Needle Mountains   Storm King Peak 1964
  Trail and Timberline
        Illustration,* "The Guardian and Mt. Silex from the Vallecito
        Side," Ralph Rosenbaum, No. 608, August 1969, p. 146.

        "Letters to the Editor,"* Martin A. Etter, No. 610,
        October 1969, p. 187.
        North face note.

"PEAK H", 13,080'   Gore Range   (Unnamed) Vail East 1970
                                 (Unnamed) Minturn 15M 1934, 13,065'
    American Alpine Journal
        "Colorado Climbing Notes, 1935,"* Carleton C. Long, Vol. 2,
        1936, p. 545.
        Possible second ascent note, Don McBride, Carleton C. Long,
        and party.

    Trail and Timberline
        "The Gore Range Outing,"* Everett Long, No. 204, October 1935,
        pp. 111-113.

        "From 'B' to 'H' in Seven Days,"* Louise Roloff, No. 357,
        September 1948, pp. 131, 138.

        "Beneath the Lettered Peaks," Harriet Morrison, No. 574,
        October 1966, pp. 169-170.

HAGAR MOUNTAIN, 13,195'   Front Range   Loveland Pass 1958
    Trail and Timberline
        Illustration, "Hal Johnson and Bill Bullard Near Summit of
        Hagar Peak, May, 1947, ...," Don Johnson, No. 362,
        February 1949, p. 25.

HAGERMAN PEAK, 13,841'   Elk Range   Snowmass Mtn. 1960
    American Alpine Journal
        "Technical Climbing in the Mountains of Colorado and Wyoming,"*
        Albert Russell Ellingwood, Vol. 1, 1930, pp. 140-147.

        "Naming America's Mountains - The Colorado Rockies,"* Francis
        P. Farquhar, Vol. 12, 1961, pp. 319-346.

    Appalachia
        "The Call of Colorado,"* Edward W. Harnden, Vol. 16,
        June 1925, pp. 158-164, 3 Illustrations.

    Chicago Mountaineering Club Newsletter
        "Colorado's Elk Mountains,"* Weldon F. Heald, Vol. 13, No. 6,
        October 1959, pp. 1-5, Front cover map.

    Climbing
        "'Northface', Hagerman Peak, Elk Mountains, Colo.," No. 11,
        January-February 1972, p. 28.
        First ascent note, Steve Shea and Chris Landry.

    The Mountaineering Journal (British)
        "American Notes: Climbing in the Snowmass Region of the Elk
        Mountains of Colorado,"* Hubert M. Walters, Vol. 2, No. 2,
        March, April, May 1934, p. 98.
        First traverse noted of the Hagerman-Snowmass ridge. See T&T,
        No. 228, November 1937, p. 126 for correct first traverse of
        the Hagerman-Snowmass ridge by Harold Clark.

Summit
   "Colorado's High-Rising Elks,"* Weldon F. Heald, Vol. 8,
   No. 11, November 1962, pp. 20-23.

Trail and Timberline
   Illustration, "Snowmass Lake and Hagerman Peak (13,412 Feet),"
   No. 42, March 1922, p. 5.

   "The Trips and the Country,"* Lucretia Vaile, No. 49,
   October 1922, pp. 4-7, 1 Illustration, 1 Illustration p. 3.

   Illustration, "Snowmass Lake and Hagerman Peak," No. 113,
   March 1928, p. 8.

   "The Hagerman Climb," E. W. Harnden, No. 120, October 1928,
   p. 12, 1 Illustration p. 2, 1 Illustration p. 11.

   Illustration, "Hagerman Peak and Snowmass Lake," Harvey T.
   Sethman, No. 172, February 1933, p. 19.

   "Snowmass and Hagerman,"* Harvey T. Sethman, No. 180,
   October 1933, pp. 145-146, Front cover illustration.
   First recorded ascent noted of the east face, Bestor Robinson,
   Robert Lewis, Donald McBride, and Harvey Sethman.
   First recorded traverse noted of the Hagerman-Snowmass ridge.
   See T&T, No. 228, November 1937, p. 126 for correct first
   traverse of the Hagerman-Snowmass ridge by Harold Clark.

   "The 1933 Climbing Season in Colorado,"* Carleton C. Long,
   No. 184, February 1934, pp. 20-23.
   (First) traverse noted of the Hagerman-Snowmass ridge. See T&T,
   No. 228, November 1937, p. 126 for correct first traverse of the
   Hagerman-Snowmass ridge by Harold Clark.

   "Clark Peak?"* Percy Hagerman, No. 228, November 1937, pp. 120,
   126.
   First traverse noted of the Hagerman-Snowmass ridge, Harold
   Clark.

   "Junior Outing,"* Rex A. Young, No. 239, November 1938,
   pp. 115-116.

   Front cover illustration, "Hagerman Peak," Standley, No. 294,
   June 1943.

   "1873 Tells 1949,"* Louisa Ward Arps, No. 365, May 1949,
   pp. 68-70.

   "1949 Snowmass Outing was A Great Success,"* Karl T.
   Neuberger, No. 370, October 1949, pp. 143, 152, Front cover
   illustration.

   Illustration, "Hagerman Peak, Reflection in Snowmass Lake,"
   Harry L. Standley, No. 388, April 1951, p. 43.

"Wet Tails in the Sunset," Paul Stewart, No. 467,
November 1957, p. 167, 1 Illustration p. 169.

"Hikes and Climbs from Crystal,"* John Beyer, No. 598,
October 1968, pp. 224-229, 1 Illustration, 1 Map.

HAGUES PEAK, 13,560'   Mummy Range, Rocky Mountain National Park
                         Trail Ridge 1957
Appalachia
"The First Ascent of A Glacier in Colorado," F. H. Chapin,
Vol. 5, December 1887, pp. 1-12, 6 Illustrations.

"Exploration,"* F. O. Carpenter, Vol. 5, December 1888, p. 234.
Ascent note, F. H. Chapin, J. R. Edmands, and C. E. Fay.

"The Peaks of Rocky Mountain National Park,"* Roger W. Toll,
Vol. 17, June 1929, pp. 252-260.

Trail and Timberline
"Fort Collins Goes Over the Top Again," Iris J. Jackson,
No. 73, October 1924, p. 7.

"The Mountain Ranges of Colorado,"* Kenneth Segerstrom,
No. 215, September 1936, pp. 109-115, 1 Map.

"Mountain Climbing and Statistics in Rocky Mountain National
Park,"* John C. Whitnah and Robert C. Peterson, No. 343,
July 1947, pp. 116-117.

HAHNS PEAK, 10,839'   North Park Range   Hahns Peak 1962
    Trail and Timberline
"Exploring the Mount Zirkel - Dome Peak Wild Area,"* Margaret
B. Chase, No. 464, August 1957, pp. 111-113, 1 Map following
p. 116.

HALLETT PEAK, 12,713'   Front Range, Rocky Mountain National Park
                         McHenrys Peak 1957
American Alpine Journal
"A First Ascent on the North Face of Hallett Peak," Ray
Northcutt, Vol. 11, 1959, pp. 233-236.
First ascent noted of the west (third) buttress, Ray Northcutt
and Harvey Carter.

"Hallett's Peak," Yvon Chouinard, Vol. 12, 1960, p. 129.
Variation note of the third buttress of the north face, Yvon
Chouinard and Ken Weeks.

"Hallett Peak," Robert Culp, Vol. 13, 1962, p. 229.
New route note on the second buttress, Tex Bossier and Robert
Culp.

"Hallett Peak, Right Wall of Third Buttress," Layton Kor,
Vol. 13, 1963, p. 492.
New route note, Butch van Tongeren and Layton Kor.

"Halletts Peak, Direct Second Buttress," Layton Kor, Vol. 14,
1965, pp. 432-433.
New route note, Tex Bossier and Layton Kor.

"Hallets (sic) Peak," Mark Hesse, Vol. 19, 1974, p. 154.
Girdle traverse route note of the second and third buttresses,
Larry Bruce and Mark Hesse.

Appalachia
"The Peaks of Rocky Mountain National Park,"* Roger W. Toll,
Vol. 17, June 1929, pp. 252-260.

"Accidents: Accident on Hallett Peak, Colorado," Benjamin G.
Ferris, Jr., Vol. 29, June 1953, p. 413.

Chicago Mountaineering Club Newsletter
"Flattop, Hallett, Otis, and Taylor Peaks,"* Barbara Heiberg,
Vol. 5, No. 5, November 1951, pp. 9-10, 1 Map p. 6.

Climbing
"Nostalgia/Part II Mundus Est Mons,"* Harvey T. Carter, No. 6,
March-April 1971, pp. 3-5.
First ascents noted of Hallett's Chimney and third buttress of
the north face.

Inside front cover illustration, "Rocky Mountain National Park,
Colo. Hallet's (sic) Peak (12,725') Reflected into Dream
Lake," Ed Cooper, No. 14, July-August 1972.

"Basecamp: Rocky Mountain National Park,"* Nos. 22 and 23,
Winter 1973-74, p. 36.
New route note to the left of the "Culp-Bossier" route,
Duncan Ferguson and Mark Hesse.
Girdle traverse note, Mark Hesse and Larry Bruce.

"View from Within: Colorado Rocky Mountain National Park,"*
Michael Covington, No. 29, March-April 1975, p. 31.
Solo free ascent note of "Northcutt-Carter" route, John Bragg.
Solo free ascent note of "Northcutt-Carter" route, Earl
Wiggins.

"Basecamp: Colorado,"* No. 37, July-August 1976, p. 4.
Ascent note of Hallett's Chimney, Duncan Ferguson and partner.

"Winter Climbing in Rocky Mountain National Park,"* Michael
Covington, No. 37, July-August 1976, pp. 7-13.
Winter ascent noted of the Jackson Johnson route, Layton Kor
and Dave Dornan.
Winter ascent noted of Hallett's Chimney, Brad Johnson and Dick
Jackson.
Winter ascent noted of the Northcutt Carter route, Dakers Gowan
(Gowans) and Mike Monger.

Harvard Mountaineering
"Climbing Notes, 1971: Rockies and the Northeast,"* Sam
Streibert, No. 19A, June 1972, pp. 53, 55.
Ascent note of the second and third buttresses.

Iowa Mountaineers Journal
"Colorado's Rockies,"* Ruth Norman, Vol. 1, No. 10,
February 1945, pp. 53-57.

"1963 Pikes Peak Crags Outing,"* Vol. 5, No. 5, 1965, p. 35.
Sixth ascent note of the second buttress of Hallett Peak,
Jackson and Johnson route.

"Pikes Peak Crags Outing,"* Harvey and Annie T. Carter, Vol. 5,
No. 5, 1965, pp. 54-59.

Off Belay
"Climbing at Rocky Mountain,"* Walt Fricke, No. 2, April 1972,
pp. 17-23, 1 Illustration, 2 Maps.

"National Parks Take Brunt of Mountaineering Traffic: Rocky
Mountain National Park, Colorado,"* No. 14, April 1974,
pp. 33-34.
Note on recorded ascents during the year.

"More on National Parks: Rocky Mountain National Park,"*
No. 21, June 1975, pp. 39, 41.
Note on recorded ascents during the year.

Summit
"On Fourth Attempt, Climbers Ascend North Face of Hallett's
Peak," Ray Northcutt, Vol. 3, No. 1, January 1957, pp. 17-21,
2 Illustrations.
First ascent noted of the west (third) buttress, Ray Northcutt
and Harvey Carter.

Trail and Timberline
Front cover water-color illustration, "Hallett Peak," Frances
Hoar, No. 291, March 1943.

"Mountain Climbing and Statistics in Rocky Mountain National
Park,"* John C. Whitnah and Robert C. Peterson, No. 343,
July 1947, pp. 116-117.

"An Ascent of Hallett's Chimney," Jim White, No. 459,
March 1957, p. 47.

"Winter Climbing: Hallett's Second Buttress," Layton Kor,
No. 495, March 1960, p. 33.
First winter ascent noted of the second buttress, Rick Tidrick
and Layton Kor.

"Climbing and Naming Hallett Peak - 1887," No. 558, June 1965,
pp. 111, 114-118, Front cover illustration.
From Mountaineering in Colorado by Frederick H. Chapin.

"Trip Report in CMC Files," Roger W. Toll, No. 558, June 1965, p. 123, Front cover illustration.

"The Antichamber: A New Route Across the Third Buttress of Halletts," Gary Spitzer, No. 566, February 1966, pp. 25-26, 32-34.
New route noted, Gary Spitzer and Warren Bleser.

"Boulder Rock Climbers: Faces of the Sixties,"* Bob Culp, No. 623, November 1970, pp. 238-244.
First ascent noted of the third buttress, Ray Northcutt and Harvey Carter.

"They're There Because ...,"* James McChristal, No. 687, March 1976, pp. 63-67.
Reprinted from The Colorado College Bulletin, May, 1975, pp. 43-45.
First ascent noted of the third buttress, Ray Northcutt and Harvey Carter.

HAMILTON PEAK, 13,658'   Sangre de Cristo Range   Blanca Peak 1967
    Trail and Timberline
        "Route to Blanca, Ellingwood and Hamilton from the Huerfano Basin,"* Rich Riefenberg, No. 637, January 1972, p. 6.

HANCOCK PEAK, 12,410'   Ruby Range   Oh-Be-Joyful 1961
    Trail and Timberline
        "Some Took the High Road,"* Stan Shepard, No. 455, November 1956, pp. 165-167.

"THE HAND", 13,150'[#]   San Juan Mountains, Sneffels Range
                        (Unnamed) Mount Sneffels 1967
American Alpine Journal
        "Climbing in the Mount Sneffels Region, Colorado,"* Dwight G. Lavender and T. Melvin Griffiths, Vol. 2, 1933, pp. 97-102, 1 Map.
        First ascent noted, Dwight G. Lavender, T. Melvin Griffiths, and Gordon Williams.

        "Southwestern Colorado Climbing Notes - 1932,"* Dwight G. Lavender, Vol. 2, 1933, p. 127.
        First ascent note, T. M. Griffiths, Gordon Williams, and Dwight G. Lavender.

The Mountaineering Journal (British)
        "Outstanding Climbing Centres in the South-Western Colorado Rockies,"* Dwight G. Lavender, Vol. 1, No. 4, June, July, August 1933, pp. 238-248.

Trail and Timberline
        "Editorial Notes,"* David Rosendale, No. 166, August 1932, p. 120.
        First ascent note, Dwight Lavender, Melvin Griffiths, and Gordon Williams.

_____

[#] Elevation figure from the American Alpine Journal.

Illustration,* "Aiguilles Northwest of Mt. Sneffels,
Photographed from Blaine Peak," D. G. Lavender, No. 171,
January 1933, p. 10.

"First Ascent Criteria,"* Carleton C. Long and Dwight G.
Lavender, No. 174, April 1933, pp. 48, 52-53.

Front cover illustration, "Traverse on Aiguille 'Hand',"
T. Melvin Griffiths, No. 175, May 1933.

HANDIES PEAK, 14,048'   San Juan Mountains   Handies Peak 1955
  <u>Appalachia</u>
    "All the 14,000's,"* Carl Melzer, Vol. 22, December 1939,
    pp. 466-479.

    "Club Excursions: Colorado Excursion, 1951,"* Jean K. Kent,
    Vol. 28, December 1951, pp. 584-589.

  <u>Mazama</u>
    "Ramble Number 21,"* A. H. Marshall, Vol. 21, No. 12,
    December 1939, pp. 55-61.

  <u>Summit</u>
    "A Leisurely Ascent of Handies Peak," Margaret Lamb, Vol. 13,
    No. 9, November 1967, pp. 22-25, 1 Illustration, 2 Maps.

  <u>Trail and Timberline</u>
    "Climbing 60,000 Feet in the San Juan,"* Carl Blaurock,
    No. 40, January 1922, pp. 2-3.

    Illustration, "Handies Peak, (Elevation, 14,103 Feet), Near
    Site of 1929 Summer Outing," Harvey T. Sethman, No. 126,
    April 1929, p. 13.

    "Handies Peak," L. R. Kendrick, No. 132, October 1929,
    pp. 6-7.

    "Editorial Notes," David Rosendale, No. 205, November 1935,
    p. 135.
    Note on register data.

    "Junior Jottings,"* No. 371, November 1949, pp. 172-173.

    "Handies, Redcloud, and Sunshine,"* Katy Wilson, No. 398,
    February 1952, p. 24.

    "Report on the 1952 San Juan Outing,"* Robert Ellingwood,
    No. 407, November 1952, pp. 159-161.

    "The Lake City Fourteens,"* Robin Simmons, No. 490,
    October 1959, pp. 141-142, 1 Illustration p. 139.

    "Silverton - Mountain Mecca,"* Art Porter, No. 620,
    August 1970, pp. 169, 171-172.

MT. HARVARD, 14,414'   Sawatch Range   Mt. Harvard 15M 1955

Alpine Journal
"The Rockies of Colorado,"* Evelio Echevarria C., Vol. 71,
May 1966, pp. 26-36, 1 Map, Bibliography.

American Alpine Journal
"Naming America's Mountains - The Colorado Rockies,"* Francis
P. Farquhar, Vol. 12, 1961, pp. 319-346.
First ascent noted, (S. F.) Sharpless and William Morris Davis.

"Club Activities: Simian Climbing Club,"* Curt Wagner,
Vol. 16, 1968, pp. 241-242.
Winter ascent note.

"Club Activities: Simian Outing Society," Rich Pestien,
Vol. 20, 1975, p. 234.
Winter attempt note.

Appalachia
"All the 14,000's,"* Carl Melzer, Vol. 22, December 1939,
pp. 466-479.

Sierra Club Bulletin
"Mountaineering Notes: Tour of the Six Highest Peaks in the
United States,"* edited by Francis P. Farquhar, Vol. 12,
No. 3, 1926, p. 307.
Ascent note on climbing the first six peaks in altitude in the
U.S., Captain John Henry Cuntz.

Trail and Timberline
"The High Peaks of the La Plata Mining Region,"* John L. J.
Hart, No. 159, January 1932, pp. 3-4, 14, 1 Illustration,
1 Map.

"The High Trails of Winter,"* Reynolds Morse, No. 194,
December 1934, pp. 163-165.

"Junior Outing,"* Anonymous, No. 227, October 1937, p. 107.

"A Conglomerate Review of the C.M.C. Summer Outing,
August 15-23, 1942 - Collegiate Range,"* Nancy Plowman, Eliot
Moses, Harold Brewer, Mary Wagner, No. 287, November 1942,
pp. 141-143, 1 Map p. 140.

"Colorado's Mountains are Higher than You Think,"* Arthur J.
McNair, No. 323, November 1945, pp. 139-142.

"Junior Fall Trips,"* Cynthia Cummings, No. 326,
February 1946, p. 27.

"Backpacking the Sawatch Range,"* Bud Boylard, No. 378,
June 1950, pp. 83-85, 90-91.

"Rocky Mountain Rambles,"* D. Williams, No. 381,
September 1950, pp. 140-141.
Reprinted from Colorado Springs Independent, Thursday,
August 3, 1950.

"New Altitudes for Some Colorado Peaks,"* Allen W. Greene,
No. 435, March 1955, pp. 57-58.

"A Climb of Harvard and Columbia,"* Russ Palmer, No. 486,
June 1959, pp. 77-78, 80.

"Harvard Lads," Hugh Kingery, No. 536, August 1963, p. 145.

"A New Harvard and Columbia Route,"* Ed H. Hilliard, No. 545,
May 1964, pp. 90-91.

"Anniversary Climbs - Mt. Harvard, Mt. Yale - August 1969,"*
Anne Sharples Frantz, No. 632, August 1971, pp. 168-170.

"HATCHET FACE",   Gore Range   (Unnamed) Willow Lakes 1970
    Trail and Timberline
        "Notes on the Gore Range, Summer, 1942,"* Carl Melzer,
        No. 284, August 1942, pp. 103-106, 1 Illustration.

HAYDEN PEAK, 13,561'   Elk Range   Hayden Peak 1960
    Chicago Mountaineering Club Newsletter
        "Colorado's Elk Mountains,"* Weldon F. Heald, Vol. 13, No. 6,
        October 1959, pp. 1-5, Front cover map.

    Climbing
        Illustration,* "Colorado's Mount Hayden (13,561') in Ski
        Country USA ... Star Peak is in the Background," Tom Merrill,
        No. 5, January 1971, p. 3.

    Trail and Timberline
        "Innocent Bystander,"* No. 259, July 1940, p. 110.
        Elevation note.

        "1873 Tells 1949,"* Louisa Ward Arps, No. 365, May 1949,
        pp. 68-70.

HAYDEN SPIRE, 12,480'   Front Range, Rocky Mountain National Park
                         McHenrys Peak 1957
    Trail and Timberline
        "Haydens Spire: The Northeast Chimney," Phil Carr, No. 508,
        April 1961, pp. 67-69, 1 Illustration.
        First ascent noted of the northeast chimney, Phil Carr and Bob
        Wellek.

        "Seven Spires: A Story of Some Climbs in Rocky Mountain
        National Park,"* Kent Keller, No. 651, March 1973, pp. 70-74.

"HEISSHORN", 13,411'   San Juan Mountains   (Unnamed) Wetterhorn Peak 1963
    The Mountaineering Journal (British)
        "Outstanding Climbing Centres in the South-Western Colorado
    Rockies,"* Dwight G. Lavender, Vol. 1, No. 4, June, July,
    August 1933, pp. 238-248.

    Trail and Timberline
        "Two New Peaks,"* Dwight Lavender, No. 132, October 1929,
    p. 6.
    (First) ascent noted, Dwight Lavender and Forrest Greenfield.

THE HEISSPITZ, 13,262'   Needle Mountains   Storm King Peak 1964
    American Alpine Journal
        "Southwestern Colorado Climbing Notes - 1932,"* Dwight G.
    Lavender, Vol. 2, 1933, pp. 128-129.
    First ascent note, Carleton Long and John Nelson.

    The Mountaineering Journal (British)
        Illustration,* "View Southwards from Point Pun in the
    Grenadiers," Carleton C. Long, Vol. 1, No. 4, June, July,
    August 1933, p. 242.

    Trail and Timberline
        "Editorial Notes,"* David Rosendale, No. 169, November 1932,
    p. 162.
    First ascent note.

        "Needle Mountaimania,"* Dave Lavender, No. 265, January 1941,
    pp. 3-4, 14-15, Front cover sketch map.

        "The Colorado Mountain Club Announces the Twenty-Eighth Annual
    Summer Outing,"* Henry Buchtel, Lewis Giesecke, Kenneth
    Segerstrom, No. 265, January 1941, pp. 9-14, 1 Map, Front cover
    sketch map.

        "Climbers Guide to Noname,"* No. 342, June 1947, pp. 97-98,
    1 Map.

        "Climber's Guide from Noname Creek,"* Henry Buchtel, No. 345,
    September 1947, pp. 143-144.

        "Revised Climbers' Guide from Noname Creek,"* William E.
    Davis, No. 502, October 1960, pp. 149-154, 1 Map.

"HERMIT PEAK", 13,322'   Sangre de Cristo Range
                         (Unnamed) Electric Peak 15M 1959
    Trail and Timberline
        "New Names in Sangres,"* No. 621, September 1970, p. 206.

HESPERUS MOUNTAIN, 13,232'   La Plata Range   La Plata 1963
    Trail and Timberline
        "The Mountain Ranges of Colorado,"* Kenneth Segerstrom,
    No. 215, September 1936, pp. 109-115, 1 Map.

Front cover illustration, "Mt. Hesperus in the La Plata
Mountains, Northwest of Durango, Colo.," Charlie Wunder,
courtesy Frontier Airlines, No. 382, October 1950.
Title information from T&T, No. 383, November 1950, p. 166.

"MT. HILDA",   Sawatch Range
   Trail and Timberline
      Illustration, "Hunky Dory Lake, Showing Camp and Mount Hilda,"
      No. 431, November 1954, p. 154.

"HIRSCHBERG PEAK", 13,312'(?)   Elk Range   (Unnamed) Pearl Pass 1961
   Trail and Timberline
      "Pearl Peak on Skis,"* Ken and Ruth Wright, No. 530,
      February 1963, pp. 31-32.

MT. OF THE HOLY CROSS, 14,005'   Sawatch Range
                                 Mount of the Holy Cross 1970
   Alpine Journal
      "The Rockies of Colorado,"* Evelio Echevarría C., Vol. 71,
      May 1966, pp. 26-36, 1 Map, Bibliography.

   American Alpine Journal
      "Technical Climbing in the Mountains of Colorado and Wyoming,"*
      Albert Russell Ellingwood, Vol. 1, 1930, pp. 140-147.

      "Naming America's Mountains - The Colorado Rockies,"* Francis
      P. Farquhar, Vol. 12, 1961, pp. 319-346.
      First ascent noted, James Terry Gardner and William H. Holmes.

      "Club Activities: Colorado College Mountain Club,"* Jim
      McChristal, Vol. 20, 1975, p. 229.
      Solo ascent note of the northeast buttress, Kurt Haire.

   Appalachia
      "The Call of Colorado,"* Edward W. Harnden, Vol. 16,
      June 1925, pp. 158-164, 1 Illustration.

      "And Now, Our Own Sacred Mountain," Vol. 19, December 1933,
      pp. 595-596.

   Canadian Alpine Journal
      "Climbing the Cross of Snow," Fritiof Fryxell, Vol. 21, 1933,
      pp. 28-32, 2 Illustrations.
      Ascent noted of the cross route, Fritiof Fryxell, Clarence
      Bendle, and Carl Ekblad.

   Mazama
      "Hither and Yon,"* A. H. Marshall, Vol. 14, No. 12,
      December 1932, pp. 32-38.

   Summit
      "Colorado's Mt. of the Holy Cross," Steve Trimble, Vol. 16,
      No. 4, May 1970, pp. 26-29, 3 Illustrations.

"The Cross of Snow," Thomas M. Jenkins, Vol. 22, No. 6,
December 1976, pp. 18-21, 44, 1 Illustration.
Ascent noted of the cross route, Jon Sudar, Stan Arnett, and
Thomas M. Jenkins.

Trail and Timberline
Illustration, "Mount of the Holy Cross," U.S. Forest Service,
No. 53, February 1923, p. 3.

"Twelfth Annual Outing,"* Constance Bouck, No. 61,
October 1923, pp. 1-2, 2 Illustrations p. 6.
Ascent noted of the cross route.

"The Mount of the Holy Cross," Fritiof Fryxell, No. 183,
January 1934, pp. 3-9, 14, 2 Illustrations.
First ascent noted, W. H. Holmes and J. T. Gardner.
Ascents of the cross route noted.

"Editorial Notes," David Rosendale, No. 183, January 1934,
pp. 10-11.
Reference note.

"Thomas Moran's Journey to the Mount of the Holy Cross in
1874," Fritiof Fryxell, No. 203, September 1935, pp. 103-105.

Front cover illustration, "Mount of the Holy Cross," No. 364,
April 1949.

Front cover illustration, "Mount of the Holy Cross," No. 427,
July 1954.

"Climb of Holy Cross," Carl Blaurock, No. 431, November 1954,
p. 156, 1 Illustration p. 154, 1 Illustration p. 155.

"Lieutenant Carpenter's Grasshopper," Gordon Alexander,
No. 523, July 1962, pp. 109-111, Front cover illustration.

"First Ascent of A Fourteener," Sean McWilliams, No. 555,
March 1965, pp. 56-57.

Illustration, "First Ascent of Holy Cross by Denver Juniors
After It Achieved the Magic Status of A Fourteen - Nov. 8,
1954," Elvis Guin, No. 567, March 1966, p. 46.

"Grasshopper Catching: Climbing Mt. of the Holy Cross? Bring
An Insect Net!" H. E. K., No. 569, May 1966, p. 89.

"Mt. Holy Cross Via the Cross," Dick Rosenow, No. 572,
August 1966, p. 138.

"A Controversy: William H. Jackson and Mount of the Holy
Cross," Robert L. Brown, No. 590, February 1968, pp. 37-41,
2 Illustrations.

MT. HOPE, 13,933'   Sawatch Range   Mount Elbert 1967
  Trail and Timberline
      "The High Peaks of the La Plata Mining Region,"* John L. J.
      Hart, No. 159, January 1932, pp. 3-4, 14, 1 Illustration,
      1 Map.

      "Some Trails of the La Plata Mining Region,"* Bruce and
      Elisabeth MacCannon, No. 159, January 1932, pp. 5-6.

      "Impressions of the Ice Mountain Outing," Lynne Horiuchi,
      No. 552, December 1964, pp. 188-189.

      "A Guide to Colorado's Almost-Fourteens,"* William A. Graves,
      No. 683, November 1975, pp. 225-227.

HORN PEAK, 13,450'   Sangre de Cristo Range   Horn Peak 1959
  Trail and Timberline
      "The Sangre de Cristo Range,"* Eva and Bill Rathbun, No. 460,
      April 1957, pp. 55-60, 64, 1 Illustration, 1 Map.

      "New Maps of the Sangre de Cristo Range,"* John L. J. Hart,
      No. 519, March 1962, pp. 32-33.

HORSETOOTH MOUNTAIN, 7,255'   Front Range   Horsetooth Reservoir 1962
  Trail and Timberline
      "A Trip to Horsetooth Mountain," Roy R. Murchison, No. 275,
      November 1941, pp. 151-152, 1 Illustration.

      "Guerilla Tactics Useful for Doggy Climbs: The Gentle Art of
      Freddy Peaking,"* Bob Michael, No. 689, May 1976, pp. 112-115.

HORSETOOTH PEAK, 10,344'   Front Range, Rocky Mountain National Park
                            Allens Park 1957
  Trail and Timberline
      "Undiscovered Jewels of Rocky Mountain National Park,"* R. D.
      Martin, No. 618, June 1970, pp. 132-134.

"THE HOUR GLASS", 13,382'   Williams Mountains   (Unnamed) Mt. Champion 1960
  Trail and Timberline
      "New Survey Figures,"* Kenneth Segerstrom, No. 171,
      January 1933, p. 12.
      First ascent note, Kenneth Segerstrom.

      "The Mountain Ranges of Colorado,"* Kenneth Segerstrom,
      No. 215, September 1936, pp. 109-115, 1 Map.

HOWARD MOUNTAIN, 12,810'   Never Summer Range, Rocky Mountain National Park
                            Mount Richthofen 1957
  Trail and Timberline
      "The Never Summers Revisited,"* Esther Holt, No. 437,
      May 1955, pp. 87-88, 98.

HUERFANO BUTTE, 6,166'   Eastern Colorado   Huerfano Butte 1969
  Trail and Timberline
      "Huerfano Butte - A Historic Site," Congressman John A.
      Martin, No. 248, August 1939, pp. 107-108, 1 Illustration.

"Huerfano Butte Monument," Caroline Sporleder Young, No. 402, June 1952, pp. 97-98, 1 Illustration, Front cover illustration.

"Historic Huerfano," James Grafton Rogers, No. 402, June 1952, p. 98.

HUMBOLDT PEAK, 14,064'   Sangre de Cristo Range   Crestone Peak 1967
  American Alpine Journal
    "Club Activities: Harvard Mountaineering Club,"* Edward C. Carman, Vol. 13, 1963, pp. 536-537.
    Winter ascent note, Dave Roberts, Don Jensen, and Bert Redmayne.

  Appalachia
    "All the 14,000's,"* Carl Melzer, Vol. 22, December 1939, pp. 466-479.

    "Club Excursions: Colorado, 1946,"* Emma Rutherford, Vol. 26, December 1946, pp. 261-264.

  Harvard Mountaineering
    "Christmas at 14,000 Feet,"* David S. Roberts, No. 16, May 1963, pp. 37-38.

  Trail and Timberline
    "Recent Trips: Humboldt Peak," No. 15, August 1919, p. 5.

    "More High Ones,"* No. 52, January 1923, pp. 12-13.

    "A Stormy Day on Humboldt," Grace M. Harvey, No. 75, December 1924, pp. 2-5, 1 Illustration.

    "A Note on Certain Elevations,"* Albert R. Ellingwood, No. 93, June 1926, pp. 4, 6.

    "Those Glorious Sangre de Cristos,"* Cedric Kaub, Russell Briggs, Evelyn Runnette, No. 236, July 1938, pp. 78-79, Front cover illustration.

    "Outing - Not: The Outing. But: Our Outing,"* E. R., No. 238, September-October 1938, pp. 99-101.

    "The Juniors and the Crestones,"* Rex Young, No. 251, November 1939, pp. 156-157.

    "Unofficial Summer Outing,"* Bobbie Buchtel, No. 359, November 1948, pp. 161-162.

    "A Poor Man's Summer Outing or Four Days of Footwork in the Crestones,"* Lester A. Michel, No. 422, February 1954, pp. 17-19.

    "Denver Junior Summer Outing,"* Jim Ross, No. 459, March 1957, pp. 39-40.

"The Sangre de Cristo Range,"* Eva and Bill Rathbun, No. 460, April 1957, pp. 55-60, 64, 1 Map.

"Humboldt Peak in April," Wilbur Arnold, No. 482, February 1959, pp. 29, 31.

"Crestone Outing,"* Wilbur Arnold, No. 521, May 1962, pp. 73-74.

"Fun at the Crestones,"* J. O. Rose, No. 526, October 1962, pp. 159-160, 166, 1 Illustration p. 167.

Illustration, "From Humboldt at Sunset," John A. Krimmel, No. 609, September 1969, p. 169.

Illustration, "Top of Humboldt," Sam Alfend, No. 611, November 1969, p. 212.

"HUNKYDORY PEAK",   Sawatch Range
    Trail and Timberline
        "Twelfth Annual Outing,"* Constance Bouck, No. 61, October 1923, pp. 1-2, 1 Illustration p. 6.

HUNTS PEAK, 13,067'   Sangre de Cristo Range   Howard 15M 1959
    Trail and Timberline
        "New Maps of the Sangre de Cristo Range,"* John L. J. Hart, No. 519, March 1962, pp. 32-33.

        "Sangre de Cristo Saga,"* Lester A. Michel, with Wilbur F. Arnold, No. 524, August 1962, pp. 123-126, 133.

HURON PEAK, 14,003'   Sawatch Range   Mt. Harvard 15M 1955
    American Alpine Journal
        "Club Activities: Colorado Mountain Club,"* Anne B. Kenyon, Vol. 10, 1957, pp. 183-184.
        Ascent note of new (54th) 14,000' peak.

    Trail and Timberline
        "The High Peaks of the La Plata Mining Region,"* John L. J. Hart, No. 159, January 1932, pp. 3-4, 14, 1 Illustration, 1 Map.

        "Some Trails of the La Plata Mining Region,"* Bruce and Elisabeth MacCannon, No. 159, January 1932, pp. 5-6.

        "Topographic Surveys Proposed," K. S., No. 186, April 1934, p. 45.

        "First Official Measurement of Many 14,000 Foot Peaks,"* John L. J. Hart, No. 446, February 1956, pp. 29-30.

        "Gala Day on Huron," Hugh W. Hetherington, No. 452, August 1956, p. 125.

        "Climb of Huron Peak," Alice Tigges, No. 453, September 1956, p. 136.

Illustration, "Juniors (and Some Seniors) on Top of Mount Huron," No. 459, March 1957, p. 43.

Front cover illustration, "On Huron Peak," William Hirth, Jr., No. 689, May 1976.

"PEAK I" ("THE SPIDER"), 12,692'   Gore Range
                                    (Unnamed) Vail East 1970
                                    (Unnamed) Minturn 15M 1934, 12,655'
    Trail and Timberline
        "A Day in the Mountains,"* Kurt Beam, No. 532, April 1963,
        pp. 67-68, 71.

        "Names on the Gores,"* William Bird Mounsey, No. 568,
        April 1966, pp. 63-65, 1 Map.

ICE MOUNTAIN, 13,920'   Sawatch Range   Mt. Harvard 15M 1955
See also THE THREE APOSTLES
    American Alpine Journal
        "Colorado Climbing Notes, 1936,"* Kenneth Segerstrom, Vol. 3,
        1937, p. 109.
        Probable fourth ascent note, Elwyn Arps and Colorado Mountain
        Club party.

    Trail and Timberline
        "How not to Climb Ice Mountain," Josiah G. Holland, No. 157,
        November 1931, pp. 171-172, 182, 4 Illustrations.
        First ascent noted, John L. J. Hart.

        "The High Peaks of the La Plata Mining Region,"* John L. J.
        Hart, No. 159, January 1932, pp. 3-4, 14, 1 Map.

        "New Survey Figures,"* Kenneth Segerstrom, No. 171,
        January 1933, p. 12.

        "Group Activities: Denver Group,"* No. 179, September 1933,
        p. 129.
        Ascent note, Carl Blaurock, L. R. Kendrick, and party.

        "Ice Mountain," Evelyn Runnette, No. 214, August 1936,
        pp. 93-95, 2 Illustrations, Front cover illustration.

        "First Official Measurement of Many 14,000 Foot Peaks,"* John
        L. J. Hart, No. 446, February 1956, pp. 29-30.

        Illustration, "The Valley Leading in to Ice Mountain,"
        No. 459, March 1957, p. 42.

        Front cover illustration,* "The Three Apostles, Ice Mountain
        in the Center," Gale Kehmeier, No. 463, July 1957.

        Illustration, "Telephoto of Ice Mountain," No. 468,
        December 1957, p. 184.

        "A Guide to Colorado's Almost-Fourteens,"* William A. Graves,
        No. 683, November 1975, pp. 225-227.

MT. IDA, 12,880'   Front Range, Rocky Mountain National Park
                    Grand Lake 1958
    Trail and Timberline
        "Thunder in the Rockies,"* Richard F. Fleck, No. 631,
        July 1971, pp. 151-157.

THE INDEX, 13,400'   Needle Mountains   Snowdon Peak 1964
  American Alpine Journal
        "Colorado Climbing Notes, 1934,"* Carleton C. Long, Vol. 2,
        1935, p. 416.
        Reconnaissance and partial ascent note, T. Melvin Griffiths,
        Frank McClintock, and H. L. McClintock.

        "Colorado Climbing Notes, 1935,"* Carleton C. Long, Vol. 2,
        1936, p. 546.
        Ascent note of the second summit, H. L. McClintock, Frank
        McClintock, and Lewis Giesecke.

        "Colorado Climbing Notes, 1937,"* Carl Blaurock, Vol. 3, 1938,
        p. 218.
        First ascent note, Melvin Griffiths and party.

  Harvard Mountaineering
        "Climbing Notes, 1964: Colorado Needles,"* Matt Hale, No. 17,
        May 1965, pp. 59-60.
        Ascent note of middle pinnacle and southern (highest)
        pinnacle, Matt Hale and Dave Roberts.

  The Mountaineering Journal (British)
        "Outstanding Climbing Centres in the South-Western Colorado
        Rockies,"* Dwight G. Lavender, Vol. 1, No. 4, June, July,
        August 1933, pp. 238-248, 1 Illustration.

  Trail and Timberline
        "The Needle Mountains Expedition,"* Carleton C. Long, No. 181,
        November 1933, pp. 155-157, 166.

        "The 1934 Climbing Season in Colorado,"* Carleton C. Long,
        No. 196, February 1935, pp. 15-18.
        Reconnaissance and ascent note of north (lower) summit, Melvin
        Griffiths, H. L. McClintock, and Frank McClintock.

        "A Route Up the Index," H. L. McClintock, No. 232, March 1938,
        pp. 27-28, 1 Illustration, Front cover illustration.
        First ascent noted of the south (highest) pinnacle, Mel
        Griffiths, Frank McClintock, and H. L. McClintock.

        "Noname Prospects,"* Mel Griffiths, No. 340, April 1947,
        pp. 56-59.

        "Climbers Guide to Noname,"* No. 342, June 1947, pp. 97-98,
        1 Map.

        "Pigeon, Turret, Peak 12, Etc. or the Fly Camp of '53,"*
        William E. Davis, No. 419, November 1953, pp. 155-158.

        "Letters to the Editor,"* Martin A. Etter, No. 610,
        October 1969, p. 187.
        North ridge note.

INDIAN LOOKOUT MOUNTAIN, 6,533'   Front Range   Lyons 1968
    Trail and Timberline
        "Foothill Climbs Near Longmont,"* Dave Taylor, No. 649,
    January 1973, pp. 3-5, 1 Illustration.

"INNOMINATA PEAK", 13,118'   Front Range, Rocky Mountain National Park
See also ISOLATION PEAK   (Unnamed) Isolation Peak 1958
    Trail and Timberline
        "A Glimpse of Wild Basin,"* Albert Russell Ellingwood,
    No. 109, November 1927, pp. 3-6.

"IRON MOUNTAIN", 12,528'   Elk Range   (Unnamed) Pearl Pass 1961
    Trail and Timberline
        "The Lighter Side,"* Hal Brewer, No. 478, October 1958,
    pp. 135, 138.

IRON NIPPLE, 13,480'   Sangre de Cristo Range   Blanca Peak 1967
    Trail and Timberline
        "The Upper Huerfano - Reflections,"* Nancy Booth, No. 624,
    December 1970, pp. 254-255, 1 Illustration.

        "Lower Peaks in the Massif,"* Jim Schofield, No. 638,
    February 1972, pp. 43-46.

ISOLATION PEAK, 13,118'   Front Range, Rocky Mountain National Park
See also "INNOMINATA PEAK" Isolation Peak 1958
    Trail and Timberline
        "Note," No. 278, February 1942, p. 14.
    Note on naming.

        "Denver Notes,"* Vera E. DeVries, No. 285, September 1942,
    p. 120.
    Ascent and naming note.

        "Junior Journeys,"* Molly Sethman, No. 298, October 1943,
    pp. 127-128.

ITALIAN MOUNTAIN, 13,378'   Elk Range   Pearl Pass 1961
    American Alpine Journal
        "The Rocky Mountains of the United States,"* Howard Palmer,
    Vol. 1, 1931, pp. 360-367.

    Chicago Mountaineering Club Newsletter
        "Colorado's Elk Mountains,"* Weldon F. Heald, Vol. 13, No. 6,
    October 1959, pp. 1-5, Front cover map.

    Trail and Timberline
        "1873 Tells 1949,"* Louisa Ward Arps, No. 365, May 1949,
    pp. 68-70.

"PEAK J", 12,942'   Gore Range   (Unnamed) Vail East 1970
                                 (Unnamed) Minturn 15M 1934, 12,921'
  American Alpine Journal
    "Colorado Climbing Notes, 1935,"* Carleton C. Long, Vol. 2,
    1936, p. 545.
    First ascent note, Everett Long, Carl Blaurock, and party.
    Second ascent note, Bob Lewis, Fred Nagel, John Nagel, and
    Gene Schaetzel.

  Chicago Mountaineering Club Newsletter
    "Ascents by Club Members,"* Stanley Midgely, Vol. 1, No. 3,
    September to December 1945, pp. 10-11.
    First ascent note, Stanley Midgely (and party).

  Trail and Timberline
    "The Gore Range Outing,"* Everett Long, No. 204, October 1935,
    pp. 111-113.
    First ascent noted, Carl Blaurock, Everett Long, and party.
    Second ascent noted, Bob Lewis, Fred Nagel, John Nagel, and
    Gene Schaetzel.

MT. JACKSON, 13,670'   Sawatch Range   Mount Jackson 1970
  Trail and Timberline
    "Mount Jackson: A Mountaineer's Mountain," Roger Fuehrer,
    No. 687, March 1976, pp. 69-70.

JACQUE PEAK, 13,205'   Gore Range   Copper Mountain 1970
  Appalachia
    "News Flashes from Camp Hale: Still Going Strong,"* José M.
    Acebo, Vol. 24, June 1943, pp. 386-388.

JAGGED MOUNTAIN, 13,824'   Needle Mountains   Storm King Peak 1964
  American Alpine Journal
    "Southwestern Colorado Climbing Notes - 1933,"* Dwight G.
    Lavender, Vol. 2, 1934, p. 257.
    First ascent note, C. C. Long, T. M. Griffiths, L. V.
    Giesecke, Dr. H. L. McClintock, and Dwight G. Lavender.

    "Colorado Climbing Notes, 1934,"* Carleton C. Long, Vol. 2,
    1935, p. 416.
    Second ascent note, William P. House and Miss Elizabeth
    Woolsey.

  Appalachia
    "Alpina,"* K. A. H., Vol. 19, December 1933, p. 594.
    First ascent note.

    "Present-Day Rock Climbing in Colorado,"* Carleton C. Long,
    Vol. 20, June 1934, pp. 132-134.
    First ascent noted, San Juan Mountaineers.

  Chicago Mountaineering Club Newsletter
    "Needles Outing of the American Alpine Club,"* Dave Bidwell,
    Vol. 7, No. 5, November 1953, pp. 10-12.

Climbing

Illustration,* "Descent Between Jagged and Leviathan Peaks,"
No. 15, September-October 1972, p. 25.

The Mountaineering Journal (British)

"Outstanding Climbing Centres in the South-Western Colorado
Rockies,"* Dwight G. Lavender, Vol. 1, No. 4, June, July,
August 1933, pp. 238-248, 1 Illustration.

"Correspondence,"* Dwight Lavender, Vol. 2, No. 1, December,
January, February 1933-34, pp. 47-51.
First ascent note.

Trail and Timberline

"The Needle Mountains Expedition,"* Carleton C. Long, No. 181,
November 1933, pp. 155-157, 166, 1 Illustration, Front cover
illustration.
First ascent noted, Dwight G. Lavender, T. Melvin Griffiths,
Lewis V. Giesecke, Dr. H. L. McClintock, and Carleton C. Long.

"The 1933 Climbing Season in Colorado,"* Carleton C. Long,
No. 184, February 1934, pp. 20-23.
First ascent note, San Juan Mountaineers.

"The 1934 Climbing Season in Colorado,"* Carleton C. Long,
No. 196, February 1935, pp. 15-18.
Second ascent note, William P. House and Miss Elizabeth
Woolsey.

"The Colorado Mountain Club Announces the Twenty-Eighth Annual
Summer Outing,"* Henry Buchtel, Lewis Giesecke, Kenneth
Segerstrom, No. 265, January 1941, pp. 9-14, 2 Illustrations,
1 Map, Front cover sketch map.

"An Ascent of Jagged Mountain," Vera DeVries, No. 274,
October 1941, pp. 139-140, 2 Illustrations.

"Noname Prospects,"* Mel Griffiths, No. 340, April 1947,
pp. 56-59.

"Climbers Guide to Noname,"* No. 342, June 1947, pp. 97-98,
1 Map, 1 Illustration p. 94.

"Climber's Guide from Noname Creek,"* Henry Buchtel, No. 345,
September 1947, pp. 143-144.

Illustration,* "Upper Basin of No-Name Creek - Peaks Left to
Right: Jagged Mtn., Peak 10, Knifepoint, and North Ridge of
Sunlight Peak," No. 419, November 1953, p. 156.

"The Needles, June 1957,"* Gene White, No. 471, March 1958,
pp. 31-35.

"Revised Climbers' Guide from Noname Creek,"* William E.
Davis, No. 502, October 1960, pp. 149-154, 1 Map.

Illustration,* "Jagged Peak, Peak Ten and Knife Point from
Scepter," No. 543, March 1964, p. 42.

"Trails of the Western Weminuche,"* William Weihofen, Ralph
Rosenbaum, and Henri Navelet, No. 608, August 1969, pp. 144-
147, Front cover illustration.

"Letters to the Editor,"* Martin A. Etter, No. 610,
October 1969, p. 187.
Note on ridges.

"Jagged," Steve Gaskill, No. 616, April 1970, pp. 85-86,
1 Illustration.

JAMES PEAK, 13,294'   Front Range   Empire 1958
  Alpine Journal
      Illustration, "The Sawatch Range from the Top of James Peak,
      13,295 Ft., Looking South-West," Evelio Echevarría C.,
      Vol. 71, May 1966, Following p. 30 (No. 11).

  American Alpine Journal
      "Colorado Climbing Notes, 1936,"* Kenneth Segerstrom, Vol. 3,
      1937, p. 108.
      Ski ascent note, A. W. Kidder.

      "Naming America's Mountains - The Colorado Rockies,"* Francis
      P. Farquhar, Vol. 12, 1961, pp. 319-346.

  Climbing
      "'Anti-Solidity', James Peak (13,294'), Colo.," No. 14, July-
      August 1972, p. 36.
      Possible first ascent note of this route on the northeast
      face, Gary Schaecher and Art Greslin.

  Trail and Timberline
      "Trailing the Colorado Mountain Club on the High Peaks,"*
      Lloyd Shaw, No. 17, January 1920, pp. 5-6.

      "The 1933 Climbing Season in Colorado,"* Carleton C. Long,
      No. 184, February 1934, pp. 20-23.
      Ascent note of the east face via middle couloir, Kenneth
      Segerstrom and Carleton C. Long.

      "Editorial Notes," Kenneth Segerstrom, No. 211, May 1936,
      p. 46.
      Ski ascent note, A. W. Kidder and Eliot B. Moses.

      "Uphill to James," Robert LeMassena, No. 378, June 1950,
      pp. 89-90.

      "A Winter Climb of James Peak," Damon Phinney, No. 505,
      January 1961, pp. 3-4, 1 Illustration.

      "The Colorado Mountaineer: CMC Winter Mountaineering School,"*
      Gregg Blomberg, No. 542, February 1964, pp. 28-29.

JOE MILLS MOUNTAIN, 11,078'   Front Range, Rocky Mountain National Park
                                McHenrys Peak 1957
    Trail and Timberline
        "Undiscovered Jewels of Rocky Mountain National Park,"* R. D.
        Martin, No. 618, June 1970, pp. 132-134.

JUPITER MOUNTAIN, 13,830'   Needle Mountains   Columbine Pass 1973
    American Alpine Journal
        "Colorado Climbing Notes, 1937,"* Carl Blaurock, Vol. 3, 1938,
        p. 218.
        Traverse note of ridge from Jupiter Mountain to Mt. Eolus,
        Jack Seerley.

    Trail and Timberline
        "Where We Went and What We Climbed,"* No. 25, October 1920,
        pp. 8-11.

        Illustration,* "Mts. Windom (Left Center) and Jupiter (Right)
        from Camp after A Light Fresh Snow had Fallen," No. 107,
        September 1927, p. 2.

        "Outing Ridge Work,"* Forest Greenfield, No. 227,
        October 1937, pp. 102-103, 105.
        Traverse noted of ridge from Jupiter - Windom - Sunlight - to
        start of Needle Ridge, Jack Heeney and party.

        "Chicago Basin Expedition,"* Al Ossinger, No. 559, July 1965,
        pp. 131-133.

"PEAK K", 12,920'   Gore Range   (Unnamed) Vail East 1970
                                   (Unnamed) Minturn 15M 1934, 12,950'
    American Alpine Journal
        "Colorado Climbing Notes, 1935,"* Carleton C. Long, Vol. 2,
        1936, p. 545.
        First ascent note, Everett Long, Carl Blaurock, and party.

    Chicago Mountaineering Club Newsletter
        "Ascents by Club Members,"* Stanley Midgely, Vol. 1, No. 3,
        September to December 1945, pp. 10-11.
        First ascent note, Stanley Midgely and party.

    Trail and Timberline
        "The Gore Range Outing,"* Everett Long, No. 204, October 1935,
        pp. 111-113.
        First ascent noted, Carl Blaurock, Everett Long, and party.

KELLER MOUNTAIN, 13,085'   Gore Range   Willow Lakes 1970
    Chicago Mountaineering Club Newsletter
        "Ascents by Club Members,"* Harold Walton, Vol. 1, No. 3,
        September to December 1945, pp. 10-11.
        Possible first ascent note on two summits about 13,050' on
        ridge running west and southwest about three quarters of a
        mile and a mile and a half from summit of Keller Mountain,
        Harold Walton.

KELSO MOUNTAIN, 13,164'   Front Range   Grays Peak 1958
    Trail and Timberline
        "High Lights on the Ten Annual Outings: Fourth Annual Outing -
        Clear Creek Basin," Grace M. Harvey, No. 43, April 1922,
        pp. 29-30.

KENDALL PEAK, 13,451'   San Juan Mountains   Howardsville 1955
    Trail and Timberline
        "Silverton - Mountain Mecca,"* Art Porter, No. 620,
        August 1970, pp. 169, 171-172.

KENNY MOUNTAIN, 9,290'   Front Range   Panorama Peak 1962
    Trail and Timberline
        "Foothill Climbs Near Longmont,"* Dave Taylor, No. 649,
        January 1973, pp. 3-5.

"KENOSHA CONE", 12,323'   Kenosha Mountains   (Unnamed) Mount Logan 1945
See SOUTH TWIN CONE PEAK

KIOWA PEAK, 13,276'   Front Range, Indian Peaks   Ward 1957
    Alpine Journal
        "The Rockies of Colorado,"* Evelio Echevarria C., Vol. 71,
        May 1966, pp. 26-36, 1 Map, Bibliography.

    Trail and Timberline
        "Our Indian Peaks,"* Karl E. Boehm, No. 497, May 1960, pp. 73-
        74.

"KISMET", 13,694'   San Juan Mountains, Sneffels Range
                    (Unnamed) Mount Sneffels 1967
    American Alpine Journal
        "Climbing in the Mount Sneffels Region, Colorado,"* Dwight G.
        Lavender and T. Melvin Griffiths, Vol. 2, 1933, pp. 97-102,
        1 Map.
        First ascent noted, Gordon Williams, Melvin Griffiths, and
        Dwight Lavender.

        "Southwestern Colorado Climbing Notes - 1932,"* Dwight G.
        Lavender, Vol. 2, 1933, pp. 127-128.
        First ascent note, Gordon Williams, T. M. Griffiths, and
        Dwight G. Lavender.

        "Colorado Climbing Notes, 1934,"* Carleton C. Long, Vol. 2,
        1935, p. 417.
        Possible second ascent note, H. M. Walters and party.

    The Mountaineering Journal (British)
        "Outstanding Climbing Centres in the South-Western Colorado
        Rockies,"* Dwight G. Lavender, Vol. 1, No. 4, June, July,
        August 1933, pp. 238-248.

    Trail and Timberline
        "Editorial Notes,"* David Rosendale, No. 166, August 1932,
        p. 120, 1 Illustration p. 116.
        First ascent note, Dwight Lavender, Melvin Griffiths, and
        Gordon Williams.

        Illustration, "Aiguille Kismet from the North," D. G.
        Lavender, No. 169, November 1932, p. 161.

        Illustration,* "Base Camp of the S.J.M. Geological Survey
        (11,060 Ft.) Kismet and Sneffels in Background," Lavender and
        Griffiths, No. 178, August 1933, p. 107.

        "1934 Summer Outing Climbs,"* Everett C. Long, No. 192,
        October 1934, pp. 131-133.

        Illustration, "Aiguille Kismet from the North," Dwight G.
        Lavender, No. 400, April 1952, p. 79.

KIT CARSON MOUNTAIN, 14,165'   Sangre de Cristo Range   Crestone Peak 1967
    American Alpine Journal
        "Technical Climbing in the Mountains of Colorado and Wyoming,"*
        Albert Russell Ellingwood, Vol. 1, 1930, pp. 140-147.

        "American Rockies - Notes, 1929,"* J. L. J. Hart, Vol. 1,
        1930, pp. 240-241.
        Fifth recorded ascent note, Colorado Mountain Club party.
        First ascent note, Albert Ellingwood and Eleanor Davis, (and
        party).
        Probable second ascent note, Carl Blaurock and William F. Ervin.
        Third ascent note, Colorado Mountain Club party.
        Fourth ascent note, first of the (south) east summit, Stephen
        H. Hart, Henry Buchtel, and party.

Appalachia
"All the 14,000's,"* Carl Melzer, Vol. 22, December 1939,
pp. 466-479.

"Club Excursions: Colorado, 1946,"* Emma Rutherford, Vol. 26,
December 1946, pp. 261-264, 1 Illustration.

Harvard Mountaineering
"Christmas at 14,000 Feet,"* David S. Roberts, No. 16,
May 1963, pp. 37-38.

Sierra Club Bulletin
"Notes and Correspondence: Colorado Mountain Club,"* Vol. 15,
No. 1, February 1930, pp. 111-112.
Ascent note, first since 1925.

Trail and Timberline
"More High Ones,"* No. 52, January 1923, pp. 12-13.

"Climbing in the Sangre de Cristo,"* Albert R. Ellingwood,
No. 81, June 1925, pp. 1-5.
First ascent noted.

"Ascent of Kit Carson," Henry Buchtel, No. 84, September 1925,
p. 4.
First ascent noted of the southeast summit, Elwyn Arps, Henry
Buchtel, and party.

"A Note on Certain Elevations,"* Albert R. Ellingwood, No. 93,
June 1926, pp. 4, 6.

"Climbing Notes,"* No. 144, October 1930, p. 9.
Fifth recorded ascent note, first since 1925, Colorado
Mountain Club party.

"Those Glorious Sangre de Cristos,"* Cedric Kaub, Russell
Briggs, Evelyn Runnette, No. 236, July 1938, pp. 78-79.

"Outing - Not: The Outing. But: Our Outing,"* E. R., No. 238,
September-October 1938, pp. 99-101.

"14,000 Feet,"* Russell Briggs, No. 246, June 1939, p. 77.

"The Juniors and the Crestones,"* Rex Young, No. 251,
November 1939, pp. 156-157, 1 Illustration.

"Kit Carson - A Name Worthy of A Peak," Fletcher W. Birney
Jr., No. 355, July 1948, pp. 104-105.

"Unofficial Summer Outing,"* Bobbie Buchtel, No. 359,
November 1948, pp. 161-162.

"Kit Carson Conquered," Wilbur F. Arnold, No. 380,
August 1950, pp. 124-126.
Southwest face ascent noted, Joe Merhar and Wilbur F. Arnold.

"After Eleven Years or How Much Can One Forget?" Dwight Hamilton, No. 398, February 1952, pp. 19-20, Front cover illustration.

"A Poor Man's Summer Outing or Four Days of Footwork in the Crestones,"* Lester A. Michel, No. 422, February 1954, pp. 17-19.

"Kit Carson by Instruments - Almost," John Devitt, No. 422, February 1954, p. 19.

"A Rugged Ten-Day Outing,"* Neil Wernette, No. 426, June 1954, pp. 83-84.

"Denver Junior Summer Outing,"* Jim Ross, No. 459, March 1957, pp. 39-40.

"The Sangre de Cristo Range,"* Eva and Bill Rathbun, No. 460, April 1957, pp. 55-60, 64, 1 Map.

"Crestone Outing,"* Wilbur Arnold, No. 521, May 1962, pp. 73-74.

"Fun at the Crestones,"* J. O. Rose, No. 526, October 1962, pp. 159-160, 166.

"A Compendium of Routes on Kit Carson," Paul Stewart, Donald J. Liska, Al Ossinger, No. 603, March 1969, pp. 45-48, 1 Illustration, 1 Map.
North ridge ascent noted, Donald Liska and party.
Ascent noted from Copper Gulch to west summit and main summit, Al Ossinger and Rich Schaefer.

"Kit Carson Peak Revisited," Al Ossinger, No. 627, March 1971, pp. 70-71, 1 Illustration.

KNIFE POINT, 13,265'   Needle Mountains   Storm King Peak 1964
American Alpine Journal
    "Colorado Climbing Notes, 1934,"* Carleton C. Long, Vol. 2, 1935, p. 416.
    First ascent note, T. Melvin Griffiths, Frank McClintock, and H. L. McClintock.

Trail and Timberline
    "The 1934 Climbing Season in Colorado,"* Carleton C. Long, No. 196, February 1935, pp. 15-18.
    First ascent note, Melvin Griffiths, H. L. McClintock, and Frank McClintock.

    Front cover illustration, "Knife Point at Head of Noname Creek," Griffiths-Williams, No. 224, June 1937.

    "Noname Prospects,"* Mel Griffiths, No. 340, April 1947, pp. 56-59.

"Climbers Guide to Noname,"* No. 342, June 1947, pp. 97-98,
1 Map, 1 Illustration p. 94.

"Climber's Guide from Noname Creek,"* Henry Buchtel, No. 345,
September 1947, pp. 116-117.

Illustration,* "Upper Basin of No-Name Creek - Peaks Left to
Right: Jagged Mtn., Peak 10, Knifepoint, and North Ridge of
Sunlight Peak," No. 419, November 1953, p. 156.

"Knife Point Idyll," John Filsinger, No. 502, October 1960,
pp. 144-145, 1 Illustration.

"Revised Climbers' Guide from Noname Creek,"* William E.
Davis, No. 502, October 1960, pp. 149-154, 1 Map.

"Those Glorious Needles," Barry Tobin, No. 543, March 1964,
pp. 51-52, 1 Illustration p. 42.

"Trails of the Western Weminuche,"* William Weihofen, Ralph
Rosenbaum, and Henri Navelet, No. 608, August 1969, pp. 144-
147.

"Letters to the Editor,"* Martin A. Etter, No. 610,
October 1969, p. 187.
West face note.

Illustration, "Knifepoint," Steve Gaskill, No. 616,
April 1970, p. 89.

KNOBTOP MOUNTAIN, 12,331'   Front Range, Rocky Mountain National Park
                            McHenrys Peak 1957
Trail and Timberline
    "Circle Trips in RMNP,"* William C. Ramaley, No. 630,
June 1971, pp. 125-128.

MT. KREUTZER, 13,120'   Sawatch Range   Mt. Harvard 15M 1955
American Alpine Journal
    "Club Activities: Colorado Mountain Club," Anne B. Kenyon,
Vol. 11, 1959, pp. 334-336.
Note on naming.

Trail and Timberline
    "Along the Trail," W. L. M., No. 475, July 1958, p. 99.
Note on naming.

    "Mt. Kreutzer," Laura Makepeace, No. 477, September 1958,
pp. 117-118.

    "Denver Group Notes,"* Sophia Tranas, No. 480, December 1958,
p. 171.
Ascent and naming note.

"THE KURTZHORN", 13,200'   Needle Mountains   (Unnamed) Storm King Peak 1964
Trail and Timberline
    "The Grenadiers in Winter,"* David S. Roberts, No. 547,
July 1964, pp. 111-117.

"PEAK L", 13,213'   Gore Range   (Unnamed) Vail East 1970
                                   (Unnamed) Minturn 15M 1934, 13,193'
    American Alpine Journal
        "Colorado Climbing Notes, 1934,"* Carleton C. Long, Vol. 2,
        1935, p. 416.
        First ascent note, Colorado Mountain Club party.

        "Colorado Climbing Notes, 1935,"* Carleton C. Long, Vol. 2,
        1936, p. 545.
        Second ascent note, Charles Moore and party.

    Trail and Timberline
        "The 1934 Climbing Season in Colorado,"* Carleton C. Long,
        No. 196, February 1935, pp. 15-18.
        First ascent note, CMC party.

        "The Gore Range Outing,"* Everett Long, No. 204, October 1935,
        pp. 111-113.
        (Second) ascent noted, Charles Moore and party.

LA PLATA PEAK, 14,336'   Sawatch Range   Mount Elbert 1967
    Alpine Journal
        "The Rockies of Colorado,"* Evelio Echevarría C., Vol. 71,
        May 1966, pp. 26-36, 1 Map, Bibliography.

    American Alpine Journal
        "The Rocky Mountains of the United States,"* Howard Palmer,
        Vol. 1, 1931, pp. 360-367.

    Appalachia
        "All the 14,000's,"* Carl Melzer, Vol. 22, December 1939,
        pp. 466-479.

        "Excursions: August Camp, 1956,"* David Wilson, Vol. 31,
        December 1956, pp. 259-261.

    Summit
        "Analysis of Mountaineering Accidents,"* Vol. 7, No. 7,
        July 1961, pp. 2-5.
        (From the American Alpine Club annual report).

    Trail and Timberline
        Illustration, "La Plata Mountain (14,332 Feet) Sawatch Range,"
        Albert Haanstad, No. 17, January 1920, p. 27.

        "The High Peaks of the La Plata Mining Region,"* John L. J.
        Hart, No. 159, January 1932, pp. 3-4, 14, 1 Map.

        "Some Trails of the La Plata Mining Region,"* Bruce and
        Elisabeth MacCannon, No. 159, January 1932, pp. 5-6.

        "14,000 Feet,"* Russell Briggs, No. 246, June 1939, p. 77.

        "Fourth of July Outing - Junior Style,"* Dorothy Sethman,
        No. 308, August 1944, p. 95, 1 Illustration.

"Colorado's Mountains are Higher than You Think,"* Arthur J. McNair, No. 323, November 1945, pp. 139-142.

"Reaching the High Spots,"* George J. Kubricht, No. 325, January 1946, pp. 3-4.

"An Early May Climb of LaPlata," Dick Stenmark, No. 391, July 1951, p. 85.

"La Plata Peak: The Ellingwood Ridge," Phil Carr, No. 493, January 1960, pp. 3-4, 11.

"A Romp Up the Ellingwood Ridge," Maurine Hoge, No. 507, March 1961, pp. 53-55.

"A New Route on La Plata," No. 557, May 1965, pp. 91-92.

"Letters to the Editor: Warning for Climbers of La Plata Peak," No. 681, September 1975, pp. 176-177.

"No Trespassing! La Plata Access & Climbing Route," No. 683, November 1975, p. 224.

"They're There Because ...,"* James McChristal, No. 687, March 1976, pp. 63-67.
Reprinted from The Colorado College Bulletin, May, 1975, pp. 43-45.
First ascent noted of the Ellingwood Ridge, Albert Ellingwood.

MT. LADY WASHINGTON, 13,281'   Front Range, Rocky Mountain National Park
                                Longs Peak 1961
   Climbing
      "'Santayana Slabs', Mount Lady Washington, South Face, Rocky Mountain National Park, Colorado," No. 6, March-April 1971, p. 21.
      First ascent note, Michael Tobias, Mark Janson, and Diane Rheinert.

"LARET",   Front Range
   Trail and Timberline
      "Climbing Notes,"* No. 143, September 1930, p. 6.
      Ski ascent note, John L. J. Hart and Graeme McGowan.

LEAD MOUNTAIN, 12,537'   Never Summer Range, Rocky Mountain National Park
                          Mount Richthofen 1957
   Trail and Timberline
      "The Trips of the Outing,"* No. 37, October 1921, pp. 2-4.

      "The Never Summers IV - Lead Mountain," Esther Holt and Bob Hubbard, No. 480, December 1958, pp. 167-168, Front cover illustration.

LEVIATHAN PEAK, 13,528'   Needle Mountains   Storm King Peak 1964
   Climbing
      Illustration,* "Descent Between Jagged and Leviathan Peaks," No. 15, September-October 1972, p. 25.

Trail and Timberline
"The Needles, June 1957,"* Gene White, No. 471, March 1958,
pp. 31-35.

"Revised Climbers' Guide from Noname Creek,"* William E.
Davis, No. 502, October 1960, pp. 149-154, 1 Map.

"Letters to the Editor,"* Martin A. Etter, No. 610,
October 1969, p. 187.
North face note.

LILY MOUNTAIN, 9,786'   Front Range   Longs Peak 1961
Appalachia
"Exploration,"* F. O. Carpenter, Vol. 5, December 1888, p. 234.
Ascent note, F. H. Chapin.

Chicago Mountaineering Club Newsletter
"Rock Climbing Practice - Lily Mountain," Jerry Wolkoff,
Hermann Jauch, Anne Stettner, and Frank Slowinski, Vol. 5,
No. 5, November 1951, pp. 8-9.

MT. LINCOLN, 14,286'   Mosquito Range   Alma 1970
Alpine Journal
"The Rockies of Colorado,"* Evelio Echevarría C., Vol. 71,
May 1966, pp. 26-36, 1 Map, Bibliography.

American Alpine Journal
"Colorado Climbing Notes, 1936,"* Kenneth Segerstrom, Vol. 3,
1937, p. 108.
Ski ascent note, Cobb, Dodge, McKenney, and Whittemore.

"Naming America's Mountains - The Colorado Rockies,"* Francis
P. Farquhar, Vol. 12, 1961, pp. 319-346.

Appalachia
"All the 14,000's,"* Carl Melzer, Vol. 22, December 1939,
pp. 466-479.

"Climbs and Trips by Members: A Colorado Vacation,"* Edmund
Bassett, Vol. 24, December 1942, pp. 257-258.

Trail and Timberline
"Recent Trips: Lincoln and Bross,"* Nos. 6 and 7, September,
October 1918, p. 4.

"The Mountain Ranges of Colorado,"* Kenneth Segerstrom,
No. 215, September 1936, pp. 109-115, 1 Map.

"Better Route to the Mt. Lincoln Group,"* Ronald L. Ives,
No. 223, May 1937, p. 57.

"Reaching the High Spots,"* George J. Kubricht, No. 325,
January 1946, pp. 3-4.

"Mosquito Range Ramble,"* Joseph W. Miller, No. 396,
December 1951, pp. 164-165.

MT. LINDSEY, 14,042'   Sangre de Cristo Range   Blanca Peak 1967
  Appalachia
    "All the 14,000's,"* Carl Melzer, Vol. 22, December 1939,
    pp. 466-479.

Trail and Timberline
    "Old Baldy," Henry Buchtel, No. 84, September 1925, pp. 7-8,
    1 Illustration p. 3.

    "Huerfano Playgrounds,"* Thomas J. Everly, No. 248,
    August 1939, pp. 103-104, 1 Illustration.

    "The Route Up Old Baldy," Hugh W. Hetherington, No. 284,
    August 1942, pp. 106, 110.

    Front cover illustration,* "Old Baldy and Blanca," Harry
    Standley, No. 297, September 1943.

    "Boulder Group Doings,"* Marie Hulse, No. 379, July 1950,
    p. 106.
    Ascent note.

    "Mount Lindsey - 14,125," No. 420, December 1953, pp. 167-168,
    176, Front cover illustration.

    "Mount Lindsey Memorial Trip," No. 425, May 1954, pp. 66, 78.

    "Mount Lindsey Dedication," No. 428, August 1954, pp. 107-112,
    2 Illustrations, Front cover illustration.

    "History of the Mount Lindsey Region," Louisa W. Arps, No. 428,
    August 1954, pp. 113-114.

    "Mount Lindsey Memorial Marker," No. 438, June 1955, p. 102.

    "Mount Lindsey Memorial Plaque Stolen," No. 440, August 1955,
    p. 138.

    "Denver Junior Summer Outing,"* Jim Ross, No. 459, March 1957,
    pp. 39-40.

    "My First Fourteen - And Its Rocks," L. O. Fortner, No. 587,
    November 1967, pp. 198-201, 2 Illustrations.

    "Climbing in the Blanca Massif,"* Roger Fuehrer, No. 637,
    January 1972, pp. 3-5, 1 Map, Front cover illustration.

    "A December Climb of Mt. Lindsey," Al Ossinger, No. 638,
    February 1972, pp. 42-43.

    "No Trespassing! Mount Lindsey Access," No. 683,
    November 1975, p. 224.

"LITTLE ARIKAREE PEAK", 12,887'(?)   Front Range, Indian Peaks
                                      (Unnamed) Monarch Lake 1958

    <u>Trail and Timberline</u>
      "A Circle Trip in the Arikarees,"* Ronald L. Ives, No. 256,
      April 1940, pp. 56-57.

LITTLE BEAR PEAK, 14,037'   Sangre de Cristo Range   Blanca Peak 1967
    <u>Appalachia</u>
      "Through San Luis Park to Sierra Blanca,"* Charles E. Fay,
      Vol. 5, May 1889, pp. 261-283, 1 Illustration (Plate XIV).
      First recorded ascent noted (referred to as West Peak),
      Charles E. Fay and J. R. Edmands.

      "All the 14,000's,"* Carl Melzer, Vol. 22, December 1939,
      pp. 466-479.

    <u>Trail and Timberline</u>
      "A Note on Certain Elevations,"* Albert R. Ellingwood, No. 93,
      June 1926, pp. 4, 6.

      "Junior Diary, July 1-4,"* No. 248, August 1939, pp. 111-112.

      "Little Bear by the West Ridge," Herb Hollister, No. 311,
      November 1944, pp. 127-128, 1 Illustration.

      "Sangre, Rain, No Tears,"* Dorothy Teague Swartz, No. 355,
      July 1948, p. 107.

      "Little Bear and Blanca,"* Bill Bueler, No. 380, August 1950,
      pp. 121-122, 1 Illustration.

      "Little Bear," Roy R. Murchison, No. 391, July 1951, pp. 83-
      84, 1 Illustration.

      "Accident on Little Bear," No. 455, November 1956, pp. 162,
      175.

      "Denver Junior Summer Outing,"* Jim Ross, No. 459, March 1957,
      pp. 39-40.

      "Climbing in the Blanca Massif,"* Roger Fuehrer, No. 637,
      January 1972, pp. 3-5, 1 Map.

      "Private Property: No Trespassing!"* Sally Richards, Nos. 679-
      680, July-August 1975, pp. 148-150.

      "No Trespassing! Little Bear Climbing Route," No. 683,
      November 1975, pp. 223-224.

LITTLE FINGER ("PEAK SEVENTEEN", TURRET NEEDLES), 13,200' Needle Mountains
See also "PEAK SEVENTEEN", TURRET NEEDLES   Snowdon Peak 1964
    <u>Trail and Timberline</u>
      "Climbers Guide to Noname,"* No. 342, June 1947, pp. 97-98,
      1 Map.

LITTLE HORN PEAK, 13,143'   Sangre de Cristo Range   Horn Peak 1959
    Trail and Timberline
        "New Maps of the Sangre de Cristo Range,"* John L. J. Hart,
        No. 519, March 1962, pp. 32-33.

        "Sangre de Cristo Saga,"* Lester A. Michel, with Wilbur F.
        Arnold, No. 525, September 1962, pp. 139-142, 150, (Continued
        from August 1962 T&T).

LITTLE MATTERHORN, 11,586'   Front Range, Rocky Mountain National Park
                              McHenrys Peak 1957
    American Alpine Journal
        "Various Notes: Chicago Mountaineering Club,"* John F.
        Fralick, Vol. 8, 1952, p. 356.
        New route note.

    Appalachia
        "The Peaks of Rocky Mountain National Park,"* Roger W. Toll,
        Vol. 17, June 1929, pp. 252-260.

        "Trips by Members: Estes Park and the Tetons,"* Vol. 26,
        December 1947, p. 514.
        Ascent note, Irvin M. Davis, Walter D. Howe, and Clinton M.
        Kelley.

    Chicago Mountaineering Club Newsletter
        "Little Matterhorn," Jack Fralick, Vol. 5, No. 5,
        November 1951, pp. 13-14, 1 Map p. 6, 1 Map p. 12.
        Ascents noted on five routes.

        "Our Western Alps,"* Don Simpson, Vol. 12, No. 6,
        November 1958, pp. 19-20.
        Possible new route noted on the southeast corner.

    Trail and Timberline
        Illustration, "Little Matterhorn - From Tourmaline Gorge,"
        Carl Blaurock, No. 173, March 1933, p. 36.

        "Little Matterhorn Scouted," Moritz Krieg, No. 236, July 1938,
        p. 81.

LITTLE PAWNEE PEAK, 12,466'   Front Range, Indian Peaks   Ward 1957
    Alpine Journal
        "The Rockies of Colorado,"* Evelio Echevarría C., Vol. 71,
        May 1966, pp. 26-36, 1 Map, Bibliography.

    Harvard Mountaineering
        "Climbing Notes, 1964: Colorado, Front Range,"* Dave Roberts,
        No. 17, May 1965, pp. 60-61.
        Winter ascent note, Dave Roberts and Burt Redmayne.

    Trail and Timberline
        "Letter to the Editor: New Peak Names,"* Evelio Echevarría C.,
        No. 572, August 1966, p. 139.

"LITTLE POWELL", 13,087'   Gore Range   (Unnamed) Mt. Powell 15M 1933
   American Alpine Journal
      "Colorado Climbing Notes, 1935,"* Carleton C. Long, Vol. 2,
      1936, p. 545.
      Ascent note.

   Trail and Timberline
      "Mt. Powell and the Gore Range,"* Kenneth Segerstrom, No. 159,
      January 1932, pp. 9-11, 1 Illustration.

      "Climbs in the Gore Range,"* Kenneth Segerstrom, No. 197,
      March 1935, pp. 32-35, 37-38, 1 Map, 1 Illustration p. 31.
      "The Gore Map - A Correction," No. 198, April 1935, p. 47.

      "The Gore Range Outing,"* Everett Long, No. 204, October 1935,
      pp. 111-113.

      "Names on the Gores,"* William Bird Mounsey, No. 568,
      April 1966, pp. 63-65, 1 Map.

"LITTLE SAWTOOTH PEAK", 12,800'(?)   Front Range, Indian Peaks
                                     (Unnamed) Monarch Lake 1958
   Trail and Timberline
      "A Circle Trip in the Arikarees,"* Ronald L. Ives, No. 256,
      April 1940, pp. 56-57.

LIZARD HEAD, 13,113'   San Miguel Range   Mount Wilson 1953
   Alpine Journal
      "Mountaineering in Southern Colorado,"* Percy W. Thomas,
      Vol. 15, August 1891, pp. 480-490.

      "Alpine Notes: Rocky Mountain Sickness,"* Percy W. Thomas,
      Vol. 17, May 1894, pp. 140-141.
      Attempt note.

      "The Rockies of Colorado,"* Evelio Echevarría C., Vol. 71,
      May 1966, pp. 26-36, 1 Map, Bibliography.
      First ascent noted, Albert R. Ellingwood and Barton Hoag.

   American Alpine Journal
      "Technical Climbing in the Mountains of Colorado and Wyoming,"*
      Albert Russell Ellingwood, Vol. 1, 1930, pp. 140-147.
      Second ascent noted, Harold Wilm and Dobson West.

      "American Rockies - Notes, 1929,"* J. L. J. Hart, Vol. 1,
      1930, p. 242, 2 Illustrations.
      Second ascent note, Harold G. Wilm and Dobson West.
      First ascent note, Albert Ellingwood and Barton Hoag.

      "The Rocky Mountains of the United States,"* Howard Palmer,
      Vol. 1, 1931, pp. 360-367.

"Naming America's Mountains - The Colorado Rockies,"* Francis
P. Farquhar, Vol. 12, 1961, pp. 319-346.
First ascent noted, Albert R. Ellingwood and J. Barton Hoag.
Second ascent noted, Harold G. Wilm and Dobson West.[#]
Third ascent noted, Dean Peabody and Winthrop Means.[#]
Fourth ascent noted, Dwight G. Lavender and John Seerly (Seerley).

Appalachia
"Alpina,"* K. A. H., Vol. 17, December 1929, p. 384.
Second ascent note, Harold G. Wilm and Dobson West.

"Colorado Climbs, 1931,"* Winthrop Means, Vol. 18,
December 1931, pp. 357-364, 2 Illustrations.
Third ascent noted, Winthrop Means and Dean Peabody.[#]
(Fourth) ascent noted, Jack Seerley and Dwight Lavender.

"Climbs by A.M.C. Members,"* K. A. H., Vol. 18, December 1931,
p. 470.
Third ascent note, Dean Peabody, Jr. and Winthrop Means.[#]

"Colorado,"* Alice R. Allan, Vol. 18, December 1931, pp. 483-
485.
Third ascent note, Dean Peabody and Winthrop Means.[#]

Climbing
"'Ellingswood's (sic) Corner', Lizard Head Peak, 13,113 Ft.,"
No. 3, September 1970, p. 23.
First winter ascent note, Art Howells, Mike Dudley, Don Doucette,
Chuck Behrensmeyer, R. J. Campbell, and Fletcher Smith.

"Nostalgia/Part II Mundus Est Mons,"* Harvey T. Carter, No. 6,
March-April 1971, pp. 3-5.
First ascent noted.

The Mountaineering Journal (British)
"Outstanding Climbing Centres in the South-Western Colorado
Rockies,"* Dwight G. Lavender, Vol. 1, No. 4, June, July,
August 1933, pp. 238-248, 1 Illustration.

Off Belay
"An Early 'Technical' Climb in Colorado: Lizard Head," No. 5,
October 1972, pp. 34-37, 39, 3 Illustrations, 1 Map.
First ascent noted, Albert Ellingwood and Barton Hoag.

Sierra Club Bulletin
"Notes and Correspondence: Colorado Mountain Club,"* Vol. 15,
No. 1, February 1930, pp. 111-112.
Second ascent note.

"Notes and Correspondence: The Colorado Mountain Club,"* David
Rosendale, Vol. 17, No. 1, February 1932, pp. 109-110.
Ascent note.

[#] The San Juan Mountaineers' Climber's Guide to Southwestern Colorado,
p. 121 lists the third ascent by Wilm, West, and Robert Ormes with
the fourth ascent by Dean Peabody and Winthrop Means.

Trail and Timberline
"The Second Ascent of Lizard Head," Harold G. Wilm, No. 130, August 1929, pp. 10-11, 3 Illustrations.
Second ascent noted, Harold G. Wilm and Dobson West.

"San Miguel Mountains,"* Dwight Lavender, No. 137, March 1930, p. 3.

"Climbing in the San Miguels,"* Dwight Lavender, No. 143, September 1930, pp. 3-4.

"The 1931 Outing Country,"* Dwight G. Lavender, No. 151, May 1931, pp. 63-66, 1 Illustration, 1 Sketch, Front cover illustration.

"The 1931 Outing," Malcolm Collier, No. 156, October 1931, pp. 151-152, Front cover illustration.

"Lizard Head," D. G. Lavender, No. 156, October 1931, pp. 158-161, 1 Illustration, 1 Illustration p. 157, Front cover illustration.
Third ascent noted, Dean Peabody, Jr. and Winthrop Means.[#]
Fourth ascent noted, Dwight G. Lavender and Jack Seerley.
Fifth ascent noted, T. M. Griffiths, Verner Gray, and Tony Ronzio.

Front cover illustration, "Lizard Head from Lower Slopes of Gladstone Peak," Dwight Lavender, No. 159, January 1932.

"First Ascent Criteria,"* Carleton C. Long and Dwight G. Lavender, No. 174, April 1933, pp. 48, 52-53.

Front cover illustration,* "El Diente, Mount Wilson, Gladstone Peak and the Lizard Head, from Black Face," Douglas Anger, No. 283, July 1942.

Illustration, "Lizard Head from the West," Standley, No. 375, March 1950, p. 39.

Front cover illustration, "Lizard Head from Wilson Peak," Don McNabb, No. 621, September 1970.

Front cover illustration,* "Window on Lizard Head and Mt. Wilson," Richard H. Balay, No. 693, September 1976.

LONE CONE, 12,613'   San Miguel Range   Lone Cone 1964
Trail and Timberline
"San Miguel Mountains,"* Dwight Lavender, No. 137, March 1930, p. 3.

"Climbing Notes,"* Dwight Lavender, No. 156, October 1931, p. 165.
First traverse note via north face and down east face, David Lavender and Dwight Lavender.

[#]See note on page 107.

Illustration, "Lone Cone from Middle Peak," Mel Griffiths, No. 586, October 1967, p. 181.

LONE EAGLE PEAK, 11,920'   Front Range, Indian Peaks   Monarch Lake 1958

Alpine Journal
"The Rockies of Colorado,"* Evelio Echevarría C., Vol. 71, May 1966, pp. 26-36, 1 Map, Bibliography.

American Alpine Journal
"Technical Climbing in the Mountains of Colorado and Wyoming,"* Albert Russell Ellingwood, Vol. 1, 1930, pp. 140-147.
First ascent noted, Carl Blaurock, Stephen H. Hart, and W. F. Ervin.

"Activities of Members,"* Vol. 1, 1930, p. 207.
First ascent note, Stephen H. Hart (and Carl A. Blaurock and William F. Ervin).

"American Rockies - Notes, 1929,"* J. L. J. Hart, Vol. 1, 1930, p. 242, 1 Illustration.
First ascent note, Carl A. Blaurock, William F. Ervin, and Stephen H. Hart.

"The North Face of Lone Eagle," Robert M. Ormes, Vol. 4, 1941, pp. 239-241, 1 Illustration.
First ascent noted, Bob Ormes, Roy Murchison, and party. See T&T, No. 275, November 1941, p. 156 for correct first ascent of the north face by Paul and Joseph Stettner.

"Lone Eagle Peak," John Sopka, Vol. 13, 1963, p. 493.
New route note, Jay Orear and John Sopka.

"Club Activities: A.A.C., Rocky Mountain Section," Cleveland M. McCarthy, Vol. 20, 1975, pp. 224-225.
Ascent note via Stettner route.

Appalachia
"Alpina,"* K. A. H., Vol. 17, December 1929, p. 384.
First ascent note, Wm. Ervin, Carl A. Blaurock, and Stephen H. Hart.

"Alpina,"* K. A. H., Vol. 18, June 1931, p. 306.
Second ascent note.

"Accidents: Lindbergh Peak, Colorado," K. A. H., Vol. 20, November 1935, p. 426.

Chicago Mountaineering Club Newsletter
"On the Face of Lone Eagle," Bill Primak, Vol. 4, No. 5, November 1950, pp. 14-15.

Sierra Club Bulletin
"Notes and Correspondence: Colorado Mountain Club,"* Vol. 15, No. 1, February 1930, pp. 111-112.
First ascent note, Carl Blaurock, William F. Ervin, and Stephen H. Hart.

Summit

"Know Your Mountains," Vol. 5, No. 8, September 1959, Inside front cover illustration.

"Lone Eagle Peak," Vol. 5, No. 8, September 1959, p. 26, 1 Map.

"Know Your Mountains," David Morison, Vol. 7, No. 7, July 1961, Inside front cover illustration.

"Lone Eagle Peak," David Morison, Vol. 7, No. 7, July 1961, pp. 12-14, 1 Illustration, 1 Map.

Illustration, "Lone Eagle Peak, 11,900 Feet, Rises Above Cascade Creek in Arapahoe National Forest, Colorado," Walden R. Joura, Vol. 17, No. 5, June 1971, p. 35.

"Know Your Mountains," Illustration by Waldon R. Joura, Vol. 20, No. 5, June 1974, p. 35.

Trail and Timberline

Sketch, "An Impression of the Peak Proposed to be Named after Colonel Lindbergh," Mrs. A. Gayle Waldrop, No. 116, June 1928, p. 5.

"Climb Up Mt. Lindbergh," as related by Carl Blaurock, No. 133, November 1929, pp. 10-11.
First ascent noted, Stephen H. Hart, William F. Ervin, and Carl Blaurock.

"Climbing Notes,"* No. 144, October 1930, p. 9, 2 Illustrations.
Second ascent note, Ernest Field.

"Notes on Nomenclature,"* K. S., No. 178, August 1933, p. 109.

"Editorial Notes," David Rosendale, No. 179, September 1933, pp. 122, 128.
Note on naming.

"Lone Eagle or Lindbergh Peak," Roy R. Murchison, No. 250, October 1939, p. 138, 2 Illustrations, Front cover illustration.

"Labor Day on Lindberg (sic) Peak," Lew Mahoney, No. 255, March 1940, p. 41.

"The Lone Eagle Lodestone," Ernest K. Field, No. 256, April 1940, p. 55, 1 Illustration.

"Lone Eagle - North Face," Bob Ormes, No. 261, September 1940, pp. 135-137, 2 Illustrations, Front cover illustration.
First ascent noted of the north face, Bob Ormes, Roy Murchison, and party. See T&T, No. 275, November 1941, p. 156 for correct first ascent of the north face by Paul and Joseph Stettner.

"Report of the 1940 Summer Outing,"* Roy Murchison, No. 261, September 1940, p. 138.
Descent note of northeast chimney, Roy Murchison and party. First ascent note of the north face, Roy Murchison, Bob Ormes, and party. See T&T, No. 275, November 1941, p. 156 for correct first ascent of the north face by Paul and Joseph Stettner.

"Some 1940 Outing Observations,"* Roy R. Murchison, No. 261, September 1940, p. 143.

"Lone Eagle," Bob Ormes, No. 275, November 1941, p. 156, 1 Illustration.
First ascent noted of the north face, Paul and Joseph Stettner.

"Tragedy on Lone Eagle Peak," Carl Blaurock, No. 296, August 1943, p. 104.

Front cover illustration, "Clouds Over Lindbergh Peak," No. 327, March 1946.

"Lone Eagle Peak," Roy R. Murchison, No. 395, November 1951, pp. 147-148, 1 Illustration, Front cover illustration.

"Looking Back,"* Roy R. Murchison, No. 453, September 1956, pp. 137-138, 1 Illustration.
Ascents noted of the knife edge ridge, north face, east chimney, west coulior, and descents of the east chimney and west face.

"The Old-Timers' Corner - Why Do Climbers Climb?" Roy R. Murchison, No. 486, June 1959, p. 80.

"Our Indian Peaks,"* Karl E. Boehm, No. 497, May 1960, pp. 73-74.

Sketch, "Lone Eagle," Gwen Meux Waldrop, No. 623, November 1970, p. 231.

"Lone Eagle Climb," Tom Tharpe, No. 652, April 1973, pp. 109-110.

Front cover illustration, "Bill Ervin & Carl Blaurock on First Ascent of Lone Eagle Peak, 1929," No. 669, September 1974.

LONGS PEAK, 14,255'   Front Range, Rocky Mountain National Park
                        Longs Peak 1961
Alpine Journal
"The Rockies of Colorado,"* Evelio Echevarría C., Vol. 71, May 1966, pp. 26-36, 1 Illustration, 1 Map, Bibliography.

"Expeditions: Spanish Pan-American Expedition, 1965-67,"* Vol. 72, November 1967, pp. 317-318.
New route note.

"Expeditions - North America: Tetons (sic)," Vol. 73,
May 1968, p. 91.
Third ascent note of the Diamond, T. Burnell and J. Evans.

"Triennial Report 1969-71 North America,"* Tom Connor,
Vol. 77, 1972, pp. 230-231.
Solo ascent note of the Diamond, Bill Forrest.

"Notes 1973 North America: The United States,"* Tom Connor,
Vol. 79, 1974, p. 257.
New route note on the Diamond, Hesse and McClure.

"Triennial Report 1972-4 North America,"* Tom Connor, Vol. 80,
1975, p. 237.
New route note on the Diamond, Dan McClure and Mark Hesse.

American Alpine Journal
"Technical Climbing in the Mountains of Colorado and Wyoming,"*
Albert Russell Ellingwood, Vol. 1, 1930, pp. 140-147.

"Seventy Years of Climbing on Longs Peak," John L. J. Hart,
Vol. 1, 1930, pp. 182-185, 1 Illustration.
Climbing routes noted.

"American Rockies - Notes, 1929,"* J. L. J. Hart, Vol. 1,
1930, p. 241.
East face solo ascent note, R. L. M. Underhill via Alexander's
route.
Winter ascent note, Jess L. Fults, A. L. Richey, and Leo
Sisler. First recorded winter ascent since 1925.

"The Rocky Mountains of the United States,"* Howard Palmer,
Vol. 1, 1931, pp. 360-367.

"Colorado Climbing Notes, 1934,"* Carleton C. Long, Vol. 2,
1935, pp. 415, 417.
New Year's Day ascent note.
Winter ascent note of the east face, Clerin Zumwalt and
Charles Hardin.
Ascent note of the Right Chimney (Ervin-Blaurock Chimney) to
Broadway and then first descent of the chimney, Elwyn Arps and
Charles Hardin.

"Colorado Climbing Notes, 1936,"* Kenneth Segerstrom, Vol. 3,
1937, p. 108.
Solo ascent note, Ernest Field.
Ascent note of the North Chimney, Charles Hardin and party.
Ascent note of Alexander's Chimney, Charles Hardin and party.
Second ascent note of Stettner's Ledges, Charles Hardin and
party.

"Colorado Climbing Notes, 1937,"* Carl Blaurock, Vol. 3, 1938,
p. 217.
New Year's Day solo ascent note, Ernest Fields (Field).

"Colorado Climbing Notes,"* Carl Blaurock, Vol. 4, 1940,
p. 141.
Fatality note.

"Longs Peak," Robert M. Ormes, Vol. 5, 1943, pp. 76-80,
3 Illustrations.

"Various Notes: Colorado Mountain Club,"* Evelyn Runnette,
Vol. 8, 1951, pp. 184-185.
New east face route note, "The Window".

"Various Notes: Chicago Mountaineering Club,"* John F.
Fralick, Vol. 8, 1952, p. 356.
Ascent note of Alexander's Chimney.

"Longs Peak, East Face," R. S. Whitney, Vol. 8, 1953, pp. 545-
546.
New route note, R. S. Whitney, Hassler Whitney, and Robert W.
Craig.

"Longs Peak," Layton H. Kor, Vol. 11, 1959, pp. 298-299.
New route note, the "Doorway", John Hough and Layton Kor.

"The Diagonal, East Face of Longs Peak," Raymond E. Northcutt,
Vol. 12, 1960, pp. 129-130.
New route note, Layton Kor and Ray Northcutt.

"The First Ascent of the Diamond, East Face of Longs Peak,"
David Rearick, Vol. 12, 1961, pp. 297-301, 2 Illustrations
following p. 354 (Plates 61, 62).
First ascent noted, David Rearick and Bob Kamps.

"Naming America's Mountains - The Colorado Rockies,"* Francis
P. Farquhar, Vol. 12, 1961, pp. 319-346.
First ascent noted, John Wesley Powell, William N. Byers,
L. W. Keplinger, Walter H. Powell, Samuel Garman, Ned E.
Farrell, and John C. Sumner.

"Club Activities: Colorado Mountain Club,"* Kenneth R. Wright,
Vol. 13, 1963, pp. 535-536.
Attempt note on the Diamond, Dale Johnson and John Wharton.
(Second) ascent note of the Diamond, Charles Roskosz and Layton
Kor.

"Longs Peak, The Diamond," Royal Robbins, Vol. 14, 1964,
pp. 195-196, 1 Illustration (Plate 96).
Second ascent note of the "Kamps-Rearick" route (D-1), Layton
Kor and Royal Robbins.
New route note, "The Jack of Diamonds", Layton Kor and Royal
Robbins.

"Longs Peak," Stanley Shepard, Vol. 14, 1964, p. 196,
1 Illustration (Plate 96).
New route note, the "Shining Slab", James Burbank and Stanley
Shepard.

"Longs Peak, A New Route on the Diamond," Pat Ament, Vol. 14, 1965, p. 431.
New route note, the "Grand Traverse", Robert Boucher and Pat Ament.

"New Routes on the East Face of Longs Peak," Layton Kor, Vol. 14, 1965, pp. 431-432.
New route note, "Grey Pillar", Tex Bossier and Layton Kor.
New route note, "Crack of Delight", Tex Bossier and Layton Kor.
New route note, "Zig Zag", Tex Bossier and Layton Kor.
New route note, the "Red Wall", Tex Bossier and Layton Kor.
New route note, the "Overhanging (Overhang) Dihedral", Pat Ament and Layton Kor.
Direct ascent note of the "Diagonal Route", Tex Bossier and Layton Kor.

"New Routes on the East Face of Longs Peak," Layton Kor, Vol. 15, 1966, pp. 145-146.
New route note, the "Stripped (Striped) Wall", Wayne Goss and Layton Kor.
New route note, the "Invisible Wall", Larry Dalke and Layton Kor.

"East Face of Longs Peak," George Hurley, Vol. 15, 1967, pp. 360-361.
New route note, the "Diamond-7", Larry Dalke, Wayne Goss, and George Hurley.
New route note, the "Hypothenuse" (Hypotenuse), Jonathan Hough and George Hurley.

"East Face of Longs Peak, Diamond," Peter H. Robinson, Vol. 15, 1967, p. 361.
New route note, the "Curving Vine", Mike Covington and Peter H. Robinson.

"Longs Peak, Diamond," Robert Bradley, Vol. 16, 1969, pp. 400-401.
New route note, "D Minor 7", Rick Petillo (Petrillo) and Bob Bradley.

"Solo on the Diamond," William Forrest, Vol. 17, 1971, pp. 285-287, 2 Illustrations following p. 298 (Plates 47, 48).
First solo ascent noted of the Diamond, William Forrest via new route, "Forrest Finish".

"New Routes in Rocky Mountain National Park,"* Walter Fricke, Vol. 17, 1971, pp. 379-380.
Ascent note of Covington's route right of the North Chimney route and Forrest's Finish to the Yellow Wall.
New route note, the "Indirettissima" (Indirectissima) on Chasm View Wall, Jock Glidden and Walter Fricke.
Variation note of "Indirettissima" (Indirectissima), Larry Dalke and Cliff Jenning.

"Diamond, Longs Peak, New Routes," Kris Walker, Vol. 18, 1973, p. 432.
Solo ascent note of new routes, "Christopher Robin" and "Waterhole N°3", Kris Walker.

"Diamond, Longs Peak," Mark Hesse, Vol. 19, 1974, p. 154.
New route note to the right of the "Westbay-Dunn" route, Dan McClure and Mark Hesse.

"Climbs in Rocky Mountain National Park, 1975,"* Michael Covington, Vol. 20, 1976, pp. 457, 459.
First free ascent note of the Diamond, Wayne Goss and Jim Logan, via "Diamond-7", "Black Dagger Chimney", "Forrest's Finish", top of "Black Dagger Chimney" to finish at Table Rock.
First all woman ascent note of the Diamond, Stephanie Alwood, Molly Higgins, and Laurie Manson, via "Diamond-7".
Free ascent note of the "Yellow Wall", James Dunn and Kris Wood.
New route note, "Dodds-Olevsky-Kasputts", Bob Dodds, Ron Olevsky, and Paul Kasputts.
New route note to the left of the "Dodds-Olevsky-Kasputts" route, George Hurley and Bob Bliss.
Variation note of the "Dodds-Olevsky-Kasputts" route, Tobin Sorenson and Bruce Adams.

Appalachia
"The Ascent of Long's Peak," F. H. Chapin, Vol. 5, June 1888, pp. 109-121, 1 Illustration, Front cover illustration.

"The Call of Colorado,"* Edward W. Harndon, Vol. 16, June 1925, pp. 158-164.

"The Peaks of Rocky Mountain National Park,"* Roger W. Toll, Vol. 17, June 1929, pp. 252-260, 1 Illustration.

"Present-Day Rock Climbing in Colorado,"* Carleton C. Long, Vol. 20, June 1934, pp. 132-134.

"Rock Climbing,"* K. A. H., Vol. 21, December 1937, p. 530.
East face ascent note, Dr. M. Beckett Howorth, Carl Blaurock, Carl Fuller, and Evelyn Runette (Runnette).

"All the 14,000's,"* Carl Melzer, Vol. 22, December 1939, pp. 466-479, 1 Illustration.

"Trips by Members: Estes Park and the Tetons,"* Vol. 26, December 1947, p. 514.
Ascent note of Mills Glacier route of the east face, Irvin M. Davis, Walter D. Howe, and Clinton M. Kelley.

"Accidents: Accident on Longs Peak," B. G. Ferris, Jr., Vol. 30, December 1955, pp. 592-593.

"National Parks: Mountaineering Activities in 1957," Kenneth A. Henderson, Vol. 32, December 1958, p. 283.
Ascents noted during the year.

"Longs Peak by Night," Richard Fleck, Vol. 33, June 1961, pp. 350-352.

"National and State Parks: The National Park Service,"
Vol. 33, December 1961, p. 563.
First ascent note of the Diamond and ascents noted during the year.

"Alpina: Longs Peak," Kenneth A. Henderson, Vol. 34, December 1962, p. 318.
Second ascent note of the Diamond, Layton Kor and Charles Roskosz.

"Climbing in General: Summary of Annual Mountaineering Reports,"* Harthon L. Bill, Vol. 36, June 1966, p. 173.
Ascents noted during the year.

"Alpina: In Colorado," Kenneth A. Henderson, Vol. 36, December 1966, p. 394.
New route notes, "Diamond Seven" and "Curving Vine".

"Alpina: One of the Longest Mountaineering Expeditions on Record,"* Vol. 37, June 1968, p. 121.
New route note, Spanish Pan-American Expedition of 1965-1967.

"Alpina: In Colorado," John A. Woodworth, Vol. 38, June 1971, p. 179.
Solo ascent note of the Diamond, Bill Forrest.

"Alpina: United States,"* John A. Woodworth, Vol. 39, December 1973, p. 144.
(Second) winter ascent note of the Diamond, Gary Neptune and Paul Parker, via the "Yellow Wall" and "D-7".

"Alpina: Colorado," John A. Woodworth, Ed., Vol. 40, December 1974, p. 116.
Ascents noted during the year.

"Alpina: Colorado," John A. Woodworth, Ed., Vol. 40, December 1975, p. 105.
Statistics of climbs.

Chicago Mountaineering Club Newsletter

"Stettners' Ledges," Vol. 1, No. 2, April to August 1945, p. 5.

"More About the Stettner Letters (sic)," contributed by Jack Fralick, Vol. 1, No. 3, September to December 1945, p. 2.

"Stettner Ledges," Jack Fralick, Unnumbered issue, July-December 1948, p. 6.

"Miscellaneous News Items," Harold Walton, Vol. 5, No. 2, March 1951, pp. 13-14.
New route note, "The Window", Harold Walton and David Hornsby. See T&T, No. 386, February 1951, pp. 15-17 for first ascent of "The Window" route by Bill Eubank and Brad Van Diver.

"Long's Peak - Trail Climbs," Allan Gonnerman, Myrtle Kolbig, Vol. 5, No. 5, November 1951, pp. 19-23, 1 Map p. 6.

"Long's Peak - West Couloir," Bob Edgerton, Vol. 5, No. 5, November 1951, pp. 23, 25, 1 Map p. 6.

"Long's Peak - East Face - Via Alexander's Chimney," George Hermach, Edmund Lowe, Vol. 5, No. 5, November 1951, pp. 25-26, 1 Map p. 6, 1 Map p. 24.

"Our First Climb - The East Face of Long's Peak!" Joel I. Connolly, Vol. 6, No. 4, November 1952, pp. 3-4.

"Stettner's Ledges," W. Primak, Vol. 10, No. 6, December 1956, pp. 14-16.

"Our Western Alps,"* Don Simpson, Vol. 12, No. 6, November 1958, pp. 19-20.
Ascents noted of Alexander's Chimney and Alexander's Traverse route.

"The Saga of Long's Peak or How to Climb A Mountain Over A Long Week-end," Erny Kuncl, Vol. 14, No. 3, June 1960, pp. 2-6.

"Ernie Kuncl Hits Mountaineering Jackpot," Vol. 14, No. 4, September 1960, pp. 6-7.
Ascents noted of Stettner's Ledges, Alexander's Chimney, and North Chimney.

"Four CMC Members Climb East Face of Longs Peak," Jim Hagan, Grover Hartsuch, Paul Hartsuch, Chuck Gramlich, Vol. 14, No. 4, September 1960, pp. 7-8.

"Long's Peak Revisited," Athan Pantsios, Vol. 22, No. 4, August-Sept.-October 1968, pp. 5-7.

"The Great Chasm Lake Shelter Expedition," Jim Mathews, Vol. 26, No. 2, Summer 1972, pp. 8-10.

Climbing
"Basecamp: Colorado," No. 3, September 1970, p. 2.
First solo ascent note of the Diamond, Bill Forrest.

"'Yellow Wall/Forrest Finish', Longs Peak, Diamond," No. 3, September 1970, p. 24.
First solo ascent note of the Diamond, Bill Forrest.

"Nostalgia/Part II Mundus Est Mons,"* Harvey T. Carter, No. 6, March-April 1971, pp. 3-5.
First ascent noted of the Chasm View Wall.

"'Circumcision', Chasm Lake Shelter, Longs Peak, Colorado,"
No. 6, March-April 1971, p. 21.
Shelter route(?), Pete Gibbs.

"Basecamp: Longs Peak," No. 10, November-December 1971, p. 4.
Second ascent note of the "Grand Traverse" route, Bill Forrest
and Ray Jardine.
Ninth ascent note of "D One", Bill Forrest and Ray Jardine.
New route note to the right of the "Jack of Diamonds", Jim Dunn
and Bill Westbay.
Solo ascent note of new route, "Waterhole No. Three", Chris
(Kris) Walker.
Ascent note of the "Yellow Wall" approached via the "Overhang
Dihedral", Steve Shea and Chris Landry.

"The Yellow Wall: A Climb of the Times," Chris Landry, No. 12,
March-April 1972, pp. 2-7, 6 Illustrations, Front cover
illustration.

"Basecamp: Colorado," No. 18, March-April 1973, p. 23,
1 Illustration.
Second (and third) winter ascent notes (of the Diamond), Gary
Neptune and Paul Parker via the "Yellow Wall" and "D-7", and
Mike Covington and Dean Ketcham (Ketchum) via "D-7".
First winter ascent note (of the Diamond), Layton Kor and Wayne
Goss, via the Enos Mills Wall.

"Basecamp: Colorado," No. 20, July-August 1973, p. 10.
Note on removal of the cables on the north face.

"Basecamp: Rocky Mountain National Park,"* Michael Covington,
Nos. 22 and 23, Winter 1973-74, p. 36.
New route note to the right side of the Diamond, Daniel McClure
and Mark Hesse.
First non bivouac ascent note of the Diamond, Michael
Covington and Billy Westbay.

"View from Within: Colorado Rocky Mountain National Park,"*
No. 28, Winter 1974-75, p. 36.
Partial free ascent note of "Diamond 7", Duncan Ferguson,
Kevin Donald, and Jim Logan.
New route note, "The Obelisk", George Hurley and Dave Rearick.
See Climbing, No. 29, March-April 1975, p. 31 for correct
names, George Hurley and Phil Fowler.
New route note, "Queen of Spades", Mark Hesse and Doug Snively.
First free ascent note of the "Diretissima" (Directissima),
Chris Reveley and Roger Briggs.
First free ascent note of "Kors Door", Larry Hamilton and Bob
Griese.

"View from Within: Colorado Rocky Mountain National Park,"*
Michael Covington, No. 29, March-April 1975, p. 31.
Second ascent note of the "Diagonal Direct", Billy Westbay and
Michael Covington.
Correction note on free ascents of the Diamond.

"Diamond," Dean Tschappat, No. 35, March-April 1976, pp. 2-8, 6 Illustrations, Front cover illustration.

"Winter Climbing in Rocky Mountain National Park,"* Michael Covington, No. 37, July-August 1976, pp. 7-13, 1 Illustration.
First winter ascent noted of the Diamond, Layton Kor and Wayne Goss, via the Enos Mills Wall.
Second winter ascent noted of the Diamond, Gary Neptune and Paul Parker, via Yellow Wall start and Diamond 7 finish.
Third winter ascent noted of the Diamond, Dean Ketchum and Michael Covington, via Diamond 7.
Fourth winter ascent noted of the Diamond, Dakers Gowan (Gowans) and Mike Monger, via Black Dagger route to Table Ledge.

"Basecamp: Colorado,"* No. 38, September-October 1976, pp. 3-5.
First complete ascent note of the "Yellow Wall", Roger Briggs and Bob Candelaria.
Free ascent note of the "Obelisk", Chris Reveley and Bill Roos.
Free ascent note of "Vertical Sanctuary", Pat Adams and Scott Woodruff. Later ascent by Steve Shea and Michael Kennedy.

"Escape from the Prism," Roger Briggs and Robert Candelaria, No. 38, September-October 1976, pp. 18-22, 7 Illustrations.

"Basecamp: Colorado,"* No. 39, November-December 1976, pp. 3-5.
New route note, "Diamond Lil", Mike Covington, Dennis Hennek, and Doug Scott.
Ascent note of the "Yellow Wall", Roger Briggs and Robert Candelaria.

Harvard Mountaineering
"Alpina Minora, 1948," G. McNear, No. 9, June 1949, pp. 86-87.
Ascent note of Stettner's Ledges.

"Climbing Notes, 1952,"* No. 11, May 1953, p. 66.
Ascent note of Alexander's Chimney, Lori Hansen and John McLeod.

"Climbing Notes, 1971: Rockies and the Northeast,"* Sam Streibert, No. 19A, June 1972, pp. 53, 55.
Ascent notes of Stettner's Ledges, the "Window", and the "Yellow Wall".

Iowa Mountaineers Journal
"Colorado's Rockies,"* Ruth Norman, Vol. 1, No. 10, February 1945, pp. 53-57, 2 Illustrations.

"1963 Pikes Peak Crags Outing,"* Vol. 5, No. 5, 1965, p. 35.
Route note on Longs Peak.

"Pikes Peak Crags Outing,"* Harvey and Annie T. Carter, Vol. 5, No. 5, 1965, pp. 54-59, 1 Illustration.

Mazama
 "A Mountaineering Marathon,"* A. H. Marshall, Vol. 13, No. 12, Decemeber 1931, pp. 63-71, 1 Illustration.

Mountain
 "Information: Longs Peak," No. 13, January 1971, p. 10.
First solo ascent note of the Diamond, Bill Forrest.

 "Information: Rocky Mountains," No. 29, September 1973, p. 15.
New route note on the Diamond, Mark Hesse and Dan McClure.

 "Information: Rocky Mountains," No. 33, March 1974, p. 10.
Note on removal of the cables.

 "Information: Rocky Mountains,"* No. 36, June 1974, p. 9.
Note on the "Black Dagger Route", Dakers Gowan (Gowans) and Mike Monger.
Note on "Diamond 1 Route", Czech team.

 "Information: Rocky Mountains," No. 39, October 1974, p. 10.
Note on free ascents of "Diamond 7". See Climbing, No. 29, March-April 1975 for correction on free ascents of the Diamond.
New route note, Doug Snively and Mark Hesse.
New route note, "Obelisk Crack" (The Obelisk), George Hurley and Phil Fowler.
Second ascent note of the "Diagonal Direct", Billy Westbay and Mike Covington.

 "Diamond Commentary," Mike Covington, No. 40, November 1974, pp. 17-20, 3 Illustrations.
Important ascents of the Diamond noted.

 "Information: The Diamond," No. 41, January 1975, p. 11.
Near complete free ascent note of "Diamond 7", Duncan Ferguson, Kevin Donald, and Jim Logan.
Note on Snively/Hesse route named "Queen of Spades".

 "Diamond Climbed Free at 5.10 by Wayne Goss and Jim Logan," Mike Covington, No. 46, November/December 1975, p. 15.
First free ascent note of the Diamond, Wayne Goss and Jim Logan.
Second free ascent note of the Diamond, Jim Dunn and Kris Wood.
First all-woman ascent note of the Diamond, Stephine (Stephanie) Alwood, Molly Higgins, and Laurie Manson via "Diamond 7".
New route note between "Obelisk" and "Curving Vine", Bob Dodds, Ron Olevsky, and Paul Kasputts. Second ascent of route, Bruce Adams and Tobin Sorenson.
New route note between "Obelisk" and "Curving Vine", George Hurley and Bob Bliss.

The Mountaineer
 "A Mountaineer in Colorado,"* Edward W. Harnden, Vol. 15, December 15, 1922, pp. 47-53.

Off Belay
    "New Routes in Rocky Mountain National Park: East Face of
    Longs Peak - The Diamond," Walt Fricke, No. 1, January-
    February 1972, p. 40, 1 Illustration.
    New solo route note, "Waterhole No. 3", Kris Walker.
    New route note, "Dunn Route", Jim Dunn and partner.
    Ascent note of "D-7", Steve Roper, Royal Robbins, and Michael
    Covington.

    "Climbing at Rocky Mountain,"* Walt Fricke, No. 2, April 1972,
    pp. 17-23, 1 Illustration, 1 Map.

    "Two New Technical Climbs in Rocky Mountain National Park,"*
    Walt Fricke, No. 5, October 1972, p. 40.
    New solo route note, "Christopher Robin", Kris Walker.

    "Winter Ascent of Longs Peak," Walt Fricke, No. 8, April 1973,
    p. 43.
    Note on the first winter ascent of the Diamond in 1967, Layton
    Kor and Wayne Goss.
    Second winter ascent note of the Diamond, Gary Neptune and
    Paul Parker.
    (Third) winter ascent note of the Diamond, Mike Covington and
    Dean Ketchum.

    "Climbing Notes from Rocky Mountain National Park," Walt
    Fricke, No. 12, December 1973, p. 39.
    New route note, "Its-Welx", Dan McClure and Mark Hess (Hesse).
    One day ascent note of "D-7", Mike Covington and Billy Westbay.

    "National Parks Take Brunt of Mountaineering Traffic: Rocky
    Mountain National Park, Colorado,"* No. 14, April 1974, pp. 33-
    34.
    Note on recorded ascents during the year.

    "Are Cables Really Necessary?" Michael Covington, No. 14,
    April 1974, p. 37, 1 Illustration.

    "Some Notes from Rocky Mountain National Park: Bad Weather and
    the Big Walls," Walt Fricke, No. 15, June 1974, pp. 31-35,
    1 Illustration.
    Fourth winter ascent of the Diamond and first winter ascent
    note of the "Black Dagger" route, Mike Munger (Monger) and
    Dakers Gowans.

    "More on National Parks: Rocky Mountain National Park,"*
    No. 21, June 1975, pp. 39, 41, 1 Illustration.
    Note on recorded ascents during the year.

    Illustration, "Climbing on 'The Diamond', the Magnificent East
    Face of Longs Peak," Chip Salaun, No. 27, June 1976, p. 33.

Sierra Club Bulletin
    "Parks and Peaks in Colorado," Vernon L. Kellogg, Vol. 3,
    No. 3, February 1901, pp. 189-199, 5 Illustrations.

"Longs Peak," Walter L. Huber, Vol. 13, No. 1, February 1928, pp. 62-64, 2 Illustrations.

"Notes and Correspondence: The Colorado Mountain Club,"* David Rosendale, Vol. 18, No. 1, February 1933, pp. 123-124.
Note on establishment of four new routes on the north face.

"The Diamond East Face of Longs Peak," Dave Rearick and Bob Kamps, Vol. 45, No. 9, December 1960, pp. 86-87.
First ascent note of the Diamond, Dave Rearick and Bob Kamps.

"Long's Peak - The Diamond," Royal Robbins, Vol. 48, No. 9, December 1963, pp. 103-104.
Second ascent note of the "Kamps-Rearick" route (D-1), Layton Kor and Royal Robbins.
New route note, "Jack of Diamonds", Layton Kor and Royal Robbins.

Summit
"'Tip Toe' on Longs Peak," Cecil M. Ouellette, Vol. 3, No. 3, March 1957, pp. 12-15, 1 Illustration, 1 Map.
New route noted, "Tip Toe", Cecil M. Ouellette and Dick Woodford.

"Know Your Mountains," Niles and Louise Werner, Vol. 6, No. 11, November 1960, Inside front cover illustration.

"Longs Peak," Vol. 6, No. 11, November 1960, pp. 14-16, 1 Illustration, 1 Map.
First ascent noted of the Diamond, Robert Kamps and Dave Rearick.

"Analysis of Mountaineering Accidents,"* Vol. 7, No. 7, July 1961, pp. 2-5.
(From the American Alpine Club annual report).

"The Summer of the Diamond," Verne Huser, Vol. 13, No. 1, January-February 1967, pp. 14-17, 24-27, 6 Illustrations.
New route noted, the Yellow Wall, Layton Kor and Charles Roskosz.
Second ascent noted of D-1, Layton Kor and Royal Robbins.
New route noted, Jack of Diamonds, Layton Kor and Royal Robbins.
New route noted, Grand Traverse, Robert Boucher and Pat Ament.
Third ascent noted of D-1, Bob Culp and Wayne Goss.
New route noted, Diamond Seven, Wayne Goss, George Hurley, and Larry Dalke.
New route noted, Curving Vine, Peter Robinson and Mike Covington.

"Ascending Two Giants,"* Vincent Prichard, Vol. 13, No. 4, May 1967, pp. 8-13, 6 Illustrations, 1 Map.

"Diamond Winter Ascent," Vol. 13, No. 5, June 1967, p. 33.
First winter ascent note of the Diamond, Layton Kor and Wayne Goss.

"Letters,"* Gary Neptune, Vol. 14, No. 10, December 1968, p. 34.
Ascent note.

"Midwinter Rescue on Longs Peak," Dee B. Crouch, M.D., Vol. 15, No. 6, July-August 1969, pp. 8-11, 1 Illustration.
Reprinted from Trail and Timberline.

"Scree: Colorado," Vol. 15, No. 8, October 1969, p. 30.
Rescue note.

"Scree: Visiting Climbers,"* Vol. 15, No. 10, December 1969,
p. 27.
Ascent note of the Diamond by two German climbers, Heinrich
Majewski and Yurgen Vogt.

"Letters," Steve Hickman, Vol. 15, No. 10, December 1969, p. 35.
Rescue note.

"Diamond Solo Ascent," Vol. 16, No. 8, October 1970, p. 31.
First solo ascent note of the Diamond, Bill Forrest.

"Longs Peak," Vol. 19, No. 6, July-August 1973, p. 12.

"Reunion of the Diamond Climbers," Pat Ament, Vol. 22, No. 3,
June 1976, pp. 30-33, 4 Illustrations.

Trail and Timberline

"Recent Trips: Longs Peak," Nos. 6 and 7, September,
October 1918, p. 5.

"The Longs Peak Register," Nos. 6 and 7, September,
October 1918, p. 5.

Illustration, "Longs Peak Across Wild Basin," George H.
Harvey, Jr., No. 16, October 1919, p. 1.

"The Resistless Urge," No. 39, December 1921, p. 3,
1 Illustration.

"High Lights on the Ten Annual Outings: Second Annual Outing -
Barthof and Long's Peak," Grace M. Harvey, No. 43, April 1922,
pp. 24-25, 1 Illustration.

Illustration, "Longs Peak after A Spring Storm," Clark
Blickensderfer, No. 44, May 1922, p. 3.

"Mountain Registers,"* Carl Blaurock, No. 52, January 1923,
p. 6.

Illustration, "Shelf Trail, Long's Peak, in July," No. 58,
July 1923, p. 3.

Illustration, "Longs Peak (14,255 Ft.)," Chas. Snow, No. 60,
September 1923, p. 5.

"A Trip Up the Northeast Face of Longs Peak," Carl Blaurock,
No. 63, December 1923, pp. 2-5, 2 Illustrations,
1 Illustration p. 9.
(Third) ascent noted of Alexander's Chimney, Mr. and Mrs.
Herman Buhl, Dudley T. Smith, John L. J. Hart, Frank Shirmer,
Herbert Wortman, and Carl Blaurock.

"Official Report," Roger W. Toll, No. 77, February 1925,
pp. 4-9, 1 Illustration.
Report of the Agnes W. Vaille fatality.

"Cable on North Side of Longs Peak," Roger W. Toll, No. 85,
October 1925, p. 4.

Illustration, "Longs Peak from Twin Sisters, May 16, 1926,"
Chas. Snow, No. 94, July 1926, p. 2.

Illustration, "Longs Peak," Clark Blickensderfer, No. 100,
January 1927, p. 6.

"A Glimpse of Wild Basin,"* Albert Russell Ellingwood,
No. 109, November 1927, pp. 3-6.

"Agnes Vaille Storm Shelter," No. 111, January 1928, pp. 1-3,
2 Illustrations.

Illustration, "Boulder Field Shelter and North Face Longs Peak.
Rocky Mountain National Park," No. 118, August 1928, p. 6.

"Crashing the American Matterhorn in Mid-Winter," A. Lynn
Richey, No. 136, February 1930, pp. 3-5, 10, 1 Illustration.

"Climbing Notes,"* No. 144, October 1930, p. 9.
New Years Day ascent note, Jess L. Fults.
Ascent note from the west, direct from the Shelf Trail.

"Club and Climbing Notes," No. 145, November 1930, p. 2.
Ascent note of the "October Chimney" on the west face, Joe
Holland and John L. J. Hart.

"Longs Peak from Wild Basin," from notes by Myron Snow and G.
Wakeham, No. 145, November 1930, p. 7, 1 Illustration p. 5,
Front cover illustration.

"Longs Peak," No. 147, January 1931, p. 9.
Register statistics.

"Denver Activities,"* No. 154, August 1931, p. 126.
North face and east face ascent notes.

Illustration, "Climbing Longs Peak," Charles F. Snow, No. 155,
September 1931, p. 141.

"Boulder Group Activities: Best Longs Peak Guide," John D.
McLucas, No. 156, October 1931, p. 163.
Speed ascent note of the east face, Everett C. Long.

"The First Ascent of the East Face of Longs Peak by Night,"
Carleton C. Long, No. 158, December 1931, pp. 193, 198.
Probable first all night ascent noted of the east face,
Everett C. Long, Melvin Wickens, Dorothy D. Collier, and
Carleton C. Long.

"Note," No. 159, January 1932, p. 8.
New Year's Day ascent note, Ernest K. Field.

"Editorial Notes,"* David Rosendale, No. 166, August 1932,
p. 120.
East face ascent note, Carl Blaurock and party.
Fatality note on the north face.

"Winter Climbing Notes," Carleton C. Long, No. 171,
January 1933, p. 9.
Winter ascent note, Everett C. Long, Hull Cook, and James Baird.

"Notes on the 1932 Climbing Season,"* Carleton C. Long,
No. 171, January 1933, p. 9.
Note on establishment of fifteen routes on the peak.

"The North Face of Longs Peak," Clerin Zumwalt, No. 172,
February 1933, pp. 20-21, 1 Illustration.
Cable route noted.
First ascent noted of "Ev's Chimney", Everett C. Long and
Melvin Wickens.
First ascent noted of the Middle Chimney (Zumies Chimney),
Everett C. Long and Clerin W. Zumwalt.
First ascent noted of "Mary's Ledges", Melvin Wickens and La
Selle Gillman. Second ascent noted, Mary Syler, Everett Long,
Hull Cook, and Clerin Zumwalt. Third ascent noted, Clerin
Zumwalt.
First ascent noted of the Dove Tail Ledges, Colonel Bruns and
William F. Ervin.

"Editorial Notes," David Rosendale, No. 177, July 1933, p. 95.
East face ascent note.

"Editorial Notes,"* David Rosendale, No. 178, August 1933,
p. 114.
East face note.

"The 1933 Climbing Season in Colorado,"* Carleton C. Long,
No. 184, February 1934, pp. 20-23.
New Years Day ascent note.
East face ascent note.

"The East Face in Winter," Clerin Zumwalt, No. 185,
March 1934, p. 35.
(First) successful winter ascent noted of the east face, Clerin
Zumwalt and Charles Hardin. See T&T, No. 77, February 1925,
pp. 4-9 for actual first winter ascent of the east face by
Agnes W. Vaille and Walter Kiener.

"A Ranger's Side of the Story," John S. McLaughlin, No. 185,
March 1934, p. 36.
(First) successful winter ascent noted of the east face, Clerin
Zumwalt and Charles Hardin. See T&T, No. 77, February 1925,
pp. 4-9 for actual first winter ascent of the east face by
Agnes W. Vaille and Walter Kiener.

"The 1934 Climbing Season in Colorado,"* Carleton C. Long, No. 196, February 1935, pp. 15-18.
First winter ascent note of the east face, Clerin Zumwalt and Charles Hardin. See T&T, No. 77, February 1925, pp. 4-9 for actual first winter ascent of the east face by Agnes W. Vaille and Walter Kiener.
New Years Day ascent note, Ernest Field and Stuart Clark.

"Editorial Notes," David Rosendale, No. 201, July 1935, p. 86.
East face ascent note.

"Climbing Notes,"* K. S., No. 214, August 1936, p. 92.
North face and east face ascent notes.

"Climbing Notes,"* K. S., No. 215, September 1936, p. 108.
Ascent note of the North Chimney, Charles B. Hardin, Ernest Field, Jack Hart, Robert C. Lewis, and Kenneth Segerstrom.
Ascent note of Alexander's Chimney, Elwyn Arps, Warren Gorrell, Ernest Field, Charles Hardin, and Miss Alene Wharton.
Second ascent note of Stettner's Ledges, Ernest Field, Warren Gorrell, Edward Watson, and Charles Hardin.

"Group Activities: Denver Group,"* Evelyn Runnette, No. 238, September-October 1938, p. 109.
Note on Stettners Ledges, Chappell Cranmer and Fritz Wiessner.

"Rock Work on Long's Peak," Ernest K. Field, No. 246, June 1939, pp. 71-72, 2 Illustrations, 1 Illustration p. 76, Front cover illustration.
Climbing routes noted.

"Report on the Fatality in the Second Chimney on Long's Peak," Ernest K. Field, No. 249, September 1939, pp. 119-120.

"Greenhorn Impressions," Bryce Newman, No. 260, August 1940, pp. 126-127.

"Note," No. 261, September 1940, p. 134.
New route note from Stettner's Ledges up to "Zumie's Thumb", Warren Gorrell Jr., Ernie Field, and Paul Hauk.

"Junior Journey's,"* Molly Sethman, No. 298, October 1943, pp. 127-128.

"Long's Peak or Bust," Dorothy Sethman, No. 298, October 1943, p. 129.

"News from Niwot," Rudolph Johnson, No. 299, November 1943, p. 141.
East face attempt note.

Front cover illustration, "Longs Peak from Trail Ridge Road," O. Roach, No. 301, January 1944.

Front cover illustration, "Longs Peak from Bear Lake," No. 316, April 1945.

"Climbing Longs Peak - Hints for Beginners," Harold M. Dunning, No. 320, August 1945, pp. 100-101.

Front cover illustration, "Longs Peak," David Stirling, No. 341, May 1947.

"Mountain Climbing and Statistics in Rocky Mountain National Park,"* John C. Whitnah and Robert C. Peterson, No. 343, July 1947, pp. 116-117.

"Summer Outings - Then and Now,"* No. 354, June 1948, pp. 88-89.

"Climbing the East Face of Longs Peak," Bob Bader, No. 358, October 1948, pp. 143-144.
Ascent of the Glacier route and Notch Chimney noted.

"This Could Happen to You," E. F. K., No. 358, October 1948, p. 151.

"An Accident on Longs Peak," No. 360, December 1948, pp. 184-185.

"Long's Peak, An Old Friend," Dwight Hamilton, No. 379, July 1950, pp. 99-101, 107, 1 Illustration.

"Records Broken on Long's Peak," Ernest K. Field, No. 382, October 1950, p. 154.

"Through the Window - Pioneer Climb of A Delicate New Route Up Longs Peak," Harold F. Walton, No. 386, February 1951, pp. 15-17, Front cover illustration.
New route noted, "the Window", Bill Eubank and Brad Van Diver.
Second ascent noted, Harold Walton and David Hornsby.

"The First Ascent of Long's Peak," L. W. Keplinger, No. 396, December 1951, pp. 159-161, Front cover illustration.
Quoted from The Trail, June 1919.
First ascent noted, Maj. J. W. Powell, Capt. W. H. Powell, Wm. N. Byers, John C. Summer (Sumner), Samuel Garman, Ned E. Farrell, and L. W. Keplinger.

"Boulder Group Notes," T. S. Gilman, No. 418, October 1953, p. 143.
Variation and fourth complete ascent note of the "Window" route, John Clark, Karl Gustafson, Skip Greene, and Lynn Ridsdale.

"A Moonlight Climb of Longs Peak," Bill Birky, No. 453, September 1956, pp. 131-132.

"Looking Back,"* Roy R. Murchison, No. 453, September 1956, pp. 137-138.

"Fun on the East Face," Baker W. Armstrong, No. 466, October 1957, pp. 150-151, 155.

"Little-Known Facts about Longs Peak," Paul Nesbit, No. 480, December 1958, p. 178.

"The Old-Timers' Corner - Longs Long Ago," Wm. L. Myatt, No. 487, July 1959, p. 98.

"The Diamond Climbed," Robert Kamps, No. 501, September 1960, pp. 123-125, 1 Illustration, Front cover illustration.
First ascent noted of the Diamond, Robert Kamps and David Rearick.

"Report of the First Ascent of the Diamond," Robert Kamps and David Rearick, No. 501, September 1960, pp. 125-126, Front cover illustration.

Front cover illustration, "Layton Kor and Charles Roskosz, the Second Team to Conquer the Diamond on Longs Peak," John Krimmel, No. 525, September 1962.

Illustration,* "Longs Peak and Mount Meeker from the South," No. 529, January 1963, p. 5.

"The Colorado Mountaineer,"* Gregg Blomberg, No. 550, October 1964, p. 166.
New route note on the Diamond, Bob Boucher and Pat Ament.

"Come Climb Longs Peak with Us!" Lorena Darby, No. 559, July 1965, p. 146.

Illustration, "Longs Peak with Chasm Lake Camp," Ruth K. Anderson, No. 561, September 1965, p. 181.

"Winter Conditions Prevail on Longs Peak," No. 562, October 1965, p. 219.

"Stettners Ledges," Dick Walker, No. 567, March 1966, pp. 43-44, 1 Illustration.

"Climbing News,"* No. 580, April 1967, p. 71.
First winter ascent note of the Diamond, Layton Kor and Wayne Goss.

"On the Granite Wall," Layton Kor, No. 582, June 1967, pp. 99-102, 1 Illustration, Front cover illustration.
First winter ascent noted of the Diamond, Layton Kor and Wayne Goss.

"High Point in the Park," Fred J. Novak, Superintendent, Rocky Mountain National Park, No. 589, January 1968, p. 3, 1 Illustration, Front cover illustration.

"1868 - First on Longs," William N. Byers, et. al., No. 589, January 1968, pp. 4-8, 1 Illustration, 1 Map, Front cover illustration.
Reprint from September 1, 1868 issue of the Rocky Mountain News.
First ascent noted, William N. Byers, Major John Wesley Powell, W. H. Powell, Jack Sumner, L. W. Keplinger, Samuel Garman, and Ned E. Farrell.

"1901 - A Swiss-American Climbs Longs," Prof. Arnold Emch, No. 589, January 1968, pp. 8-15, 1 Illustration, 2 Sketches, Front cover illustration.
Chapter from Reise und Kulturbilder aus den Vereiningten Staaten von Amerika.

"1967 - A Night on Longs Peak," Ed Wallick, No. 589, January 1968, pp. 16-20, 2 Illustrations, Front cover illustration.

"Most Vertical Point in the Park," Jerry Phillips, Wild Basin Ranger, Rocky Mountain National Park, No. 589, January 1968, pp. 21-22, 1 Illustration, Front cover illustration.
1967 Diamond climbs noted.

"1967 - Walls, Flowers, and Birds," Jonathan Hough, No. 589, January 1968, pp. 23-25, Front cover illustration.
Variation ascent noted of D-7, "The Over-Thirty-Hang", Jonathan Hough and George Hurley.

"Letter to the Editor - Longs Peak Anniversary Climb," Martha Keplinger Cook, No. 600, December 1968, pp. 268-269.

"Midwinter Rescue on Longs Peak," Dee B. Crouch, M.D., No. 603, March 1969, pp. 41-44, 1 Illustration.

"The Diamond," Jonathan Hough, No. 615, March 1970, pp. 52-59, 2 Illustrations, Front cover illustration.

"Boulder Rock Climbers: Faces of the Sixties,"* Bob Culp, No. 623, November 1970, pp. 238-244.
First ascent noted of Hornbein Crack, Tom Hornbein and Cary Huston.
First ascent noted of the Diagonal, Ray Northcutt and Layton Kor.
First winter ascent noted of the Diamond (Enos Mills Wall route), Layton Kor and Wayne Goss.

"Lightning on Longs Peak," Al Ossinger, No. 629, May 1971, pp. 105-106, 1 Illustration.

"Thunder in the Rockies,"* Richard F. Fleck, No. 631, July 1971, pp. 151-157.

"The Rigors and Joys of Winter Climbing,"* Stan Stephan, No. 643, July 1972, pp. 143-145, 1 Illustration.

"Ski Touring Tragedy Near Longs Peak," Walt Fricke, No. 653, May 1973, p. 121.
Reprinted from Off Belay Magazine, April 1972.

"Longs Peak Cables Removed," No. 657, September 1973, p. 233.

"Are Cables Really Necessary?" Mike Covington, No. 665, May 1974, pp. 123-124.

"Longs Peak Bicentennial Climb," Dar Schafer and Jerry Weskalneis, No. 696, December 1976, pp. 227-228.

LOOKOUT MOUNTAIN, 10,715'   Front Range, Rocky Mountain National Park
                             Allens Park 1957
Trail and Timberline
    "Undiscovered Jewels of Rocky Mountain National Park,"* R. D. Martin, No. 618, June 1970, pp. 132-134.

    "Guerilla Tactics Useful for Doggy Climbs: The Gentle Art of Freddy Peaking,"* Bob Michael, No. 689, May 1976, pp. 112-115.

LOST RANGER PEAK, 11,932'   North Park Range   Mount Ethel 1955
Trail and Timberline
    "North Park and Mt. Zirkle,"* No. 202, August 1935, p. 95.

LULU MOUNTAIN, 12,228'   Never Summer Range, Rocky Mountain National Park
                          Fall River Pass 1958
Trail and Timberline
    "The Trips of the Outing,"* No. 37, October 1921, pp. 2-4.

"PEAK M", 13,080'   Gore Range   (Unnamed) Vail East 1970
     American Alpine Journal
          "Colorado Climbing Notes, 1935,"* Carleton C. Long, Vol. 2,
          1936, p. 545.
          Ascent note.

     Trail and Timberline
          "The Gore Range Outing,"* Everett Long, No. 204, October 1935,
          pp. 111-113.

MAHANA PEAK, 12,632'   Front Range, Rocky Mountain National Park
                        Isolation Peak 1958
     Trail and Timberline
          "A Glimpse of Wild Basin,"* Albert Russell Ellingwood,
          No. 109, November 1927, pp. 3-6.

"THE MAIDEN", 8,549'[#]   Front Range   (Unnamed) Eldorado Springs 1965
     Climbing
          "East Ridge, the Maiden," Dick Bird, No. 3, September 1970,
          pp. 22, 24.
          First ascent noted of the east ridge, Dave Robertson, Dale
          Johnson, Cary Huston, and Phil Robertson.

          "Nostalgia/Part II Mundus Est Mons,"* Harvey T. Carter, No. 6,
          March-April 1971, pp. 3-5.
          First ascent noted of the south side route.

     Summit
          Illustration, "A Favorite Pastime for Climbers in the Boulder
          Area of Colorado, is Rappelling Off the Maiden," courtesy of
          Holubar, Boulder, Colorado, Vol. 4, No. 3, March 1958, p. 11.

          "Maiden," Larry Johnson, Vol. 19, No. 3, April 1973, pp. 26-
          27, 1 Illustration.

     Trail and Timberline
          "The Maiden," LeRoy Holubar, No. 393, September 1951, pp. 107-
          109, 1 Illustration, Front cover illustration.
          First ascent noted, Roy Peak and Mark Taggart.
          Second ascent noted, Herb and Jan Conn.
          Third ascent noted, Brad Van Diver, Don Gibson, and Bob
          Betterley.
          Ascent noted, LeRoy Holubar and party.

          "Two New Routes on the Maiden," Dale L. Johnson, No. 440,
          August 1955, pp. 139-142, Front cover illustration.
          First ascent noted of the (north) west overhang, Dale L.
          Johnson.
          First ascent noted of the east ridge, Dale L. Johnson, Dave
          Robertson, Phil Robertson, and Cary Huston.
          First ascent noted of the south face, Harvey T. Carter and
          Clifford Smith.

_____
[#]Elevation of South Boulder Peak.

MARBLE MOUNTAIN, 13,266'   Sangre de Cristo Range   Crestone Peak 1967
   Appalachia
      "Club Excursions: Colorado, 1946,"* Emma Rutherford, Vol. 26, December 1946, pp. 261-264.

   Trail and Timberline
      "The Sangre de Cristo Range,"* Eva and Bill Rathbun, No. 460, April 1957, pp. 55-60, 64, 1 Map.

      "Crestone Outing,"* Wilbur Arnold, No. 521, May 1962, pp. 73-74.

      "Sangre de Cristo Saga,"* Lester A. Michel, with Wilbur F. Arnold, No. 525, September 1962, pp. 139-142, 150, (Continued from August 1962 T&T).

"MT. MARCY", 13,510'   Sangre de Cristo Range
                       (Unnamed) Electric Peak 15M 1959
   Trail and Timberline
      "New Names in Sangres,"* No. 621, September 1970, p. 206.

MAROON BELLS, Elk Range   Maroon Bells 1960
See also NORTH MAROON PEAK and (SOUTH) MAROON PEAK
   Appalachia
      "Excursions: August Camp, 1956,"* David Wilson, Vol. 31, December 1956, pp. 259-261, 1 Illustration.

      "Accidents: The Accident on Maroon Bells, Colorado," Charles S. Houston, Vol. 31, December 1956, pp. 265-266.

   Climbing
      "Basecamp: Colorado,"* No. 5, January 1971, p. 2.
      Accident note.

   Off Belay
      Illustration, "Maroon Bells, Colorado," Keith Gunnar, No. 7, February 1973, pp. 28-29.

   Summit
      "Suggestions for Climbing in the Maroon Bells," Mountain Rescue Service and Aspen Ski Club, Vol. 12, No. 6, July-August 1966, pp. 28-29.

   Trail and Timberline
      Front cover illustration, "Lower Maroon," Robert C. Black, III, No. 211, May 1936.

      Illustration, "Our Maroon Bells?" No. 339, March 1947, p. 41.

      Front cover illustration, "Maroon Bells in Winter," Lee Iverson, No. 470, February 1958.

      Illustration, "Maroon Bells from the North Fork of the Crystal River," Gwen Toepfer, No. 585, September 1967, p. 163.

(SOUTH) MAROON PEAK, 14,156'   Elk Range   Maroon Bells 1960
See also MAROON BELLS

Alpine Journal
"The Rockies of Colorado,"* Evelio Echevarría C., Vol. 71,
May 1966, pp. 26-36, 1 Illustration, 1 Map, Bibliography.

American Alpine Journal
"Technical Climbing in the Mountains of Colorado and Wyoming,"*
Albert Russell Ellingwood, Vol. 1, 1930, pp. 140-147.

"Colorado Climbing Notes, 1936,"* Kenneth Segerstrom, Vol. 3,
1937, p. 109.
Ascent note from the east via the ice couloir between the
north and south peaks, Elwyn Arps and O. P. Settles.

"Various Notes: Colorado Mountain Club,"* Evelyn Runnette,
Vol. 8, 1951, pp. 184-185.
Note on snow and ice route.

"Naming America's Mountains - The Colorado Rockies,"* Francis
P. Farquhar, Vol. 12, 1961, pp. 319-346.
Possible first ascent noted, C. P. Wilsson.

Appalachia
"The Call of Colorado,"* Edward W. Harnden, Vol. 16,
June 1925, pp. 158-164, 2 Illustrations.

"All the 14,000's,"* Carl Melzer, Vol. 22, December 1939,
pp. 466-479.

Chicago Mountaineering Club Newsletter
"Colorado's Elk Mountains,"* Weldon F. Heald, Vol. 13, No. 6,
October 1959, pp. 1-5, Front cover map.

Climbing
"Basecamp: Aspen,"* No. 10, November-December 1971, p. 4.
Accident note.

"Basecamp: Rockies,"* No. 11, January-February 1972, p. 11.
First winter ascent note of the east face, Fritz Stammberger
and Mike Pokress.

The Mountaineer
"A Mountaineer in Colorado,"* Edward W. Harnden, Vol. 15,
December 15, 1922, pp. 47-53.

The Mountaineering Journal (British)
"American Notes: Climbing in the Snowmass Region of the Elk
Mountains of Colorado,"* Hubert M. Walters, Vol. 2, No. 2,
March, April, May 1934, p. 98.
Traverse note of the Maroon Bells.

Summit
"Colorado's High-Rising Elks,"* Weldon F. Heald, Vol. 8,
No. 11, November 1962, pp. 20-23, Inside front cover
illustration.

"The Maroon Bells,"* Stewart Green, Vol. 16, No. 5, June 1970, pp. 16-17, 1 Illustration.

Trail and Timberline
"The Trips and the Country,"* Lucretia Vaile, No. 49, October 1922, pp. 4-7.

"The Maroon Bells,"* Donald McBride, No. 180, October 1933, pp. 143-144, 1 Illustration, 1 Illustration p. 139.

"Climbing Notes,"* K. S., No. 214, August 1936, p. 92. Ascent note of the couloir between the north and south peaks, Elwyn Arps and O. P. Settles.

"Junior Outing,"* Rex A. Young, No. 239, November 1938, pp. 115-116.

"The Maroon Traverse from Snowmass Lake,"* Roy R. Murchison, No. 322, October 1945, p. 128.

"1949 Snowmass Outing was A Great Success,"* Karl T. Neuberger, No. 370, October 1949, pp. 143, 152.

"Hi-Peak Ascents of 1949 Summer Outing,"* Bob Steele, No. 371, November 1949, pp. 164-165.

"High Adventure on South Maroon Peak," Bob Bear, No. 467, November 1957, p. 166, 1 Illustration p. 168.

"Long Day on South Maroon," Allen Auten, No. 478, October 1958, pp. 133-134, 138, 142, 1 Illustration p. 136.

"The Lighter Side,"* Hal Brewer, No. 478, October 1958, pp. 135, 138, 1 Illustration p. 136.

Front cover illustration,* "Aerial View of North and South Maroon Peaks (Photo Taken in Early Spring)," Gale Kehmeier, No. 489, September 1959.

"Seventeen on South," Lester Michel, No. 503, November 1960, pp. 169-171, 1 Illustration.

MT. MASSIVE, 14,421'   Sawatch Range   Mount Massive 1967
Alpine Journal
"The Rockies of Colorado,"* Evelio Echevarría C., Vol. 71, May 1966, pp. 26-36, 1 Map, Bibliography.

American Alpine Journal
"The Rocky Mountains of the United States,"* Howard Palmer, Vol. 1, 1931, pp. 360-367.

Appalachia
"A Visit to the Higher Mountains of California and Colorado,"* Allen H. Bent, Vol. 13, October 1914, pp. 103-114, 2 Illustrations.

"The Call of Colorado,"* Edward W. Harnden, Vol. 16,
June 1925, pp. 158-164.

"Forty-Eight State Summits,"* A. H. Marshall, Vol. 21,
December 1936, pp. 167-182.

"All the 14,000's,"* Carl Melzer, Vol. 22, December 1939,
pp. 466-479.

Mazama
"Hitting the High Spots,"* A. H. Marshall, Vol. 12, No. 12,
December 1930, pp. 44-56, 1 Illustration.

Sierra Club Bulletin
"Mountaineering Notes: Tour of the Six Highest Peaks in the
United States,"* edited by Francis P. Farquhar, Vol. 12,
No. 3, 1926, p. 307.
Ascent note on climbing the first six peaks in altitude in
the U.S., Captain John Henry Cuntz.

Trail and Timberline
"Massive or Gannett," No. 42, March 1922, p. 11.

"Climbing Notes,"* No. 217, November 1936, p. 133.
Elevation note.

Front cover illustration, "Mt. Massive," H. L. Standley,
No. 306, June 1944.

"Massive It Is," No. 352, April 1948, p. 51.

"A Vote of Thanks to the Juniors,"* John and Mary Hitch,
No. 356, August 1948, pp. 115-116.

"Backpacking the Sawatch Range,"* Bud Boylard, No. 378,
June 1950, pp. 83-85, 90-91.

"Confessions of A Solo Climber or How I Recanted My Heresy,"*
Wilbur F. Arnold, No. 389, May 1951, pp. 51-55.

Front cover illustration, "Mount Massive from Arkansas
Valley," Fred Barton, No. 462, June 1957.

Poem, "On Mount Massive," Edward P. Bailey, Jr., No. 683,
November 1975, p. 233.

MATTERHORN PEAK, 13,590'   San Juan Mountains   Uncompahgre Peak 1963
Appalachia
"Club Excursions: Colorado Excursion, 1951,"* Jean K. Kent,
Vol. 28, December 1951, pp. 584-589.

Trail and Timberline
Illustration,* "Wetterhorn, Matterhorn and Coxcomb Peaks, All
to be Climbed During the 1929 Summer Outing," U.S. Forest
Service, No. 127, May 1929, p. 7.

Illustration,* "Wetterhorn and Matterhorn in Uncompahgre National Forest, Colorado," U.S. Forest Service, No. 368, August 1949, p. 119.

Illustration,* "Looking Toward Matterhorn and Wetterhorn from Uncompahgre, Mt. Sneffels in Background," Mike Sadusky, No. 485, May 1959, p. 67.

"Fly Camps on the Yankee Boy Outing,"* Barbara Evert, No. 635, November 1971, pp. 222-223.

McCAULEY PEAK, 13,554'   Needle Mountains   Columbine Pass 1973
    Trail and Timberline
        "Where We Went and What We Climbed,"* No. 25, October 1920,
        pp. 8-11, 1 Illustration.

        Illustration,* "Mts. Grizzly (13,695, Left) and McCauley
        (13,551, Right) Seen from Summit of Jupiter," George H.
        Harvey, Jr., No. 104, May 1927, p. 5.

        Illustration,* "Mts. Grizzly and McCauley Seen from Summit of
        Jupiter," No. 107, September 1927, p. 21.

        Illustration,* "Grizzly and McCauley Peaks from Top of
        Jupiter," George Harvey, No. 223, May 1937, p. 55.

McCLELLAN MOUNTAIN, 13,587'   Front Range   Grays Peak 1958
    Trail and Timberline
        "The Tale,"* No. 310, October 1944, pp. 117-121.

        "The Four Fourteen Foible,"* William L. Myatt, No. 545,
        May 1964, pp. 87-88.

McCURDY MOUNTAIN, 12,168'   Tarryall Range   McCurdy Mountain 1956
    Trail and Timberline
        "Backpacking the McCurdy Park Trail," Ed Wallick, No. 550,
        October 1964, pp. 155-157, 1 Illustration, Front cover
        illustration.

McGREGOR MOUNTAIN, 10,486'   Front Range, Rocky Mountain National Park
                              Estes Park 1961
    Off Belay
        "More on National Parks: Rocky Mountain National Park,"*
        No. 21, June 1975, pp. 39, 41.
        Note on recorded ascents during the year on McGregor Slab.

    Trail and Timberline
        "The McGregor Shield," Mike Stults, No. 572, August 1966,
        pp. 132-133, 136-138.

McHENRYS PEAK, 13,327'   Front Range, Rocky Mountain National Park
                          McHenrys Peak 1957
    American Alpine Journal
        "Technical Climbing in the Mountains of Colorado and Wyoming,"*
        Albert Russell Ellingwood, Vol. 1, 1930, pp. 140-147.

"McHenry's Peak, Northeast Face," Lawrence Hamilton, Vol. 20, 1975, p. 139.
Ascent note of buttress of the northeast face, Dakers Gowans and Lawrence Hamilton.

Appalachia
"The Peaks of Rocky Mountain National Park,"* Roger W. Toll, Vol. 17, June 1929, pp. 252-260.

Chicago Mountaineering Club Newsletter
"McHenry's Peak," Hans Heuer, Jane Jahn, Merritt Kastens, Harriet Mantel, Vol. 5, No. 5, November 1951, pp. 15-17, 1 Map p. 6.

Climbing
"View from Within: Colorado Rocky Mountain National Park,"* No. 28, Winter 1974-75, p. 36.
New route note, "Dog Star" on northeast face, Larry Hamilton and Dakers Gowans.

Summit
"Exploring New Routes in Rocky Mountain National Park,"* Philip C. Ritterbush, Vol. 5, No. 2, February 1959, pp. 10-13, 20-21, 1 Illustration, 1 Map.
First traverse noted of the Arrowhead-McHenrys ridge, Prentiss Sawyer, Charles Sawyer, Charles Ehlert, and Philip C. Ritterbush.

Trail and Timberline
"Some First Ascent Possibilities in Colorado,"* Kenneth Segerstrom, No. 165, July 1932, pp. 103-104.

Front cover illustration, "McHenry's from Thatchtop," Earl Davis, No. 249, September 1939.

Illustration, "McHenry's and Cleaver Ridge," Mtn. States Aviation, No. 249, September 1939, p. 127.

"Mountain Climbing and Statistics in Rocky Mountain National Park,"* John C. Whitnah and Robert C. Peterson, No. 343, July 1947, pp. 116-117.

"On not Climbing McHenry (sic) Peak," B. F. McHenry, No. 558, June 1965, pp. 109-110.
Copy of letter by B. F. McHenry from George H. Knifton's scrapbook.

"Ms. McHenrys Resists: Love Affair with A Mountain," Bill Hirth, No. 675, March 1975, pp. 51-54, 1 Illustration.

"September 1922: The Naming of Stone Man Pass," Gilbert H. Osgood, No. 677, May 1975, pp. 97-99, 2 Illustrations.

McNAMEE PEAK, 13,760'   Mosquito Range   Climax 1970
Appalachia
Illustration,* "Fremont Pass - Peaks Left to Right: Clinton, MacNamee (sic), Democrat, Buckskin, and Arkansas," L. Larmore, Vol. 26, June 1946, Following p. 32.

MEADEN PEAK, 10,879'   Elkhead Mountains   Meaden Peak 1962
  Trail and Timberline
    "Forest Service Bulletins: Meaden Peak Named," No. 163,
    May 1932, p. 68.

MEADOW MOUNTAIN, 11,632'   Front Range, Rocky Mountain National Park
                           Allens Park 1957
  Trail and Timberline
    "Undiscovered Jewels of Rocky Mountain National Park,"* R. D.
    Martin, No. 618, June 1970, pp. 132-134.

MEADOW MOUNTAIN (ARKANSAS MOUNTAIN), 11,853'   Elk Range
                                               Snowmass Mtn. 1960
  Trail and Timberline
    "Hikes and Climbs from Crystal,"* John Beyer, No. 598,
    October 1968, pp. 224-229, 1 Map.

MT. MEEKER, 13,911'   Front Range, Rocky Mountain National Park
                      Allens Park 1957
  Climbing
    "View from Within: Colorado Rocky Mountain National Park,"*
    Michael Covington, No. 29, March-April 1975, p. 31.
    New route note on the north face, Chip Salaun and Bill
    Alexander.

    "Winter Climbing in Rocky Mountain National Park,"* Michael
    Covington, No. 37, July-August 1976, pp. 7-13.
    Solo winter ascent noted of gully left of the Flying Buttress,
    Dean Ketchum.

  Trail and Timberline
    "Mountain Climbing and Statistics in Rocky Mountain National
    Park,"* John C. Whitnah and Robert C. Peterson, No. 343,
    July 1947, pp. 116-117.

    "Mount Meeker," Allen W. Greene, No. 421, January 1954,
    pp. 7-8, Front cover illustration.

    "Boulder Notes,"* Margaret M. Bivans, No. 437, May 1955,
    p. 96.
    Winter ascent note.

    Illustration,* "Longs Peak and Mount Meeker from the South,"
    No. 529, January 1963, p. 5.

    "The Rigors and Joys of Winter Climbing,"* Stan Stephan,
    No. 643, July 1972, pp. 143-145.

    "A Guide to Colorado's Almost-Fourteens,"* William A. Graves,
    No. 683, November 1975, pp. 225-227.

METHODIST MOUNTAIN, 11,655'   Sangre de Cristo Range   Bonanza 15M 1959
  Trail and Timberline
    "Sangre de Cristo Saga,"* Lester A. Michel, with Wilbur F.
    Arnold, No. 524, August 1962, pp. 123-126, 133.

"MT. MEUX" (LONE EAGLE PEAK ?), 11,920'   Front Range, Indian Peaks
                                           (Unnamed) Monarch Lake 1958
    Trail and Timberline
        Illustration, "Fair Glacier, Mt. Meux, Peck Glacier and Crater
        Lake," Harry M. Vars, No. 79, April 1925, p. 4.

MIDDLE PEAK, 12,595'   San Miguel Range   Dolores Peak 1953
    Trail and Timberline
        "The Lesser Climbs,"* Mark Bostwick, No. 586, October 1967,
        pp. 181-182, 1 Map.

MIDDLE TRINITY PEAK, 13,805'   Needle Mountains   Storm King Peak 1964
See also TRINITY PEAKS
    Chicago Mountaineering Club Newsletter
        "Grenadiers 1962,"* John C. Ohrenschall, Vol. 17, No. 2,
        April 1963, pp. 1-4.

        "The Trinity Peaks and Vestal Peak,"* Frank Babb, Vol. 24,
        No. 1, March 1970, pp. 13-14.

    Trail and Timberline
        "The Colorado Mountain Club Announces the Twenty-Eighth Annual
        Summer Outing,"* Henry Buchtel, Lewis Giesecke, Kenneth
        Segerstrom, No. 265, January 1941, pp. 9-14, 1 Map, Front
        cover sketch map.

        "Garlic Gulch Episode,"* L. V. Giesecke, No. 274,
        October 1941, pp. 143-145.
        First ascent noted on CMC outing.

        "The Grenadiers, 1962,"* John C. Ohrenschall, No. 534,
        June 1963, pp. 107-109.

MILWAUKEE PEAK, 13,522'   Sangre de Cristo Range   Crestone Peak 1967
    Trail and Timberline
        "Crestone Outing,"* Wilbur Arnold, No. 521, May 1962, pp. 73-
        74.

        "Sangre de Cristo Saga,"* Lester A. Michel, with Wilbur F.
        Arnold, No. 525, September 1962, pp. 139-142, 150, (Continued
        from August 1962 T&T).

MINERAL POINT, 11,025'   Elk Range   Snowmass Mtn. 1960
    Trail and Timberline
        "Hikes and Climbs from Crystal,"* John Beyer, No. 598,
        October 1968, pp. 224-229, 1 Map.

MISSOURI MOUNTAIN, 14,067'   Sawatch Range   Mt. Harvard 15M 1955
    American Alpine Journal
        "Club Activities: Colorado Mountain Club,"* Anne B. Kenyon,
        Vol. 10, 1956, pp. 149-150.
        Ascent note by C.M.C. party to place register on new 14,000'
        peak.

    Trail and Timberline
        "Missouri Mountain - Number 53," No. 439, July 1955, p. 122.

"First Official Measurement of Many 14,000 Foot Peaks,"* John
L. J. Hart, No. 446, February 1956, pp. 29-30.

MONITOR PEAK, 13,695'   Needle Mountains   Storm King Peak 1964
  American Alpine Journal
      "Southwestern Colorado Climbing Notes - 1933,"* Dwight G.
      Lavender, Vol. 2, 1934, p. 257.
      Attempt and reconnoiter note.

      "Colorado Climbing Notes, 1935,"* Carleton C. Long, Vol. 2,
      1936, p. 546.
      First ascent note, H. L. McClintock, Frank McClintock, and
      Lewis Giesecke.

      "The East Face of Monitor Peak," Jack Fralick, Vol. 7,
      April 1948, pp. 5-14, 1 Illustration.
      First ascent noted of the east face, Joe Stettner, John Speck,
      and Jack Fralick.

      "Various Notes: Chicago Mountaineering Club, 1947,"* Harry
      Lumby, Vol. 7, April 1948, pp. 107-108.
      First ascent note of the east face, Joe Stettner, Jack
      Fralick, and John Speck.

      "Monitor Peak, East Face, Needle Mountains," John F. Fralick,
      Vol. 16, 1969, p. 400.
      Second ascent note of the east face via more direct route,
      Paul Stettner, Jr. and Larry Dalke.

  Chicago Mountaineering Club Newsletter
      "Our Climb of Monitor Peak - August 9-10, 1947," Jack Fralick,
      Vol. 2, No. 4, July to December 1947, pp. 11-14.
      First ascent noted of the east face, Jack Fralick, Joe
      Stettner, and John Speck.

      "Needles Outing of the American Alpine Club,"* Dave Bidwell,
      Vol. 7, No. 5, November 1953, pp. 10-12.

      Front cover illustration, "Monitor in the Needle Mountains,"
      Vol. 14, No. 2, April 1960.

      Front cover illustration, "Monitor in the Needle Mountains,"
      Vol. 15, No. 5, December 1961.

      "CMC News - Paul Stettner Jr.," Vol. 23, No. 3, July-August-
      September 1969, p. 16.
      Second ascent note of the east face, Paul Stettner Jr. and
      Larry Dalke.

  Harvard Mountaineering
      "Climbing Notes, 1964: Colorado Needles,"* Matt Hale, No. 17,
      May 1965, pp. 59-60.
      Ascent note, Matt Hale and Dave Roberts.

Iowa Mountaineers Journal
 "East Face of Monitor Peak," Joe Stettner, Vol. 2, No. 2,
 Summer 1948, pp. 57-63, 98, 5 Illustrations.
 First ascent noted of the east face, Joe Stettner, Jack
 Fralick, and John Speck.

The Mountaineering Journal (British)
 "Outstanding Climbing Centres in the South-Western Colorado
 Rockies,"* Dwight G. Lavender, Vol. 1, No. 4, June, July,
 August 1933, pp. 238-248, 2 Illustrations.

 "Correspondence,"* Dwight Lavender, Vol. 2, No. 1, December,
 January, February 1933-34, pp. 47-51.
 Attempt note.

Trail and Timberline
 "The Needle Mountains Expedition,"* Carleton C. Long, No. 181,
 November 1933, pp. 155-157, 166.
 Attempt noted.

 Illustration, "Monitor Peak from Ruby Lake," Everett C. Long,
 No. 223, May 1937, p. 59.

 "San Juan Testimony,"* H. L. McClintock, No. 224, June 1937,
 p. 69, 1 Illustration.

 "Noname Prospects,"* Mel Griffiths, No. 340, April 1947,
 pp. 56-59, 2 Illustrations.

 "Climbers Guide to Noname,"* No. 342, June 1947, pp. 97-98,
 1 Map.

 "Climber's Guide from Noname Creek,"* Henry Buchtel, No. 345,
 September 1947, pp. 143-144.

 "East Face of Monitor Peak," Jack Fralick, No. 347,
 December 1947, pp. 191-195, 1 Illustration, Front cover
 illustration.
 First ascent noted, Joseph Stettner, John Speck, and Jack
 Fralick.

 Front cover illustration, "Monitor Peak from Top of Sunlight,"
 Alice B. Rawson, No. 419, November 1953.

 "The Needles, June 1957,"* Gene White, No. 471, March 1958,
 pp. 31-35.

 Illustration, "Monitor Peak from Top of Sunlight," Alice
 Rawson, No. 494, February 1960, p. 21.

 "Revised Climbers' Guide from Noname Creek,"* William E.
 Davis, No. 502, October 1960, pp. 149-154, 1 Map.

"East Face of Monitor Peak," Jack Fralick, No. 607,
July 1969, pp. 126-127, 1 Illustration.
Second ascent noted of the east face, Paul Stettner, Jr. and
Larry Dalke.

"THE MONOLITH", 13,500'[#]   San Juan Mountains, Sneffels Range
                            (Unnamed) Mount Sneffels 1967
   American Alpine Journal
      "Colorado Climbing Notes, 1934,"* Carleton C. Long, Vol. 2,
      1935, p. 417.
      First ascent note, Lewis Giesecke and Carleton C. Long.

   The Mountaineering Journal (British)
      "Outstanding Climbing Centres in the South-Western Colorado
      Rockies,"* Dwight G. Lavender, Vol. 1, No. 4, June, July,
      August 1933, pp. 238-248.

   Trail and Timberline
      Illustration,* "South from 'The Hand'. Aiguilles Monolith and
      Blue Needle to the Left. Block Tops of Gilpin to the Right,"
      D. G. Lavender, No. 169, November 1932, p. 158.

      "1934 Summer Outing Climbs,"* Everett C. Long, No. 192,
      October 1934, pp. 131-133.
      First ascent noted, Lewis Giesecke and Carleton Long.

      Illustration,* "South from 'The Hand'. Aiguilles Monolith and
      Blue Needle to the Left. Block Tops of Gilpin to the Right,"
      Dwight G. Lavender, No. 400, April 1952, p. 80.

MUMMY MOUNTAIN, 13,425'   Mummy Range, Rocky Mountain National Park
                          Estes Park 1961
   Appalachia
      "Exploration,"* F. O. Carpenter, Vol. 5, December 1888, p. 234.
      Ascent note of the west peak, F. H. Chapin, J. R. Edmands, and
      C. E. Fay.

   Trail and Timberline
      "Mountain Climbing and Statistics in Rocky Mountain National
      Park,"* John C. Whitnah and Robert C. Peterson, No. 343,
      July 1947, pp. 116-117.

MUSIC MOUNTAIN, 13,355'   Sangre de Cristo Range   Crestone Peak 1967
   Trail and Timberline
      "The Sangre de Cristo Range,"* Eva and Bill Rathbun, No. 460,
      April 1957, pp. 55-60, 64, 1 Map.

      "Colorado Climbs: Music Mountain," Wilbur Arnold, No. 594,
      June 1968, pp. 146-148, 1 Map.

_____
[#]Elevation figure from The San Juan Mountaineers' Climber's Guide
to Southwestern Colorado.

"PEAK N", 13,150'   Gore Range   (Unnamed) Mt. Powell 15M 1933
    American Alpine Journal
        "Colorado Climbing Notes, 1935,"* Carleton C. Long, Vol. 2,
        1936, p. 545.
        Ascent note.

    Trail and Timberline
        "The 1933 Climbing Season in Colorado,"* Carleton C. Long,
        No. 184, February 1934, pp. 20-23.
        Attempt note.

        "The Gore Range Outing,"* Everett Long, No. 204, October 1935,
        pp. 111-113.

NAVAJO PEAK, 13,409'   Front Range, Indian Peaks   Monarch Lake 1958
    American Alpine Journal
        "Technical Climbing in the Mountains of Colorado and Wyoming,"*
        Albert Russell Ellingwood, Vol. 1, 1930, pp. 140-147.

        "Colorado Climbing Notes, 1937,"* Carl Blaurock, Vol. 3, 1938,
        p. 218.
        First ascent note of the northeast face, party of six.

    Chicago Mountaineering Club Newsletter
        "North Face of the 'Big Sister' and Navajo," Rolf Buehler,
        Vol. 4, No. 5, November 1950, pp. 12-13.

    Summit
        "Arapaho Glacier Country,"* Weldon F. Heald, Vol. 9, No. 10,
        November 1963, pp. 20-23, 1 Illustration p. 23.
        See the following corrections to the above article:
        "Letters," John M. Clark, Vol. 9, No. 11, December 1963, p. 31.
        "Letters," David Parkhurst, Vol. 10, No. 1, January-
        February 1964, p. 36, 1 Illustration.

        "On the North Face of Navajo," Jonathan Turk, Vol. 17, No. 3,
        April 1971, pp. 32-33, 35.

        "Letters," Chuck Cofer, Vol. 17, No. 5, June 1971, p. 33.
        Rescue note.

    Trail and Timberline
        "The 1918 Outing,"* Nos. 6 & 7, September, October 1918,
        pp. 1-4.

        "Hunting New Glaciers," Lee P. Brown, No. 56, May 1923,
        pp. 2-4, 1 Illustration.

        "Wild, Rugged, Crater Lake Country Will be Opened by U.S.
        Forest Figure-Eight Trails," A. Gayle Waldrop, No. 62,
        November 1923, pp. 1-3, 1 Illustration.

        "Navajo Peak - First Peak Climb of the Season," No. 105,
        June 1927, pp. 3-5, 2 Illustrations.

Illustration, "Isabelle Glacier and Navajo Peak," No. 131, September 1929, p. 8.

"Navajo Peak: Ascent of the East Face," Vera E. DeVries, No. 227, October 1937, pp. 106, 108-109, 1 Illustration. First ascent noted of the east face, Carl Blaurock, Moritz Kreig, Everett Long, Louise Johnson, Marian Cook, and Vera DeVries.

Illustration, "Isabelle Glacier and Navajo Peak," No. 270, June 1941, p. 86.

"The Long Lake Region,"* A. Gayle Waldrop, No. 281, May 1942, pp. 69-70, 1 Illustration.

"Reminiscences," Vera DeVries, No. 281, May 1942, pp. 71-72, 1 Illustration. First ascent noted of the east face.

"Our Indian Peaks,"* Karl E. Boehm, No. 497, May 1960, pp. 73-74.

"Adventure, Culture and Prunes,"* Susan Gibbs, No. 555, March 1965, pp. 58-59.

"About Wind," Theron Miller, No. 652, April 1973, p. 105.

"NAYLOR PEAK",   Front Range
    Trail and Timberline
        "The High Trails of Winter,"* Reynolds Morse, No. 194, December 1934, pp. 163-165.

MT. NEBO, 13,205'   Needle Mountains   Storm King Peak 1964
    Trail and Timberline
        Illustration, "Headwaters of Vallecito Creek, Dominated by Mt. Nebo," Ralph Rosenbaum, No. 608, August 1969, p. 145.

NEEDLE RIDGE, 13,480'   Needle Mountains   Storm King Peak 1964
    American Alpine Journal
        "Various Notes: Chicago Mountaineering Club, 1947,"* Harry Lumby, Vol. 7, April 1948, pp. 107-108. First traverse note from west to east, Joe Stettner, Margurette Sharp, Donald Gruber, and Edmund Lowe.

        "Club Activities: Chicago Mountaineering Club,"* Grover Hartsuch, Vol. 12, 1960, pp. 166-167. Traverse note.

    Chicago Mountaineering Club Newsletter
        "Wrong Mountain Climbed, by New Route! Needle Ridge - August 7, 1947," Joseph Stettner, Vol. 2, No. 4, July to December 1947, p. 15. First west to east climb of ridge noted, Peggy Sharp, Donald Gruber, Edmund Lowe, and Joseph Stettner.

Trail and Timberline
    "San Juan Testimony,"* H. L. McClintock, No. 224, June 1937,
    p. 68.

    "Needle Mountain Notes,"* David Lavender, No. 225, July 1937,
    pp. 80-81, 1 Illustration.
    First east to west traverse noted, Mel Griffiths and Bob
    Ormes.

    "Noname Prospects,"* Mel Griffiths, No. 340, April 1947,
    pp. 56-59.

    "Climbers Guide to Noname,"* No. 342, June 1947, pp. 97-98,
    1 Map.

THE NEEDLES, 10,068'   Front Range, Rocky Mountain National Park
                        Estes Park 1961
    Trail and Timberline
    "Guerilla Tactics Useful for Doggy Climbs: The Gentle Art of
    Freddy Peaking,"* Bob Michael, No. 689, May 1976, pp. 112-115.

MT. NEVA, 12,814'   Front Range   Monarch Lake 1958
    American Alpine Journal
    "Mount Neva, East Face, Indian Peak Range," Bruce Adams,
    Vol. 19, 1974, p. 153.
    East face ascent note, Bart Chandler and Bruce Adams.

    Trail and Timberline
    "Climbing Notes,"* K. S., No. 214, August 1936, p. 92.
    Note on register data.

NEW YORK PEAK, 12,811'   Elk Range   New York Peak 1960
    Climbing
    "Basecamp: Winter Climbing,"* No. 6, March-April 1971, p. 3.
    Attempt note, Rob Gerdey and party.

MT. NIMBUS, 12,706'   Never Summer Range, Rocky Mountain National Park
                       Mount Richthofen 1957
    Trail and Timberline
    "Never Summer Backpack,"* Esther Holt, No. 397, January 1952,
    pp. 9-11.

"NO NAME PEAK", 12,720'(?)   Front Range, Indian Peaks
                             (Unnamed) Monarch Lake 1958
    Trail and Timberline
    "A Circle Trip in the Arikarees,"* Ronald L. Ives, No. 256,
    April 1940, pp. 56-57.

NORTH ARAPAHO PEAK, 13,502'   Front Range, Indian Peaks   Monarch Lake 1958
    Alpine Journal
    "The Rockies of Colorado,"* Evelio Echevarría C., Vol. 71,
    May 1966, pp. 26-36, 1 Map, Bibliography.
    First recorded ascent noted, E. André, J. Bartz, and J. Baer.

Chicago Mountaineering Club Newsletter
"Mt. Arapahoe," Bill Primak, Vol. 4, No. 5, November 1950, pp. 13-14.

Summit
"Arapaho Glacier Country,"* Weldon F. Heald, Vol. 9, No. 10, November 1963, pp. 20-23, 1 Illustration.
See the following corrections to the above article:
"Letters," John M. Clark, Vol. 9, No. 11, December 1963, p. 31.
"Letters," David Parkhurst, Vol. 10, No. 1, January-February 1964, p. 36.

Trail and Timberline
"Up the Arapahoes in January,"* No. 18, March 1920, p. 4.

"An Attack on Arapahoe Peak from the North," Frances Thompson, No. 23, August 1920, p. 7.

"Boulder Bunch Leads A Horde Up the Arapahoes,"* Frances Thompson, No. 35, August 1921, p. 6.

Illustration,* "Arapahoe Peaks and Glacier," Geo. H. Harvey, Jr., No. 48, September 1922, p. 7.

"Winter Climbing Notes,"* No. 158, December 1931, p. 188.
Note on winter ascents, Ernest M. Greenman.

"Climbing Notes,"* No. 217, November 1936, p. 132.
New route attempt note via east arete, Robert C. Lewis, Jr. and Kenneth Segerstrom.

Front cover illustration, "Diamond Lake and Arapaho Peak," Jesse M. Cleveland, Jr., No. 466, October 1957.

"Our Indian Peaks,"* Karl E. Boehm, No. 497, May 1960, pp. 73-74.

"NORTH BLANCA PEAK",   Sangre de Cristo Range
                              (Unnamed) Blanca Peak 1967
   Trail and Timberline
      "Climbing in the Sangre de Cristo,"* Albert R. Ellingwood, No. 81, June 1925, pp. 1-5.

NORTH EOLUS, 14,039'   Needle Mountains   Storm King Peak 1964
   Appalachia
      "Excursions: Colorado Trip,"* E. Folger Taylor and Walter D. Howe, Vol. 23, December 1940, pp. 257-259, 1 Illustration following p. 262.

      "The Old and New West in the Needle Mountains,"* Duncan A. MacInnes, Vol. 23, June 1941, pp. 374-379.

Chicago Mountaineering Club Newsletter
   "Needles Outing of the American Alpine Club,"* Dave Bidwell, Vol. 7, No. 5, November 1953, pp. 10-12.

Harvard Mountaineering
"Climbing Notes, 1964: Colorado Needles,"* Matt Hale, No. 17,
May 1965, pp. 59-60.
Ascent note, Matt Hale and Dave Roberts.

The Mountaineering Journal (British)
Illustration,* "View Southwards from Point Pun in the
Grenadiers," Carleton C. Long, Vol. 1, No. 4, June, July,
August 1933, p. 242.

Trail and Timberline
"Mt. Eolus and Mt. 'North Eolus',"* Grace M. Harvey, No. 107,
September 1927, p. 8.

"Four in One Day,"* Dr. Corwin S. Clarke, No. 107,
September 1927, p. 18.

"San Juan Testimony,"* Harvey Sethman, No. 224, June 1937,
pp. 68-70, 1 Illustration, 1 Illustration p. 67.

"Needle Mountain Notes,"* David Lavender, No. 225, July 1937,
pp. 80-81.

"Noname Prospects,"* Mel Griffiths, No. 340, April 1947,
pp. 56-59, 1 Illustration.

"Climbers Guide to Noname,"* No. 342, June 1947, pp. 97-98,
1 Map.

"NORTH FACE",   Needle Mountains
  Chicago Mountaineering Club Newsletter
    "North Face," Robin Orear, Vol. 24, No. 1, March 1970, p. 8.

NORTH MAROON PEAK, 14,014'   Elk Range   Maroon Bells 1960
See also MAROON BELLS
  Alpine Journal
    "The Rockies of Colorado,"* Evelio Echevarría C., Vol. 71,
    May 1966, pp. 26-36, 1 Illustration, 1 Map, Bibliography.

  American Alpine Journal
    "Technical Climbing in the Mountains of Colorado and Wyoming,"*
    Albert Russell Ellingwood, Vol. 1, 1930, pp. 140-147.

  Appalachia
    "All the 14,000's,"* Carl Melzer, Vol. 22, December 1939,
    pp. 466-479.

    "Accidents: Accident on Maroon Peak, West Elk Mountains,
    Colorado," Robert C. Lewis, Jr., Vol. 29, December 1952,
    pp. 270-272.

    "Alpina: In the Elk Mountains," John A. Woodworth, Vol. 38,
    December 1971, p. 183.
    Solo winter ascent note, Fritz Stammberger.

Chicago Mountaineering Club Newsletter
"Camping at Maroon Bell Lakes,"* Grover Hartsuch, Vol. 10, No. 5, October 1956, pp. 11-12.

"Colorado's Elk Mountains,"* Weldon F. Heald, Vol. 13, No. 6, October 1959, pp. 1-5, Front cover map.

Climbing
"Basecamp: Winter Climbing,"* No. 6, March-April 1971, p. 3. Solo first winter ascent note, Fritz Stammberger.

"Nostalgia/Part II Mundus Est Mons,"* Harvey T. Carter, No. 6, March-April 1971, pp. 3-5. Winter siege note of the north face.

"Basecamp: Winter Climbs,"* No. 8, July-August 1971, p. 14. Winter attempt note, Fritz Stammberger and Frank Whetmore. Solo winter ascent note, Fritz Stammberger.

"Basecamp: Colorado,"* No. 9, September-October 1971, p. 3. Solo climb and ski descent note of the north face, Fritz Stammberger.

"First Ski Descent of North Maroon Bell," Fritz Stammberger, No. 9, September-October 1971, pp. 4-5, 1 Illustration.

"Basecamp: Aspen,"* No. 10, November-December 1971, p. 4. Accident note.

"Basecamp: Colorado,"* No. 38, September-October 1976, pp. 3-5. Note on northeast ridge route.

The Mountaineering Journal (British)
"American Notes: Climbing in the Snowmass Region of the Elk Mountains of Colorado,"* Hubert M. Walters, Vol. 2, No. 2, March, April, May 1934, p. 98. Traverse note of the Maroon Bells.

Off Belay
"Ski Descents of Difficult Routes: North Maroon Bell," No. 1, January-February 1972, p. 42. Ski descent note of the north face, Fritz Stammberger.

Summit
"Colorado's High-Rising Elks,"* Weldon F. Heald, Vol. 8, No. 11, November 1962, pp. 20-23, Inside front cover illustration.

"Hard Hat Saves Climber," Vol. 12, No. 4, May 1966, p. 32.

"The Maroon Bells,"* Stewart Green, Vol. 16, No. 5, June 1970, pp. 16-17, 1 Illustration.

Trail and Timberline
"The Trips and the Country,"* Lucretia Vaile, No. 49, October 1922, pp. 4-7.

"More High Ones,"* No. 52, January 1923, pp. 12-13.

"North Maroon Peak," Dr. Ferdinand Belz, No. 120,
October 1928, pp. 6-7, 1 Illustration.

"The Maroon Bells,"* Donald McBride, No. 180, October 1933,
pp. 143-144, 1 Illustration, 1 Illustration p. 139.

"Junior Outing,"* Rex A. Young, No. 239, November 1938,
pp. 115-116.

"Report on the North Maroon Peak Trip, Labor Day, 1940,"
Elwyn Arps, No. 262, October 1940, pp. 157-159.

"Ski Ascent,"* Whitney Borland, No. 277, January 1942,
pp. 181-183.

"The Maroon Traverse from Snowmass Lake,"* Roy R. Murchison,
No. 322, October 1945, p. 128.

"1873 Tells 1949,"* Louisa Ward Arps, No. 365, May 1949,
pp. 68-70, 1 Illustration following p. 70.

Illustration, "North Maroon Peak: March, 1949," No. 368,
August 1949, p. 112.

"Hi-Peak Ascents of 1949 Summer Outing,"* Bob Steele, No. 371,
November 1949, pp. 164-165.

"My Favorite Mountain," Hugh W. Hetherington, No. 449,
May 1956, pp. 76-78, 1 Illustration.

Front cover illustration,* "Aerial View of North and South
Maroon Peaks (Photo Taken in Early Spring)," Gale Kehmeier,
No. 489, September 1959.

"NORTH MILWAUKEE PEAK", 13,400'   Sangre de Cristo Range
                                    (Unnamed) Crestone Peak 1967
   Trail and Timberline
      Front cover illustration,* "North Milwaukee and Crestone
      Needle," Sam Alfend, No. 611, November 1969.

"NORTH TRAVERSE PEAK", 13,079'   Gore Range   (Unnamed) Willow Lakes 1970
   Trail and Timberline
      "Backpacking in the Gore Range,"* Shirli Voigt, No. 667,
      July 1974, pp. 177-180, 1 Map.

NORTH TWIN THUMB, 13,400'   Needle Mountains   Storm King Peak 1964
See also TWIN THUMBS
   American Alpine Journal
      "Various Notes: Chicago Mountaineering Club, 1947,"* Harry
      Lumby, Vol. 7, April 1948, pp. 107-108.
      Ascent note via north face of the east ridge, Joe Stettner,
      Edith Stettner, Alma Eberli, Max Eberli, and Arthur Tielsch.

"A.A.C. and C.M.C. Joint Outing, Needle Mountains, Colorado,
July 19 - August 9, 1953,"* Henry L. McClintock, Vol. 9, 1954,
pp. 169-171, 1 Illustration following p. 126.

Chicago Mountaineering Club Newsletter
"Climbing the North Thumb - August 14, 1947," Joseph Stettner,
Vol. 2, No. 4, July to December 1947, p. 16.
New route noted.

The Mountaineering Journal (British)
"Correspondence,"* Dwight Lavender, Vol. 2, No. 1, December,
January, February 1933-34, pp. 47-51.
First ascent note.

Trail and Timberline
"The Needle Mountains Expedition,"* Carleton C. Long, No. 181,
November 1933, pp. 155-157, 166.
Possible first ascent noted, San Juan Mountaineers.

"The 1933 Climbing Season in Colorado,"* Carleton C. Long,
No. 184, February 1934, pp. 20-23.
Possible first ascent note, San Juan Mountaineers.

NOTCHTOP MOUNTAIN, 12,129'   Front Range, Rocky Mountain National Park
                               McHenrys Peak 1957
American Alpine Journal
"Notchtop Mountain, East Face," Lawrence Hamilton, Vol. 20,
1975, p. 138.
First ascent note, "White Room" route, Roger Briggs and
Lawrence Hamilton.
Ascent note of northeast corner of rib of the east face,
Dakers Gowans and Lawrence Hamilton.

"Notchtop," Michael Covington, Vol. 20, 1976, p. 460.
New route note on the north face, Doug Snively and Michael
Covington.

"Notchtop Mountain, East Face, Religion," Lawrence Hamilton,
Vol. 20, 1976, p. 461.
Free ascent note, Keith Bell and Lawrence Hamilton.

Appalachia
"The Peaks of Rocky Mountain National Park,"* Roger W. Toll,
Vol. 17, June 1929, pp. 252-260.

"Rock Climbing,"* K. A. H., Vol. 21, December 1937, p. 530.
Attempt note on rock chimney, Dr. M. Beckett Howorth and Carl
Fuller.

Chicago Mountaineering Club Newsletter
"Notch Top," Fritz Coester, Vol. 5, No. 5, November 1951,
p. 11, 1 Map p. 6.

Climbing
"Basecamp: Rocky Mountain National Park,"* Nos. 22 and 23,
Winter 1973-74, p. 36.
New route note, "Religion" on the south face, Larry Hamilton
and Keith Bell.

"View from Within: Colorado Rocky Mountain National Park,"*
No. 28, Winter 1974-75, p. 36.
New route note, "White Room" on the southeast face, Larry
Hamilton and Roger Briggs.
Free ascent note, "Optimus", Larry Hamilton and John Byrd.
New route note, "If She Were My Daughter", Larry Hamilton and
Dakers Gowans.

"Winter Climbing in Rocky Mountain National Park,"* Michael
Covington, No. 37, July-August 1976, pp. 7-13,
3 Illustrations.
Solo winter ascent noted of the Spiral route, Michael
Covington.
First winter ascent noted of the north face, Michael
Covington and Dean Ketchum.
Ascent noted of the north face, Doug Snively and Michael
Covington.
Winter ascent noted of the south ridge, Duncan Ferguson and
John Markel.

Iowa Mountaineers Journal
"Colorado's Rockies,"* Ruth Norman, Vol. 1, No. 10,
February 1945, pp. 53-57.

Off Belay
"Climbing at Rocky Mountain,"* Walt Fricke, No. 2, April 1972,
pp. 17-23, 1 Illustration, 2 Maps.

"More on National Parks: Rocky Mountain National Park,"*
No. 21, June 1975, pp. 39, 41.
Note on recorded ascents during the year.

Trail and Timberline
Illustration, "'Notchtop' in Winter, Rocky Mountain National
Park," William F. Ervin, No. 17, January 1920, p. 23.

"Circle Trips in RMNP,"* William C. Ramaley, No. 630,
June 1971, pp. 125-128.

"Seven Spires: A Story of Some Climbs in Rocky Mountain
National Park,"* Kent Keller, No. 651, March 1973, pp. 70-74.

OGALALLA PEAK, 13,138'   Front Range, Indian Peaks   Isolation Peak 1958
  Summit
      "Arapaho Glacier Country,"* Weldon F. Heald, Vol. 9, No. 10,
      November 1963, pp. 20-23, 1 Illustration top left p. 20.
      See the following corrections to the above article:
      "Letters," John M. Clark, Vol. 9, No. 11, December 1963, p. 31.
      "Letters," David Parkhurst, Vol. 10, No. 1, January-
      February 1964, p. 36.

  Trail and Timberline
      "A Glimpse of Wild Basin,"* Albert Russell Ellingwood,
      No. 109, November 1927, pp. 3-6.

      "Junior Journeys,"* Molly Sethman, No. 298, October 1943,
      pp. 127-128.

      "Buchanan Pass - Mt. Ogalalla Backpack Trip," George W. Kelly,
      No. 308, August 1944, p. 96.

      "Our Indian Peaks,"* Karl E. Boehm, No. 497, May 1960, pp. 73-
      74.

OH-BE-JOYFUL PEAK, 12,400'   Ruby Range   Oh-Be-Joyful 1961
  Trail and Timberline
      "Some Took the High Road,"* Stan Shepard, No. 455,
      November 1956, pp. 165-167.

OHIO PEAK, 12,271'   West Elk Range   Mt. Axtell 1961
  Trail and Timberline
      "The Mountain Ranges of Colorado,"* Kenneth Segerstrom,
      No. 215, September 1936, pp. 109-115, 1 Map.

MT. OLYMPUS, 8,808'   Front Range   Panorama Peak 1962
  Trail and Timberline
      "Guerilla Tactics Useful for Doggy Climbs: The Gentle Art of
      Freddy Peaking,"* Bob Michael, No. 689, May 1976, pp. 112-115.

"OMINOUS PINNACLE", 13,000'   Needle Mountains
                               (Unnamed) Storm King Peak 1964
  American Alpine Journal
      "Ascents in the San Juan Needles,"* George I. Bell, Vol. 13,
      1962, pp. 230-231.
      First ascent note, Graham Matthews and George I. Bell.

  Trail and Timberline
      "Some Ascents in the San Juan Needles,"* George Bell, No. 518,
      February 1962, pp. 19-21, 1 Illustration.
      First ascent noted, Graham Matthews and George Bell.

OPHIR NEEDLES, 12,070'   San Juan Mountains   Ophir 1955
  Climbing
      "'Mail Chute', Post Office Wall, Ophir Needles, Colo.,"
      No. 10, November-December 1971, p. 28.
      First ascent note, Tom and Wayne Merrill.

"'South Face', Post Office Wall, Ophir Needles, Colo.,"
No. 10, November-December 1971, p. 28.
First ascent note, Henry Barber and Tom Stinson.

"'Hot Wee Wee', South Face, Ophir Needles, Colo.," No. 11,
January-February 1972, p. 26.
First ascent note, Henry Barber and Jim Dixon.

"'Joe's Overhang', South Side, Ophir Needles, Colo.," No. 11,
January-February 1972, p. 28.
First ascent note, Henry Barber, John Butler, and Dana Bartlett.

ORMES PEAK, 9,727'   Rampart Range   Cascade 1961
   Trail and Timberline
      "Group Activities: Pikes Peak Group,"* Mildred May, No. 179,
      September 1933, p. 130.
      Note on naming.

MT. ORTON, 11,724'   Front Range, Rocky Mountain National Park
                      Allens Park 1957
   Trail and Timberline
      "A Glimpse of Wild Basin,"* Albert Russell Ellingwood,
      No. 109, November 1927, pp. 3-6.

      "Mountain Climbing and Statistics in Rocky Mountain National
      Park,"* John C. Whitnah and Robert C. Peterson, No. 343,
      July 1947, pp. 116-117.

MT. OSO, 13,684'   Needle Mountains   Emerald Lake 1973
   Alpine Journal
      "The Rockies of Colorado,"* Evelio Echevarría C., Vol. 71,
      May 1966, pp. 26-36, 1 Map, Bibliography.

OTIS PEAK, 12,486'   Front Range, Rocky Mountain National Park
                      McHenrys Peak 1957
   Appalachia
      "The Peaks of Rocky Mountain National Park,"* Roger W. Toll,
      Vol. 17, June 1929, pp. 252-260.

   Chicago Mountaineering Club Newsletter
      "Flattop, Hallett, Otis, and Taylor Peaks,"* Barbara Heiberg,
      Vol. 5, No. 5, November 1951, pp. 9-10, 1 Map p. 6.

   Iowa Mountaineers Journal
      "Colorado's Rockies,"* Ruth Norman, Vol. 1, No. 10,
      February 1945, pp. 53-57.

   Trail and Timberline
      "Circle Trips in RMNP,"* William C. Ramaley, No. 630,
      June 1971, pp. 125-128.

OTTER MOUNTAIN, 12,766'   Front Range   Georgetown 1957
   Trail and Timberline
      "The Tale,"* No. 310, October 1944, pp. 117-121.

"MT. OTTO", 12,851'   Sangre de Cristo Range   (Unnamed) Howard 15M 1959
    Trail and Timberline
        "New Names in Sangres,"* No. 621, September 1970, p. 206.

MT. OURAY, 13,971'   Sawatch Range   Bonanza 15M 1959
    Trail and Timberline
        "Note," No. 247, July 1939, p. 94.
        Note on first scheduled ascent by the CMC via westerly ridge.

        "A Guide to Colorado's Almost-Fourteens,"* William A. Graves,
        No. 683, November 1975, pp. 225-227.

OUZEL PEAK, 12,716'   Front Range, Rocky Mountain National Park
                       Isolation Peak 1958
    Trail and Timberline
        "A Glimpse of Wild Basin,"* Albert Russell Ellingwood,
        No. 109, November 1927, pp. 3-6.

        "Junior Journeys,"* Molly Sethman, No. 298, October 1943,
        pp. 127-128.

MT. OWEN, 13,058'   Ruby Range   Oh-Be-Joyful 1961
    Trail and Timberline
        "The Mountain Ranges of Colorado,"* Kenneth Segerstrom,
        No. 215, September 1936, pp. 109-115, 1 Map.

        "Pittsburgh on the Slate,"* Louisa Ward Arps, No. 450,
        June 1956, pp. 87-90.

        "Some Took the High Road,"* Stan Shepard, No. 455,
        November 1956, pp. 165-167.

MT. OWEN, 13,387'   Sangre de Cristo Range   Electric Peak 15M 1959
    Trail and Timberline
        "New Maps of the Sangre de Cristo Range,"* John L. J. Hart,
        No. 519, March 1962, pp. 32-33.

MT. OXFORD, 14,153'   Sawatch Range   Mt. Harvard 15M 1955
    American Alpine Journal
        "Naming America's Mountains - The Colorado Rockies,"* Francis
        P. Farquhar, Vol. 12, 1961, pp. 319-346.

    Appalachia
        "All the 14,000's,"* Carl Melzer, Vol. 22, December 1939,
        pp. 466-479.

    Trail and Timberline
        "A New 14,000 Foot Peak," No. 155, September 1931, p. 142.

        "The High Peaks of the La Plata Mining Region,"* John L. J.
        Hart, No. 159, January 1932, pp. 3-4, 14, 1 Map.

        "Some Trails of the La Plata Mining Region,"* Bruce and
        Elisabeth MacCannon, No. 159, January 1932, pp. 5-6,
        1 Illustration.

"First Ascent of Mt. Oxford," J. L. J. Hart, No. 178,
August 1933, p. 112.

"The 1933 Climbing Season in Colorado,"* Carleton C. Long,
No. 184, February 1934, pp. 20-23.
Ascent note, Francis M. Froelicher and party.

"Surveying the La Plata Mining Region,"* Ronald L. Ives,
No. 192, October 1934, p. 139, 1 Map.
"A Correction," No. 196, February 1935, p. 22.
Map correction.

"Innocent Bystander,"* No. 259, July 1940, p. 110.
Elevation note.

"A Conglomerate Review of the C.M.C. Summer Outing,
August 15-23, 1942 - Collegiate Range,"* Nancy Plowman, Eliot
Moses, Harold Brewer, Mary Wagner, No. 287, November 1942,
pp. 141-143, 1 Map p. 140, Front cover illustration.

"Colorado's Mountains are Higher than You Think,"* Arthur J.
McNair, No. 323, November 1945, pp. 139-142.

"Junior Jottings,"* No. 371, November 1949, pp. 172-173.

"First Official Measurement of Many 14,000 Foot Peaks,"* John
L. J. Hart, No. 446, February 1956, pp. 29-30.

"PEAK P", 12,965'   Gore Range   (Unnamed) Vail East 1970
    American Alpine Journal
        "Colorado Climbing Notes, 1935,"* Carleton C. Long, Vol. 2,
        1936, p. 545.
        First ascent note, Bob Lewis, Fred Nagel, John Nagel, and
        Gene Schaetzel.

    Trail and Timberline
        "The Gore Range Outing,"* Everett Long, No. 204, October 1935,
        pp. 111-113.
        First ascent noted, Bob Lewis, Fred Nagel, John Nagel, and
        Gene Schaetzel.

        Illustration,* "Upper Slate Lake, Gore Range, with Peaks Q
        (Left) and P (Right) Behind," Hugh E. Kingery, No. 569,
        May 1966, p. 80.

PACIFIC PEAK, 13,950'   Tenmile Range   Breckenridge 1970
    Trail and Timberline
        Illustration,* "Ten Mile Range Between Mt. Fletcher and
        Pacific Peak," Curt E. Krieser, No. 326, February 1946, p. 19.

        "Mountain Club Scales Pacific Peak," Helen Rich, No. 396,
        December 1951, p. 162.
        Reprinted from The Summit County Journal, Breckenridge,
        Colorado, August 31, 1951.

        "A Guide to Colorado's Almost-Fourteens,"* William A. Graves,
        No. 683, November 1975, pp. 225-227.

PAGODA MOUNTAIN, 13,497'   Front Range, Rocky Mountain National Park
                            Isolation Peak 1958
    American Alpine Journal
        "Technical Climbing in the Mountains of Colorado and Wyoming,"*
        Albert Russell Ellingwood, Vol. 1, 1930, pp. 140-147.

    Appalachia
        "The Peaks of Rocky Mountain National Park,"* Roger W. Toll,
        Vol. 17, June 1929, pp. 252-260.

    Chicago Mountaineering Club Newsletter
        "Traverse of Chief's Head and Pagoda,"* Jack Fralick, Vol. 5,
        No. 5, November 1951, pp. 18-19, 1 Map p. 6.

    Climbing
        "Basecamp,"* No. 32, September-October 1975, p. 33.
        Ascent note of the "Nose" in the center of the west face,
        Jeff Bevan and Dan Hare.

    Trail and Timberline
        "A Glimpse of Wild Basin,"* Albert Russell Ellingwood,
        No. 109, November 1927, pp. 3-6.

        "Some First Ascent Possibilities in Colorado,"* Kenneth
        Segerstrom, No. 165, July 1932, pp. 103-104.

"Climbing Notes,"* K. S., No. 215, September 1936, p. 115.
Note on unclimbed north face.

"Chief's Head - Pagoda,"* Roy R. Murchison, No. 249,
September 1939, pp. 121-122, 2 Illustrations.

"Mountain Climbing and Statistics in Rocky Mountain National
Park,"* John C. Whitnah and Robert C. Peterson, No. 343,
July 1947, pp. 116-117.

PAIUTE PEAK, 13,088'   Front Range, Indian Peaks   Monarch Lake 1958
    Trail and Timberline
        "Climbing Notes,"* No. 143, September 1930, p. 6.
    Ridge traverse note from Pawnee Peak to Paiute Peak, Hubert M.
    Walters and Frank Allen.

        "Some First Ascent Possibilities in Colorado,"* Kenneth
    Segerstrom, No. 165, July 1932, pp. 103-104.

        "The Long Lake Region,"* A. Gayle Waldrop, No. 281, May 1942,
    pp. 69-70.

        "Our Indian Peaks,"* Karl E. Boehm, No. 497, May 1960, pp. 73-
    74.

PALISADE MOUNTAIN, 8,264'   Front Range   Drake 1962
    Trail and Timberline
        "Guerilla Tactics Useful for Doggy Climbs: The Gentle Art of
    Freddy Peaking,"* Bob Michael, No. 689, May 1976, pp. 112-115.

PALMYRA PEAK, 13,319'   San Juan Mountains   Telluride 1955
    Trail and Timberline
        Front cover drawing, "Mt. Palmyra - San Juans," Mary Hope
    Robinson, No. 596, August 1968.

PARKVIEW MOUNTAIN, 12,296'   Rabbit Ears Range   Parkview Mountain 1956
    Trail and Timberline
        "The Mountain Ranges of Colorado,"* Kenneth Segerstrom,
    No. 215, September 1936, pp. 109-115, 1 Map.

MT. PARNASSUS, 13,574'   Front Range   Grays Peak 1958
    Trail and Timberline
        "Ski Trip to Mount Parnassus in June," Karl Neubuerger,
    No. 347, November 1947, p. 183.

        "Parnassus and Bard Peaks,"* Esther L. Holt, No. 499,
    July 1960, pp. 102-103, 1 Illustration.

PARRY PEAK, 13,391'   Front Range   Empire 1958
    Trail and Timberline
        "Our Mountains in Winter,"* No. 138, April 1930, p. 12.

        "An Ascent of Parry Peak on Skis from West Portal," Graeme
    McGowan, No. 142, August 1930, pp. 3-4, 11, 1 Illustration.

Front cover illustration, "Parry Peak," Graeme McGowan,
No. 206, December 1935.

"Summit Lake to Adolph's (Winter Park),"* Edward F. Taylor,
No. 304, April 1944, pp. 39-40, 45, 1 Illustration.

"Up Mamma, Pappa, and Baby Peaks,"* Esther Holt, No. 386,
February 1951, pp. 18-19.

"MT. PARSENN",   Front Range
   Trail and Timberline
     Illustration, "View from Mt. Parsenn Looking Northeast," Erl
     Ellis, No. 151, May 1931, p. 68.

PAWNEE PEAK, 12,943'   Front Range, Indian Peaks   Monarch Lake 1958
   Alpine Journal
     "The Rockies of Colorado,"* Evelio Echevarría C., Vol. 71,
     May 1966, pp. 26-36, 1 Map, Bibliography.

   Chicago Mountaineering Club Newsletter
     "Club Outing in the Arapahoes,"* Ray J. Gatz, Vol. 4, No. 5,
     November 1950, pp. 8-9.

   Harvard Mountaineering
     "Climbing Notes, 1964: Colorado, Front Range,"* Dave Roberts,
     No. 17, May 1965, pp. 60-61.
     Winter ascent note, Dave Roberts and Burt Redmayne.

   Trail and Timberline
     "Climbing Notes,"* No. 143, September 1930, p. 6.
     Ridge traverse note from Pawnee Peak to Paiute Peak, Hubert
     M. Walters and Frank Allen.

     "The Long Lake Region,"* A. Gayle Waldrop, No. 281, May 1942,
     pp. 69-70.

     "Our Indian Peaks,"* Karl E. Boehm, No. 497, May 1960, pp. 73-
     74.

PEAK 1, 12,805'   Tenmile Range   Frisco 1970
   Trail and Timberline
     "Ten Mile Range Traverse,"* Carl Melzer, No. 326,
     February 1946, pp. 19-23.

"PEAK 2" (TENMILE PEAK), 12,933'   Tenmile Range   (Unnamed) Frisco 1970
See TENMILE PEAK

PEAK TWO, 13,475'   Needle Mountains   Storm King Peak 1964
   Chicago Mountaineering Club Newsletter
     "Peak Two," Lilias Jones, Vol. 24, No. 1, March 1970, p. 6.

     "Peak Two," Emily Smith, Vol. 24, No. 1, March 1970, pp. 11-12.

     "Peak Two - East Face," John Sellers, Vol. 24, No. 1,
     March 1970, p. 16.

"Peak Two - Easy Route," Les Orear, Vol. 24, No. 1,
March 1970, p. 16.

PEAK 3, 12,676'   Tenmile Range   Frisco 1970
    Trail and Timberline
        "Ten Mile Range Traverse,"* Carl Melzer, No. 326,
        February 1946, pp. 19-23.

PEAK THREE, 13,478'   Needle Mountains   Storm King Peak 1964
    Chicago Mountaineering Club Newsletter
        "Peak Three," Filmore Baltierra, Vol. 24, No. 1, March 1970,
        p. 8, 1 Illustration p. 15.

        "East Ridge of Peak Three," Jay Orear, Vol. 24, No. 1,
        March 1970, p. 8, 1 Illustration p. 15.

PEAK 4, 12,866'   Tenmile Range   Frisco 1970
    Trail and Timberline
        "Ten Mile Range Traverse,"* Carl Melzer, No. 326,
        February 1946, pp. 19-23.

PEAK FOUR, 13,410'   Needle Mountains   Storm King Peak 1964
    The Mountaineering Journal (British)
        Illustration,* "Southeast from Heisspitz," Carleton C. Long,
        Vol. 1, No. 4, June, July, August 1933, p. 241.

    Trail and Timberline
        "The Colorado Mountain Club Announces the Twenty-Eighth Annual
        Summer Outing,"* Henry Buchtel, Lewis Giesecke, Kenneth
        Segerstrom, No. 265, January 1941, pp. 9-14, 1 Map, Front cover
        sketch map.

        "Garlic Gulch Episode,"* L. V. Giesecke, No. 274,
        October 1941, pp. 143-145.
        First ascent noted on CMC outing.

        "Climbers Guide to Noname,"* No. 342, June 1947, pp. 97-98,
        1 Map.

        "Climber's Guide from Noname Creek,"* Henry Buchtel, No. 345,
        September 1947, pp. 143-144.

        "Revised Climbers' Guide from Noname Creek,"* William E.
        Davis, No. 502, October 1960, pp. 149-154, 1 Map.

PEAK 5, 12,855'   Tenmile Range   Frisco 1970
    Trail and Timberline
        "Ten Mile Range Traverse,"* Carl Melzer, No. 326,
        February 1946, pp. 19-23.

PEAK FIVE, 13,283'   Needle Mountains   Storm King Peak 1964
    Trail and Timberline
        "The Colorado Mountain Club Announces the Twenty-Eighth Annual
        Summer Outing,"* Henry Buchtel, Lewis Giesecke, Kenneth
        Segerstrom, No. 265, January 1941, pp. 9-14, 1 Map, Front cover
        sketch map.

"Garlic Gulch Episode,"* L. V. Giesecke, No. 274,
October 1941, pp. 143-145.
First ascent noted on CMC outing.

"Climbers Guide to Noname,"* No. 342, June 1947, pp. 97-98,
1 Map.

"Revised Climbers' Guide from Noname Creek,"* William E.
Davis, No. 502, October 1960, pp. 149-154, 1 Map.

PEAK 6, 12,573'   Tenmile Range   Breckenridge 1970
   Trail and Timberline
      "Ten Mile Range Traverse,"* Carl Melzer, No. 326,
      February 1946, pp. 19-23.

PEAK SIX, 13,705'   Needle Mountains   Storm King Peak 1964
   American Alpine Journal
      "Southwestern Colorado Climbing Notes - 1933,"* Dwight G.
      Lavender, Vol. 2, 1934, p. 257.
      Second ascent note, San Juan Mountaineers.

   The Mountaineering Journal (British)
      "Correspondence,"* Dwight Lavender, Vol. 2, No. 1, December,
      January, February 1933-34, pp. 47-51.
      (Second) ascent note, San Juan Mountaineers.

   Trail and Timberline
      "The Needle Mountains Expedition,"* Carleton C. Long, No. 181,
      November 1933, pp. 155-157, 166.
      (Second) ascent noted, San Juan Mountaineers.

      "The 1933 Climbing Season in Colorado,"* Carleton C. Long,
      No. 184, February 1934, pp. 20-23.
      Possible second ascent note, San Juan Mountaineers.
      First ascent note, Percy Hagerman (and Harold Clark).

      "The Colorado Mountain Club Announces the Twenty-Eighth Annual
      Summer Outing,"* Henry Buchtel, Lewis Giesecke, Kenneth
      Segerstrom, No. 265, January 1941, pp. 9-14, 1 Illustration,
      1 Map, Front cover sketch map.

      "Climbers Guide to Noname,"* No. 342, June 1947, pp. 97-98,
      1 Map.

      "Revised Climbers' Guide from Noname Creek,"* William E.
      Davis, No. 502, October 1960, pp. 149-154, 1 Map.

      "Trails of the Western Weminuche,"* William Weihofen, Ralph
      Rosenbaum, and Henri Navelet, No. 608, August 1969, pp. 144-
      147.

PEAK 7, 12,665'   Tenmile Range   Breckenridge 1970
   Trail and Timberline
      "Ten Mile Range Traverse,"* Carl Melzer, No. 326,
      February 1946, pp. 19-23.

PEAK SEVEN, 13,682'   Needle Mountains   Storm King Peak 1964
    Trail and Timberline
        "The Colorado Mountain Club Announces the Twenty-Eighth Annual
        Summer Outing,"* Henry Buchtel, Lewis Giesecke, Kenneth
        Segerstrom, No. 265, January 1941, pp. 9-14, 1 Illustration,
        1 Map, Front cover sketch map.

        "Garlic Gulch Episode,"* L. V. Giesecke, No. 274,
        October 1941, pp. 143-145.
        First ascent noted on CMC outing.

PEAK 8, 12,987'   Tenmile Range   Breckenridge 1970
    Trail and Timberline
        "Ten Mile Range Traverse,"* Carl Melzer, No. 326,
        February 1946, pp. 19-23.

PEAK EIGHT, 13,228'   Needle Mountains   Storm King Peak 1964
    American Alpine Journal
        "Club Activities: Harvard Mountaineering Club,"* David S.
        Roberts, Vol. 14, 1964, pp. 243-244.
        Probable first ascent note.

    Harvard Mountaineering
        "Climbing Notes, 1963: Colorado, Needle Mountains,"* Dave
        Roberts, No. 17, May 1965, pp. 55-56.
        Possible first ascent note, Don Jensen and Dave Roberts.

    Trail and Timberline
        "The Colorado Mountain Club Announces the Twenty-Eighth Annual
        Summer Outing,"* Henry Buchtel, Lewis Giesecke, Kenneth
        Segerstrom, No. 265, January 1941, pp. 9-14, 1 Map, Front cover
        sketch map.

        "The Grenadiers in Winter,"* David S. Roberts, No. 547,
        July 1964, pp. 111-117, 1 Illustration.
        First ascent noted, David S. Roberts and Don Jensen.

PEAK 9, 13,195'   Tenmile Range   Breckenridge 1970
    Trail and Timberline
        "Ten Mile Range Traverse,"* Carl Melzer, No. 326,
        February 1946, pp. 19-23.

PEAK NINE, 13,402'   Needle Mountains   Storm King Peak 1964
    Trail and Timberline
        "The Colorado Mountain Club Announces the Twenty-Eighth Annual
        Summer Outing,"* Henry Buchtel, Lewis Giesecke, Kenneth
        Segerstrom, No. 265, January 1941, pp. 9-14, 1 Map, Front cover
        sketch map.

        "Letters to the Editor,"* Martin A. Etter, No. 610,
        October 1969, p. 187.
        East face note.

PEAK 10, 13,633'   Tenmile Range   Breckenridge 1970
   Trail and Timberline
      "Ten Mile Range Traverse,"* Carl Melzer, No. 326,
      February 1946, pp. 19-23.

PEAK TEN, 13,392'   Needle Mountains   Storm King Peak 1964
   The Mountaineering Journal (British)
      Illustration,* "Southeast from Heisspitz," Carleton C. Long,
      Vol. 1, No. 4, June, July, August 1933, p. 241.

   Trail and Timberline
      "The Colorado Mountain Club Announces the Twenty-Eighth Annual
      Summer Outing,"* Henry Buchtel, Lewis Giesecke, Kenneth
      Segerstrom, No. 265, January 1941, pp. 9-14.

      "Noname Prospects,"* Mel Griffiths, No. 340, April 1947,
      pp. 56-59.

      "Climbers Guide to Noname,"* No. 342, June 1947, pp. 97-98,
      1 Map, 1 Illustration p. 94.

      "Climber's Guide from Noname Creek,"* Henry Buchtel, No. 345,
      September 1947, pp. 143-144.

      Illustration,* "Upper Basin of No-Name Creek - Peaks Left to
      Right: Jagged Mtn., Peak 10, Knifepoint, and North Ridge of
      Sunlight Peak," No. 419, November 1953, p. 156.

      "Revised Climbers' Guide from Noname Creek,"* William E.
      Davis, No. 502, October 1960, pp. 149-154, 1 Map.

      Illustration,* "Jagged Peak, Peak Ten and Knife Point from
      Scepter," No. 543, March 1964, p. 42.

PEAK ELEVEN, 13,460'   Needle Mountains   Storm King Peak 1964
   American Alpine Journal
      "Southwestern Colorado Climbing Notes - 1933,"* Dwight G.
      Lavender, Vol. 2, 1934, p. 257.
      First ascent note, San Juan Mountaineers.

   The Mountaineering Journal (British)
      Illustration,* "View Southwards from Point Pun in the
      Grenadiers," Carleton C. Long, Vol. 1, No. 4, June, July,
      August 1933, p. 242.

      "Correspondence,"* Dwight Lavender, Vol. 2, No. 1, December,
      January, February 1933-34, pp. 47-51.
      First ascent note, San Juan Mountaineers.

   Trail and Timberline
      "The Needle Mountains Expedition,"* Carleton C. Long, No. 181,
      November 1933, pp. 155-157, 166, 1 Illustration.
      First ascent noted, San Juan Mountaineers.

"The 1933 Climbing Season in Colorado,"* Carleton C. Long,
No. 184, February 1934, pp. 20-23.
Possible first ascent note, San Juan Mountaineers.

"Climbers Guide to Noname,"* No. 342, June 1947, pp. 97-98,
1 Map.

"Revised Climbers' Guide from Noname Creek,"* William E.
Davis, No. 502, October 1960, pp. 149-154, 1 Map.

"PEAK TWELVE", 13,120'   Needle Mountains   (Unnamed) Storm King Peak 1964
    American Alpine Journal
        "Southwestern Colorado Climbing Notes - 1933,"* Dwight G.
        Lavender, Vol. 2, 1934, p. 257.
        Probable first ascent note, San Juan Mountaineers.

    The Mountaineering Journal (British)
        "Correspondence,"* Dwight Lavender, Vol. 2, No. 1, December,
        January, February 1933-34, pp. 47-51.
        First ascent note, San Juan Mountaineers.

    Trail and Timberline
        "The Needle Mountains Expedition,"* Carleton C. Long, No. 181,
        November 1933, pp. 155-157, 166.
        Probable first ascent noted, San Juan Mountaineers.

        "The 1933 Climbing Season in Colorado,"* Carleton C. Long,
        No. 184, February 1934, pp. 20-23.
        Possible first ascent note, San Juan Mountaineers.

        "Climbers Guide to Noname,"* No. 342, June 1947, pp. 97-98,
        1 Map.

        "Pigeon, Turret, Peak 12, Etc. or the Fly Camp of '53,"*
        William E. Davis, No. 419, November 1953, pp. 155-158.

        "Revised Climbers' Guide from Noname Creek,"* William E.
        Davis, No. 502, October 1960, pp. 149-154, 1 Map.

PEAK THIRTEEN ("SCEPTER", "SPECTOR"), 13,705'   Needle Mountains
                                                 Storm King Peak 1964
    Chicago Mountaineering Club Newsletter
        "Impromptu Climb of Scepter - August 11, 1947," Groves
        Kilbourn, Vol. 2, No. 4, July to December 1947, p. 17.

        "Needles Outing of the American Alpine Club,"* Dave Bidwell,
        Vol. 7, No. 5, November 1953, pp. 10-12.

    The Mountaineering Journal (British)
        Illustration,* "View Southwards from Point Pun in the
        Grenadiers," Carleton C. Long, Vol. 1, No. 4, June, July,
        August 1933, p. 242.

        Illustration,* "View South from Heisspitz," Carleton C. Long,
        Vol. 1, No. 4, June, July, August 1933, p. 242.

Trail and Timberline
   "Climbers Guide to Noname,"* No. 342, June 1947, pp. 97-98,
   1 Map.

   "Climber's Guide from Noname Creek,"* Henry Buchtel, No. 345,
   September 1947, pp. 143-144.

   "Revised Climbers' Guide from Noname Creek,"* William E.
   Davis, No. 502, October 1960, pp. 149-154, 1 Map.

   "Letters to the Editor,"* Martin A. Etter, No. 610,
   October 1969, p. 187.
   East face note.
   Note on 1600 foot north facing ridge directly north ½ mile of
   Peak Thirteen.

PEAK FIFTEEN (TURRET NEEDLES), 13,680'   Needle Mountains
See also TURRET NEEDLES   Snowdon Peak 1964
   The Mountaineering Journal (British)
      Illustration,* "View Southwards from Point Pun in the
      Grenadiers," Carleton C. Long, Vol. 1, No. 4, June, July,
      August 1933, p. 242.

   Trail and Timberline
      "Climbers Guide to Noname,"* No. 342, June 1947, pp. 97-98,
      1 Map.

      "Confessions of A Solo Climber or How I Recanted My Heresy,"*
      Wilbur F. Arnold, No. 389, May 1951, pp. 51-55.
      Arnold possibly mistakenly identified Peak Fifteen as Peak
      Sixteen. See T&T, No. 393, September 1951, pp. 113-114 for
      explanation.

      "New York Basin Ascents,"* Henry L. McClintock, No. 393,
      September 1951, pp. 113-114.
      First ascent noted, Joe Merhar, Chris Schoredos, Frank
      McClintock, and Henry L. McClintock.

PEAK SIXTEEN (TURRET NEEDLES), 13,480'   Needle Mountains
See also TURRET NEEDLES   Snowdon Peak 1964
   Trail and Timberline
      "Climbers Guide to Noname,"* No. 342, June 1947, pp. 97-98,
      1 Map.

      "New York Basin Ascents,"* Henry L. McClintock, No. 393,
      September 1951, pp. 113-114.
      First ascent noted, Joe Merhar, Chris Schoredos, Frank
      McClintock, and Henry L. McClintock.

"PEAK SEVENTEEN" (LITTLE FINGER, TURRET NEEDLES), 13,200'   Needle Mountains
See also LITTLE FINGER, TURRET NEEDLES   (Unnamed) Snowdon Peak 1964
   Trail and Timberline
      "New York Basin Ascents,"* Henry L. McClintock, No. 393,
      September 1951, pp. 113-114, 1 Illustration.
      First ascent noted, Joe Merhar, Chris Schoredos, Frank
      McClintock, and Henry L. McClintock.

"PEAK EIGHTEEN", 13,472'   Needle Mountains   (Unnamed) Columbine Pass 1973
    American Alpine Journal
        "Colorado Climbing Notes, 1934,"* Carleton C. Long, Vol. 2,
        1935, p. 416.
        Probable first ascent note, John Nelson and Everett Long.

    Trail and Timberline
        "The 1934 Climbing Season in Colorado,"* Carleton C. Long,
        No. 196, February 1935, pp. 15-18.
        First ascent note, Everett Long and John Nelson.

        "Denver Junior Summer Outing,"* Louise Jackson, No. 443,
        November 1955, pp. 190-191.

        "Chicago Basin Expedition,"* Al Ossinger, No. 559, July 1965,
        pp. 131-133.

"PEAK 12,694'", 12,666'   Front Range   (Unnamed) Byers Peak 1957
                                          (Unnamed) Fraser 15M 1926, 12,694'
    Trail and Timberline
        "Suggestions for Two Good 'Summit' Ski Trips Near Denver,"*
        Karl Neubuerger, No. 290, February 1943, pp. 20-21.

"PEAK 12,738'", 12,578'   Gore Range   (Unnamed) Vail Pass 1970
                                         (Unnamed) Dillon 15M 1929, 12,738'
    Trail and Timberline
        Illustration, "Peak 12,738," Carl Melzer, No. 284,
        August 1942, p. 105.

"PEAK 12,750'", 12,752'   Front Range   (Unnamed) Loveland Pass 1958
                                          (Unnamed) Montezuma 15M 1933, 12,750'
    Trail and Timberline
        "The Winter Outing - 1943: Zipfelberger Cabin - Loveland Pass
        Area,"* Bill Steele, No. 292, April 1943, pp. 49-50.

"PEAK 12,850'",   Gore Range
    Chicago Mountaineering Club Newsletter
        "Ascents by Club Members,"* Stanley Midgely, Vol. 1, No. 3,
        September to December 1945, pp. 10-11.
        First ascent note, Stanley Midgely, 1935.

"PEAK 13,053'" ("MT. SOLITUDE"), 13,075'   Gore Range
                                            (Unnamed) Vail East 1970
                                            (Unnamed) Minturn 15M 1934, 13,053'
    Chicago Mountaineering Club Newsletter
        "Ascents by Club Members,"* Stanley Midgely, Vol. 1, No. 3,
        September to December 1945, pp. 10-11.
        First ascent note, Stanley Midgely.

    Trail and Timberline
        "Behind the Front - The Gore Range," Stanley W. Midgely, Jr.,
        No. 296, August 1943, pp. 101-104.
        (First) ascent noted, Stanley Midgely.

"PEAK 13,135'", 13,135'   Elk Range   (Unnamed) Pearl Pass 1961
    Trail and Timberline
        "'F' is for Fun, Friends and Fiasco,"* Dick Walker, No. 676,
    April 1975, pp. 73, 75.

"PEAK 13,200'" ("MT. VALHALLA"), 13,180'   Gore Range
See also "MT. VALHALLA" in ADDENDA p. 258.(Unnamed) Willow Lakes 1970
                                        (Unnamed) Dillon 15M 1929, 13,200'
    Chicago Mountaineering Club Newsletter
        "Ascents by Club Members,"* Stanley Midgely, Vol. 1, No. 3,
    September to December 1945, pp. 10-11.
    First ascent note, Stanley Midgely, 1943.

"PEAK 13,330'" ("EAST THORN"), 13,333'   Gore Range
                                    (Unnamed) Willow Lakes 1970
                                    (Unnamed) Dillon 15M 1929, 13,330'

    Trail and Timberline
        "Notes on the Gore Range, Summer, 1942,"* Carl Melzer,
    No. 284, August 1942, pp. 103-106.

        "Rock Climbing in the Gore Range,"* Mark P. Addison, No. 457,
    January 1957, pp. 3-4, 13, 2 Maps.

"PEAK 13,500'", 13,615'   Tenmile Range   (Unnamed) Breckenridge 1970
                                    (Unnamed) Mt. Lincoln 15M 1938, 13,600'
    Trail and Timberline
        "Ten Mile Range Traverse,"* Carl Melzer, No. 326,
    February 1946, pp. 19-23.

"PEAK 13,515'", 13,515'   Needle Mountains   (Unnamed) Snowdon Peak 1964
    Trail and Timberline
        "Letters to the Editor,"* Martin A. Etter, No. 610,
    October 1969, p. 187.
    North ridge note.

"PEAK 13,550'" ("FORSEE"), 13,400'   Elk Range
                                (Unnamed) Snowmass Mtn. 1960
    Trail and Timberline
        "Hikes and Climbs from Crystal,"* John Beyer, No. 598,
    October 1968, pp. 224-229, 1 Map.

"PEAK 13,550'" (PETTINGELL PEAK), 13,553'   Front Range
                                (Unnamed) Loveland Pass 1958
                                (Unnamed) Montezuma 15M 1933, 13,550'
    Trail and Timberline
        "Suggestions for Two Good 'Summit' Ski Trips Near Denver,"*
    Karl Neubuerger, No. 290, February 1943, pp. 20-21.

        "The Winter Outing - 1943: Zipfelberger Cabin - Loveland Pass
    Area,"* Bill Steele, No. 292, April 1943, pp. 49-50.

"PEAK 13,555'", 13,555'   Sangre de Cristo Range
                    (Unnamed) Blanca Peak 1967
    Trail and Timberline
        "Lower Peaks in the Massif,"* Jim Schofield, No. 638,
    February 1972, pp. 43-46.

"PEAK 13,828'", 13,828'   Sangre de Cristo Range
                          (Unnamed) Blanca Peak 1967
    Trail and Timberline
        "Lower Peaks in the Massif,"* Jim Schofield, No. 638,
        February 1972, pp. 43-46.

"PEAK 13,841'", 13,841'   San Juan Mountains
                          (Unnamed) Pole Creek Mountain 1964
    American Alpine Journal
        "P 13,841, North Face," Jeff Lowe, Vol. 18, 1973, pp. 432-433.
        Ascent note of the north face, Larry Derby and Jeff Lowe.

PEARL MOUNTAIN, 13,362'   Elk Range   Pearl Pass 1961
    Chicago Mountaineering Club Newsletter
        "Colorado's Elk Mountains,"* Weldon F. Heald, Vol. 13, No. 6,
        October 1959, pp. 1-5, Front cover map.

    Trail and Timberline
        "On Skis in the Elks,"* Bob Beverly, No. 446, February 1956,
        pp. 23-26, 1 Map.

        "Pearl Peak on Skis,"* Ken and Ruth Wright, No. 530,
        February 1963, pp. 31-32, 2 Illustrations, Front cover
        illustration.

PEELER PEAK, 12,227'   Ruby Range   Oh-Be-Joyful 1961
    Trail and Timberline
        "Some Took the High Road,"* Stan Shepard, No. 455,
        November 1956, pp. 165-167.

"THE PENGUIN", 12,900'#   San Juan Mountains, Sneffels Range
                          (Unnamed) Mount Sneffels 1967
    American Alpine Journal
        "Colorado Climbing Notes, 1934,"* Carleton C. Long, Vol. 2,
        1935, pp. 416, 417.
        First ascent note, Dwight Lavender and Jack Seerley.
        Second ascent note, Charles Kane, Robert Ormes, and T. Melvin
        Griffiths.

    The Mountaineering Journal (British)
        "Outstanding Climbing Centres in the South-Western Colorado
        Rockies,"* Dwight G. Lavender, Vol. 1, No. 4, June, July,
        August 1933, pp. 238-248.

    Trail and Timberline
        Illustration,* "Aiguilles Northwest of Mt. Sneffels,
        Photographed from Blaine Peak," D. G. Lavender, No. 171,
        January 1933, p. 10.

        "1934 Summer Outing Climbs,"* Everett C. Long, No. 192,
        October 1934, pp. 131-133.
        First ascent noted, Dwight Lavender and John Seerley.

#Elevation figure from the American Alpine Journal.

"The 1934 Climbing Season in Colorado,"* Carleton C. Long,
No. 196, February 1935, pp. 15-18.
Second ascent note, Charles Kane, Robert Ormes, and Melvin
Griffiths.
First ascent note, Dwight Lavender and Jack Seerley.

"PETIT GREPON", 11,800'   Front Range, Rocky Mountain National Park
                          (Unnamed) McHenrys Peak 1957
    American Alpine Journal
    "Petit Grepon, South Face," William J. Buckingham, Vol. 13,
    1962, pp. 229-230.
    First ascent note via south face, Arthur Davidson and William
    J. Buckingham.

    "New Routes in Rocky Mountain National Park,"* Walter Fricke,
    Vol. 17, 1971, pp. 379-380.
    Ascent note of the "Culp-Beal" route.

    Climbing
    "Basecamp: Rocky Mountain National Park,"* Nos. 22 and 23,
    Winter 1973-74, p. 36.
    First all free, all clean ascent note of the "Culp-Beall"
    (Culp-Beal) route on the south face, Daniel McClure and Bob
    Hritz.

    Off Belay
    "Climbing at Rocky Mountain,"* Walt Fricke, No. 2, April 1972,
    pp. 17-23, 1 Illustration, 2 Maps.

    Trail and Timberline
    "The Petit Grepon," Ron Cox, No. 471, March 1958, p. 41,
    1 Illustration.

PETTINGELL PEAK, 13,553'   Front Range   Loveland Pass 1958
See "PEAK 13,550'"

"PH FACTOR", 13,024'   Gore Range   (Unnamed) Willow Lakes 1970
    Trail and Timberline
    "Backpacking in the Gore Range,"* Shirli Voigt, No. 667,
    July 1974, pp. 177-180, 1 Map.

"PHOTOGRAPHIC RIDGE", 13,596'   Needle Mountains
                          (Unnamed) Mountain View Crest 1973
    Appalachia
    "Excursions: Colorado Trip,"* E. Folger Taylor and Walter D.
    Howe, Vol. 23, December 1940, pp. 257-259, 1 Illustration
    following p. 262.

    Trail and Timberline
    "Where We Went and What We Climbed,"* No. 25, October 1920,
    pp. 8-11.

    "Photographic Ridge," Harry L. Standley, No. 107,
    September 1927, p. 16.

PIGEON PEAK, 13,972'   Needle Mountains   Snowdon Peak 1964
  American Alpine Journal
    "Technical Climbing in the Mountains of Colorado and Wyoming,"*
    Albert Russell Ellingwood, Vol. 1, 1930, pp. 140-147.

    "Colorado Climbing Notes, 1935,"* Carleton C. Long, Vol. 2,
    1936, p. 546.
    Second ascent and traverse note, H. L. McClintock, Frank
    McClintock, and Lewis Giesecke. Actual third ascent. See T&T,
    No. 672, December 1974, pp. 284-288 for first ascent by William
    S. Cooper and John V. Hubbard. Second ascent by Albert R.
    Ellingwood and Barton Hoag.

    "Colorado Climbing Notes, 1937,"* Carl Blaurock, Vol. 3,
    1938, p. 218.
    Ascent note, Elwyn Arps and party.

  Appalachia
    "Colorado Climbs, 1931,"* Winthrop Means, Vol. 18,
    December 1931, pp. 357-364, 1 Illustration.
    Attempt note.

    "Colorado,"* Alice R. Allan, Vol. 18, December 1931, pp. 483-
    485.
    Attempt note.

    "The Old and New West in the Needle Mountains,"* Duncan A.
    MacInnes, Vol. 23, June 1941, pp. 374-379, 1 Illustration.

  Harvard Mountaineering
    "Climbing Notes, 1964: Colorado Needles,"* Matt Hale, No. 17,
    May 1965, pp. 59-60.
    Ascent note, Matt Hale and Dave Roberts.

  The Mountaineering Journal (British)
    Illustration,* "View Southwards from Point Pun in the
    Grenadiers," Carleton C. Long, Vol. 1, No. 4, June, July,
    August 1933, p. 242.

    Illustration,* "View South from Heisspitz," Carleton C. Long,
    Vol. 1, No. 4, June, July, August 1933, p. 242.

  Trail and Timberline
    Illustration,* "Turret and Pigeon from Emerald Lake," Dr. Wm.
    C. Crisp, No. 25, October 1920, p. 18.

    Illustration,* "Mts. Pigeon and Turret, Seen from Emerald
    Lake, Near Camp on 1927 Annual Outing," William F. Ervin,
    No. 103, April 1927, p. 3.

    Front cover illustration,* "Ridge North of Pigeon and Turret,"
    Wm. F. Ervin, courtesy American Alpine Journal, No. 153,
    July 1931.

"The Second Ascent of Turret Peak,"* Carleton C. Long, No. 156, October 1931, p. 166.
Attempt noted on south face of Pigeon Peak.

Illustration,* "Mt. Eolus (Left), Turret Peak (Center), and Pigeon Peak (Right)," Percy Hagerman, No. 178, August 1933, p. 110.

Front cover illustration,* "Pigeon and Turret Peaks from Emerald Lake," No. 223, May 1937.

Illustration,* "Turret and Pigeon Peaks from Animas Mtn.," Everett C. Long, No. 223, May 1937, p. 57.

"San Juan Testimony,"* Harvey Sethman, No. 224, June 1937, pp. 68-70.
(Second) ascent noted, Ellingwood and Hoag in 1920.

"Needle Mountain Notes,"* David Lavender, No. 225, July 1937, pp. 80-81.
Fourth ascent (actual fifth ascent) noted, David Lavender and party.
Earlier ascent (fourth ascent) of the southeast side, Dr. H. L. McClintock, Gordon Williams, Mary McClintock, and Frank McClintock.

"Pigeon and Turret Trip,"* Elwyn Arps, No. 227, October 1937, p. 104, 1 Illustration, Front cover illustration.

"Noname Prospects,"* Mel Griffiths, No. 340, April 1947, pp. 56-59, 2 Illustrations.

"Climbers Guide to Noname,"* No. 342, June 1947, pp. 97-98, 1 Map.

"Climber's Guide from Noname Creek,"* Henry Buchtel, No. 345, September 1947, pp. 143-144.

"Pigeon and Turret or the Fly Camp of 1947,"* Louise Roloff, No. 345, September 1947, pp. 144-145.

"Pigeon, Turret, Peak 12, Etc., or the Fly Camp of '53,"* William E. Davis, No. 419, November 1953, pp. 155-158.

"Pigeon Peak from Ruby Basin," Robert M. Smith, No. 502, October 1960, pp. 142-143, 155, Front cover illustration.

"Revised Climbers' Guide from Noname Creek,"* William E. Davis, No. 502, October 1960, pp. 149-154, 1 Map, Front cover illustration.

"Colorado Mountain Club History: William S. Cooper - Explorer of the Needles and Grenadiers,"* William M. Bueler, No. 672, December 1974, pp. 284-288.
First ascent noted, William S. Cooper and John V. Hubbard.

"A Guide to Colorado's Almost-Fourteens,"* William A. Graves,
No. 683, November 1975, pp. 225-227.

PIKES PEAK, 14,109'   Pikes Peak Region   Pikes Peak 1951
Alpine Journal
"The Rockies of Colorado,"* Evelio Echevarría C., Vol. 71,
May 1966, pp. 26-36, 1 Map, Bibliography.

American Alpine Journal
"American Rockies - Notes, 1929,"* J. L. J. Hart, Vol. 1,
1930, p. 241.
Adaman Club ascent note.

"The Rocky Mountains of the United States,"* Howard Palmer,
Vol. 1, 1931, pp. 360-367.

"Colorado Climbing Notes, 1934,"* Carleton C. Long, Vol. 2,
1935, p. 415.
New Years Day ascent note.

"Colorado Climbing Notes, 1937,"* Carl Blaurock, Vol. 3, 1938,
p. 217.
Adaman Club ascent note.

"Naming America's Mountains - The Colorado Rockies,"* Francis
P. Farquhar, Vol. 12, 1961, pp. 319-346.
First ascent noted, Edwin James, Wilson, and Verplank.

"Club Activities: Iowa Mountaineers," Phil Fowler and John
Ebert, Vol. 14, 1964, pp. 244-245.
New route note, "Crater-Bastion Route" on the east side.

Appalachia
"An Ascent of Pike's Peak, 1879," Henry L. Stearns, Vol. 3,
June 1882, pp. 33-40.

"Early American Mountaineers,"* Allen H. Bent, Vol. 13,
May 1913, pp. 45-67.

"All the 14,000's,"* Carl Melzer, Vol. 22, December 1939,
pp. 466-479.

"Bloomer Girl of the Rockies," Weldon F. Heald, Vol. 32,
June 1959, pp. 349-351.
First ascent noted by a woman, Julia Archibald Holmes.

Climbing
"'Bigger Bagger', Pikes Peak, Bottomless Pit," No. 2,
July 1970, p. 24.
First complete ascent note, Don Doucette, Mike Dudley, and
Steve Cheney (Cheyney).
"Corrections," No. 3, September 1970, p. 21.
Note on route name correction.

"Nostalgia/Part II Mundus Est Mons,"* Harvey T. Carter, No. 6,
March-April 1971, pp. 3-5.
First ascent noted of Bastion.

"Basecamp: Pike's Peak," No. 9, September-October 1971, p. 2.
500th ascent note, Prof. Edwin H. Paget.

"'Direct East Face Variation', Giant, Bigger Bagger,
Bottomless Cirque, Pikes Peak, Colo.," No. 11, January-
February 1972, p. 26.
First ascent note, Muff Cheyney and Billy Westbay.

Iowa Mountaineers Journal
    "1963 Pikes Peak Crags Outing,"* Vol. 5, No. 5, 1965, p. 35.
First ascent note of Proline route (N).
Third ascent note of ABC route.

    "Pikes Peak Crags Outing,"* Harvey and Annie T. Carter, Vol. 5,
No. 5, 1965, pp. 54-59.

Mazama
    "'Pike's Peak or Bust'," Vera Joyce Nelson, Vol. 34, No. 13,
December 1952, pp. 50-51.

Summit
    "The Peak Called Pikes," Weldon F. Heald, Vol. 4, No. 5,
May 1958, pp. 10-11.
First ascent noted, Dr. Edwin James and party of two.

    Inside front cover illustration, "Know Your Mountains," U.S.
Air Force photo, Vol. 10, No. 7, September 1964.

    "Pikes Peak Region,"* Major James E. Banks, U.S.A.F., Vol. 10,
No. 7, September 1964, pp. 14-15, 1 Illustration.

Trail and Timberline
    "Climbing Pikes Peak in the Winter of 1876," Henry K. Palmer,
No. 39, December 1921, pp. 2-3.
Published in The Interior, Feb. 1876.

    "The Barr Trail," Dr. F. E. Johnson, No. 50, November 1922,
p. 7, 1 Illustration, 1 Illustration p. 3, 1 Illustration p. 9.

    "Pikes Peak Notes," Fred Morath, No. 53, February 1923, p. 4.
Ascent note, Fred and Ed Morath, Fred Barr, Harry Standley, and
Willis Magee. (First Adaman Club ascent).

    "Major Long's Expedition to Colorado," Roger W. Toll, No. 64,
January 1924, pp. 2-5.
First ascent noted, Dr. Edwin James and party of two.

    "A Pikes Peak Watch Party," Fred P. Morath, No. 76,
January 1925, pp. 1-3, 1 Illustration.

    Illustration, "Pikes Peak from Austin's Bluffs, Colorado
Springs," Harry L. Standley, No. 86, November 1925, p. 2.

Illustration, "Pikes Peak from Mt. Manitou," Hubert Strang,
No. 98, November 1926, p. 5.

Illustration, "Pikes Peak from the North," H. L. Standley,
No. 109, November 1927, p. 2.

Illustration, "Pikes Peak," H. L. Standley, No. 121,
November 1928, p. 2.

Illustration, "Near the Summit of Pikes Peak at Early Morning
of June 17, 1928," No. 121, November 1928, p. 6.
Title information from p. 7.

"Zebulon Montgomery Pike," Stephen H. Hart, No. 125,
March 1929, pp. 3-6, 1 Map.

Illustration, "Pikes Peak from Across Ute Pass," H. L.
Standley, No. 133, November 1929, p. 6.

Illustration, "Pikes Peak from Manitou," No. 133,
November 1929, p. 8.

"The 1933 Climbing Season in Colorado,"* Carleton C. Long,
No. 184, February 1934, pp. 20-23.
New Year's Day ascent note.

"The 1934 Climbing Season in Colorado,"* Carleton C. Long,
No. 196, February 1935, pp. 15-18.
AdAmAn Club ascent note, New Year's Day.

"Climbing Notes,"* No. 217, November 1936, p. 133.
Elevation note.

Front cover illustration, "Pikes Peak Through Gateway to
Garden of the Gods," No. 253, January 1940.

"The Geologic History of the Pikes Peak Region," June M.
Common, No. 288, December 1942, pp. 151-152, Front cover
illustration.

"The 1944 Adaman Trip," Carl Blaurock, No. 301, January 1944,
pp. 5, 11, 1 Illustration.

"The AdAmAn Club," Harry L. Standley, No. 309, September 1944,
pp. 103-104.

"The Peak Above," Mary Shirer, No. 309, September 1944,
pp. 109-110.

"Reaching the High Spots,"* George J. Kubricht, No. 325,
January 1946, pp. 3-4.

"Pike's 'Pinical'," Zebulon Montgomery Pike, No. 333,
September 1946, pp. 143-145, Front cover illustration.
Excerpts from the 1810 edition of Diary of An Expedition Made
Under the Order of the War Department by Captain Z. M. Pike in
the Years 1806 and 1807, to Explore the Internal Parts of Louisiana.

"A Summit Greeting," Vernon Twombley, No. 338, February 1947, pp. 17-18, 1 Illustration.

Front cover illustration, "Pikes Peak," Harry L. Standley, No. 340, April 1947.

"Rock Climbing on Pikes Peak," Stanley Boucher, No. 341, May 1947, pp. 79-80, 1 Illustration.

"An Exagbination into Sundry Doings of the C.C.C.M.C.: First Semester,"* Stanley Boucher, No. 351, March 1948, pp. 43-44.
"Correction," No. 352, April 1948, p. 51.
Note on title correction.

Front cover illustration, "Pikes Peak from Ute Pass," H. L. Standley, No. 358, October 1948.

Front cover illustration, "Pikes Peak from Across Ute Pass," Harry L. Standley, No. 388, April 1951.

"My Past on the Peak," Robert W. Ellingwood, No. 395, November 1951, pp. 143-144.

"Rock Climbing in the Pikes Peak Region," Ray W. Phillips, No. 422, February 1954, p. 20.

Illustration, "Pikes Peak Over Gateway Rocks, from the Mesa," Paul Nesbit, No. 503, November 1960, p. 161.

"Skiing Off the Top," Walt Kuenning, No. 505, January 1961, pp. 7-8, 1 Illustration.

"Pikes Peak - July 14, 1820," Louisa Ward Arps, No. 520, April 1962, pp. 53-54.
First ascent noted, Edwin James, Verplank, and Zachariah Wilson.

"The Account of the Climb," Edwin James, No. 520, April 1962, pp. 54-61, 2 Illustrations.
Reprint as edited by Reuben Gold Thwaities from Early Western Travels, 1748-1846, Cleveland, Ohio, Arthur H. Clark Co., 1905.
First ascent noted, Edwin James and party of two.

"Something Different on Pikes Peak," Art Porter, No. 615, March 1970, pp. 72-74, 1 Illustration, 1 Map.

"Ladies Climb Pikes Peak - Circa 1920," Agnes S. Hall, No. 622, October 1970, pp. 210-216.

"Ladies Climb Pikes Peak - Circa 1970," Jean Vine, No. 622, October 1970, p. 217.

"The AdAmAn Club: The First Fifty Years," Wilbur F. Arnold,
No. 650, February 1973, pp. 60-62.
First recorded winter ascent noted, Ed Morath, Fred Morath,
Fred W. Barr, Harry L. Standley, and Willis Magee. See T&T,
No. 653, May 1973, p. 146 for correct first winter ascents.
See also T&T, No. 39, December 1921, pp. 2-3 for early winter
ascent.

"Letters to T&T," John L. J. Hart, No. 653, May 1973, p. 146.
Note on winter ascents.

"Private Property: No Trespassing!"* Sally Richards, Nos. 679-
680, July-August 1975, pp. 148-150.

"Pikes Peak," William M. Bueler, No. 682, October 1975, p. 215.

PILOT KNOB, 13,738'   San Juan Mountains   Ophir 1955
  American Alpine Journal
     "Southwestern Colorado Climbing Notes - 1932,"* Dwight G.
  Lavender, Vol. 2, 1933, p. 129.
  New route note, Charles Kendrick, Scott, Dave Lavender,
  Giesecke, and Dwight G. Lavender, via final cliff on the west
  face.
  Traverse note of the lower (southern) summit to the high
  summit and descent of the east face, Father H. M. Walters,
  Charles Kendrick, and Dwight G. Lavender.

  Trail and Timberline
     "1932 Summer Outing,"* Jack Kendrick, No. 162, April 1932,
  pp. 47, 57-58, 1 Illustration.

     "Opportunities for Climbing Afforded by the Ice Lake Basin
  Outing,"* D. G. Lavender, No. 164, June 1932, p. 91.

     "Six First Ascents on the '32 Outing,"* Dwight G. Lavender,
  No. 168, October 1932, pp. 139-140, 149-150, 1 Illustration,
  1 Illustration p. 145.
  First ascent noted, Bob Scott, Lewis Giesecke, Dave Lavender,
  Dwight Lavender, and Charles Kendrick. See T&T, No. 173,
  March 1933, p. 41 for first ascent correction.

     "Climbing Notes,"* D. G. L., No. 173, March 1933, p. 41.
  First ascent correction note.

     "Exploring Ice Lake Basin,"* Allen W. Greene, No. 474,
  June 1958, pp. 75-76, 87.

POINT PUN, 13,150'   Needle Mountains   Snowdon Peak 1964
  American Alpine Journal
     "Southwestern Colorado Climbing Notes - 1932,"* Dwight G.
  Lavender, Vol. 2, 1933, p. 128.
  First ascent note, Carleton Long and John Nelson.

Trail and Timberline
  "Editorial Notes,"* David Rosendale, No. 169, November 1932,
  p. 162.
  First ascent note, Carleton C. Long (and John Nelson).

  "An Unusually High Timberline," C. C. L., No. 177, July 1933,
  p. 94.
  First ascent noted, Carleton C. Long and (John) Nelson.

  "Needle Mountaimania,"* Dave Lavender, No. 265, January 1941,
  pp. 3-4, 14-15.

  "Grenadier Reminiscences,"* Carleton C. Long, No. 266,
  February 1941, pp. 29-31.
  (First) ascent noted, Carleton C. Long and John Nelson.

"POPE'S NOSE", 11,120'   San Juan Mountains   (Unnamed) Emerald Lake 1973
  American Alpine Journal
    "Pope's Nose, Southwest Face, San Juan Range," James Galvin,
    Vol. 17, 1971, p. 381.
    First ascent note of the southwest face, Mike Burdick, Jim
    Yurchenco, and James Galvin.

  Climbing
    "'Chalice Wall', Pope's Nose, San Juan's, Colorado," No. 5,
    January 1971, p. 22.
    First ascent note, Jim Yurchenco, Jim Galvin, and Mike Burdick.

    "Papal Rock Test," Mike Burdick, No. 8, July-August 1971,
    pp. 11-13, 4 Illustrations.

POTATO HILL, 11,871'   San Juan Mountains   Engineer Mountain 1960
  Trail and Timberline
    "First Ascent Criteria,"* Carleton C. Long and Dwight G.
    Lavender, No. 174, April 1933, pp. 48, 52-53.

POTOSI PEAK, 13,786'   San Juan Mountains, Sneffels Range   Ironton 1955
  Appalachia
    Illustration, "Potosi Peak," Frederick H. Chapin, Vol. 6,
    December 1890, (Plate 9) following p. 154.

  The Mountaineering Journal (British)
    "Outstanding Climbing Centres in the South-Western Colorado
    Rockies,"* Dwight G. Lavender, Vol. 1, No. 4, June, July,
    August 1933, pp. 238-248, 1 Illustration.

  Trail and Timberline
    Illustration, "Potosi Peak (13,790) from Teakettle Mountain,"
    D. G. Lavender, No. 169, November 1932, p. 158.

    Illustration, "Potosi Peak (13,790) from Teakettle Mountain,"
    Dwight G. Lavender, No. 400, April 1952, p. 80.

    Illustration, "Potosi Peak from the Valley Above Camp,"
    No. 407, November 1952, p. 166.

Front cover illustration, "Sneffels Country - Potosi Peak from Teakettle Mountain," D. G. Lavender, No. 512, August 1961.

Front cover illustration, "Potosi Peak," No. 534, June 1963.

Front cover illustration,* "Cirque Peak, Teakettle and Potosi from Cirque Shoulder," Sam Alfend, No. 539, November 1963.

Illustration, "Potosi Peak," Hugh E. Kingery, No. 625, January 1971, p. 11.

MT. POWELL, 13,534'   Gore Range   Mt. Powell 15M 1933

Alpine Journal
"The Rockies of Colorado,"* Evelio Echevarría C., Vol. 71, May 1966, pp. 26-36, 1 Map, Bibliography.

American Alpine Journal
"Colorado Climbing Notes, 1935,"* Carleton C. Long, Vol. 2, 1936, p. 545.
Ascent note, Carl Blaurock, Rudolph Johnson, and party.
Ascent note, Charles Moore and party which brought back records of Major Powell's first ascent with Ned Farrell in 1868 and his second ascent with the Hayden Survey in 1873.

Trail and Timberline
"New Regions,"* No. 140, June 1930, p. 16.

"Mt. Powell," W. H. Holmes, No. 155, September 1931, p. 140.
First ascent noted, Major Powell and Ned Farrell in 1868.
(Second) ascent noted, W. H. Holmes (and Hayden Survey party).

"Note," No. 157, November 1931, p. 182.
Third ascent note, party of surveyors (U.S.G.S.). Actual fourth ascent. See T&T, No. 159, January 1932, pp. 9-11 for record of early ascents.

"Mt. Powell and the Gore Range,"* Kenneth Segerstrom, No. 159, January 1932, pp. 9-11, 1 Illustration.
First ascent noted, Major Powell and Ned Farrell.
Second ascent noted, Major J. W. Powell, Tom Bancroft, F. T. (J. T.) Gardner, F. V. Hayden, J. D. Whitney, and party.
Third ascent noted, Stewart and party.
Fourth ascent noted, C. D. Mitchell, R. E. Brislawn, and H. T. Weaver of the U.S. Geological Survey, and G. A. Graham.

"An Early Climb of Mt. Powell," Percy Hagerman, No. 161, March 1932, p. 35.
(Third) ascent noted, P. B. Stewart, Wolcott Stewart, Percy Hagerman, and Lowry Hagerman.
(First) ascent noted, Ned E. Farrell and J. W. Powell.
(Second) ascent noted, J. F. (J. T.) Gardner, J. V. (F. V.) Hayden, W. H. Holmes, W. D. (J. D.) Whitney, Jim Craven, Tom Bancroft, and party.

"Climbs in the Gore Range,"* Kenneth Segerstrom, No. 197, March 1935, pp. 32-35, 37-38, 1 Map.
"The Gore Map - A Correction," No. 198, April 1935, p. 47.

"The Gore Range Outing,"* Everett Long, No. 204, October 1935, pp. 111-113, 1 Illustration.
Ascent noted, Carl Blaurock and party.
Ascent noted, Charles Moore and party which brought back records of Major Powell's first ascent with Ned Farrell in 1868 and his second ascent with the Hayden Survey in 1873.

"The Mountain Ranges of Colorado,"* Kenneth Segerstrom, No. 215, September 1936, pp. 109-115, 1 Map.

"Climbing Notes,"* K. S., No. 215, September 1936, p. 116.
Seventh ascent note, Carl Erickson and Kenneth Segerstrom.

"Group Activities: Denver Group,"* Evelyn Runnette, No. 215, September 1936, p. 118.
(Seventh) ascent note, Kenneth Segerstrom and Carl Erickson.

"Powell Ascents," compiled by Carl Melzer, No. 284, August 1942, p. 102.
See T&T, No. 159, January 1932, pp. 9-11 for correct record of early ascents.

"Notes on the Gore Range, Summer, 1942,"* Carl Melzer, No. 284, August 1942, pp. 103-106, Front cover illustration.
Sixth ascent (probable eighth ascent) noted, Carl and Bob Melzer.

"A Weekend in the Gore Range: August 21-22, 1943,"* Curt E. Krieser, No. 315, March 1945, pp. 31-32, 1 Illustration.

"Summer Outings - Then and Now,"* No. 354, June 1948, pp. 88-90, 1 Illustration.

Illustration,* "Panorama from Little Powell - (Powell and Eagle's Nest to the Right)," No. 356, August 1948, p. 115.

"From 'B' to 'H' in Seven Days,"* Louise Roloff, No. 357, September 1948, pp. 131, 138.

"Opening Up the Gores - New Approach to Mount Powell," Allen Greene, No. 462, June 1957, pp. 83-84.

"Junior Summer Outing, 1962,"* Dave Abbott and Chip Bishop, No. 532, April 1963, pp. 69-71.

"Names on the Gores,"* William Bird Mounsey, No. 568, April 1966, pp. 63-65, 1 Map.

"The Gorgeous Gore,"* Beth Lalonde, No. 574, October 1966, pp. 167-168.

"Backpacking in the Gore Range,"* Shirli Voigt, No. 667,
July 1974, pp. 177-180, 1 Map.

POWELL PEAK, 13,208'   Front Range, Rocky Mountain National Park
                        McHenrys Peak 1957
  American Alpine Journal
    "Powell Peak, East Face," Lawrence Hamilton, Vol. 20, 1975,
    p. 139.
    New route note on the east face, John Byrd, Dakers Gowans, and
    Lawrence Hamilton.

  Climbing
    "View from Within: Colorado Rocky Mountain National Park,"*
    No. 28, Winter 1974-75, p. 36.
    New route note, "Snark" on the east face, Larry Hamilton, John
    Byrd, and Dakers Gowans.

PRECIPICE PEAK, 13,144'   San Juan Mountains   Wetterhorn Peak 1963
  Trail and Timberline
    "An Outing is Born,"* Allen W. Greene, No. 564, December 1965,
    pp. 245-249, 1 Illustration p. 254, 1 Illustration p. 257.

MT. PRINCETON, 14,197'   Sawatch Range   Poncha Springs 15M 1956
  American Alpine Journal
    "Naming America's Mountains - The Colorado Rockies,"* Francis
    P. Farquhar, Vol. 12, 1961, pp. 319-346.

  Appalachia
    "All the 14,000's,"* Carl Melzer, Vol. 22, December 1939,
    pp. 466-479.

  Chicago Mountaineering Club Newsletter
    "Sneaking Up on Colorado Peaks by Way of Texas,"* Groves
    Kilbourn, Vol. 17, No. 1, February 1964, pp. 4-5.

  Trail and Timberline
    "Trailing the Colorado Mountain Club on the High Peaks,"*
    Lloyd Shaw, No. 17, January 1920, pp. 5-6.

    "A George-eous Trip," No. 35, August 1921, p. 5.

    "The High Trails of Winter,"* Reynolds Morse, No. 194,
    December 1934, pp. 163-165.

    "Junior Outing,"* Anonymous, No. 227, October 1937, p. 107.

    "14,000 Feet,"* Russell Briggs, No. 246, June 1939, p. 77.

    "Princeton Boys in the Rockies," Louisa Ward Arps, No. 283,
    July 1942, pp. 94-96, 1 Illustration.
    First recorded ascent noted, William Libbey Jr.

"A Conglomerate Review of the C.M.C. Summer Outing,
August 15-23, 1942 - Collegiate Range,"* Nancy Plowman, Eliot
Moses, Harold Brewer, Mary Wagner, No. 287, November 1942,
pp. 141-143, 1 Map p. 140.

"Reaching the High Spots,"* George J. Kubricht, No. 325,
January 1946, pp. 3-4.

"Backpacking the Sawatch Range,"* Bud Boylard, No. 378,
June 1950, pp. 83-85, 90-91.

"First Overnight,"* Esther Holt, No. 382, October 1950,
pp. 151-152.

Front cover illustration, "On the Summit of Mt. Princeton,"
No. 555, March 1965.

"The Rigors and Joys of Winter Climbing,"* Stan Stephan,
No. 643, July 1972, pp. 143-145.

PROSPECT MOUNTAIN, 8,900'   Front Range   Longs Peak 1961
  Appalachia
    "The Peaks of Rocky Mountain National Park,"* Roger W. Toll,
    Vol. 17, June 1929, pp. 252-260.

"PTARMIGAN TOWERS", 12,324'[#]   Front Range, Rocky Mountain National Park
                        (Unnamed) McHenrys Peak 1957
  American Alpine Journal
    "Ptarmigan Towers, East Side," Lawrence Hamilton, Vol. 20,
    1976, p. 460.
    Ascent note of "Tundra Turkey Crack" on Tower 2, Tom Gries and
    Lawrence Hamilton.
    Ascent note of northeast corner of Tower 4, Tom Gries and
    Lawrence Hamilton.

"PURGATORY POINT", 13,536'[+]   San Juan Mountains, Sneffels Range
                        (Unnamed) Mount Sneffels 1967
  American Alpine Journal
    "Colorado Climbing Notes, 1934,"* Carleton C. Long, Vol. 2,
    1935, p. 417.
    Reconnaissance note.

  The Mountaineering Journal (British)
    "Outstanding Climbing Centres in the South-Western Colorado
    Rockies,"* Dwight G. Lavender, Vol. 1, No. 4, June, July,
    August 1933, pp. 238-248.

PURPLE MOUNTAIN, 12,958'   Ruby Range   Oh-Be-Joyful 1961
See "SLATE MOUNTAIN"

[#]Elevation of Ptarmigan Mountain.

[+]Elevation figure from the American Alpine Journal.

PYRAMID PEAK, 14,018'   Elk Range   Maroon Bells 1960
  Appalachia
      "The Call of Colorado,"* Edward W. Harnden, Vol. 16,
      June 1925, pp. 158-164.

      "All the 14,000's,"* Carl Melzer, Vol. 22, December 1939,
      pp. 466-479.

  Chicago Mountaineering Club Newsletter
      "Camping at Maroon Bell Lakes,"* Grover Hartsuch, Vol. 10,
      No. 5, October 1956, pp. 11-12.

      "Colorado's Elk Mountains,"* Weldon F. Heald, Vol. 13, No. 6,
      October 1959, pp. 1-5, Front cover map.

  Climbing
      "'West Flank', Pyramid Peak, 14,000 Ft., Elk Mtns., Colorado,"
      No. 4, November 1970, p. 23.
      First winter ascent note, Fritz Stammberger and Gordon
      Whitmire (Whitmer).

      "Basecamp: Winter Climbing,"* No. 6, March-April 1971, p. 3.
      Second winter ascent note, first by N.N.E. ridge, Harvey T.
      Carter, Robert Sullivan, and Ted Pelletier.

      "Nostalgia/Part II Mundus Est Mons,"* Harvey T. Carter, No. 6,
      March-April 1971, pp. 3-5.
      First ascent noted of the north face.

      Inside front cover illustration, "Pyramid Peak, Colorado,"
      David Hiser, No. 18, March-April 1973.

      "Basecamp: Colorado,"* No. 37, July-August 1976, p. 4,
      1 Illustration.
      Winter ascent note of the north face, Lou Dawson, Mike
      Kennedy, and Michael Pokress.

  Summit
      "Colorado's High-Rising Elks,"* Weldon F. Heald, Vol. 8,
      No. 11, November 1962, pp. 20-23, 1 Illustration.

  Trail and Timberline
      Illustration, "Pyramid Peak (14,000 Ft.), Elk Mountains,
      Colo.," Wm. F. Ervin, No. 110, December 1927, p. 9.

      "Pyramid Peak," John J. Seerley, Jr., No. 120, October 1928,
      pp. 10-11.

      "The Pyramid Trip," Corwin S. Clarke, No. 180, October 1933,
      pp. 139, 148.

      "Pyramid Peak," Evelyn Runnette, No. 225, July 1937, p. 83,
      1 Illustration p. 82.

"Clark Peak?"* Percy Hagerman, No. 228, November 1937, pp. 120, 126.
Probable first ascent noted of Pyramid Peak, Percy Hagerman and Harold Clark.

"Junior Outing,"* Rex A. Young, No. 239, November 1938, pp. 115-116.

Front cover illustration, "Pyramid Peak in the Elk Mountains," William F. Ervin, No. 295, July 1943.

"Juniors Move to Maroon Lake at End of Outing to Climb Steep Pyramid," Dorothy Sethman, No. 322, October 1945, pp. 129-130, 1 Illustration.

"1873 Tells 1949,"* Louisa Ward Arps, No. 365, May 1949, pp. 68-70, 1 Illustration following p. 70.

Illustration, "On Trail to Buckskin Pass, Looking South - Pyramid Peak Spur," No. 368, August 1949, p. 113.

"They're There Because ...,"* James McChristal, No. 687, March 1976, pp. 63-67.
Reprinted from The Colorado College Bulletin, May, 1975, pp. 43-45.
First ascent noted of the north face, Harvey T. Carter (and party).

"Longs Peakers on Pyramid," Dave Taylor and Pat Maynard, No. 696, December 1976, pp. 230-231, Front cover illustration.

"PEAK Q" ("MT. TRIDENT"), 13,230'   Gore Range   (Unnamed) Vail East 1970
See also "MT. TRIDENT"
    American Alpine Journal
        "Colorado Climbing Notes, 1934,"* Carleton C. Long, Vol. 2,
        1935, pp. 415-416.
        Second ascent note, Colorado Mountain Club party.

    Trail and Timberline
        "The 1933 Climbing Season in Colorado,"* Carleton C. Long,
        No. 184, February 1934, pp. 20-23.
        First ascent note, Kenneth Segerstrom, Edmund Cooper, and
        Burbank Buffum.

        "The 1934 Climbing Season in Colorado,"* Carleton C. Long,
        No. 196, February 1935, pp. 15-18.
        Second ascent note, CMC party.
        First ascent note, Kenneth Segerstrom, Edmund Cooper, and
        Burbank Buffum.

        "Climbs in the Gore Range,"* Kenneth Segerstrom, No. 197,
        March 1935, pp. 32-35, 37-38, 1 Map.
        First ascent noted, Edmund Cooper, Burbank Buffum, and Kenneth
        Segerstrom.
        "The Gore Map - A Correction," No. 198, April 1935, p. 47.

        Illustration,* "Upper Slate Lake, Gore Range, with Peaks Q
        (Left) and P (Right) Behind," Hugh E. Kingery, No. 569,
        May 1966, p. 80.

QUANDARY PEAK, 14,265'   Tenmile Range   Breckenridge 1970
    Alpine Journal
        "The Rockies of Colorado,"* Evelio Echevarría C., Vol. 71,
        May 1966, pp. 26-36, 1 Map, Bibliography.

    American Alpine Journal
        "Colorado Climbing Notes, 1934,"* Carleton C. Long, Vol. 2,
        1935, p. 415.
        Probable first complete ski ascent note (along with Mt.
        Bierstadt) of 14,000 foot peak, Donald McBride and party.

    Appalachia
        "All the 14,000's,"* Carl Melzer, Vol. 22, December 1939,
        pp. 466-479.

    Trail and Timberline
        "Editorial Notes,"* David Rosendale, No. 193, November 1934,
        p. 151.
        Ski ascent note, Donald McBride.

        "Winter Climbs," Donald McBride, No. 193, November 1934,
        p. 154, 1 Illustration.

        "The High Trails of Winter,"* Reynolds Morse, No. 194,
        December 1934, pp. 163-165.

"The 1934 Climbing Season in Colorado,"* Carleton C. Long,
No. 196, February 1935, pp. 15-18.
First complete ski ascent note (along with Mt. Bierstadt) of
14,000 foot peak, Donald McBride and party.

"The Mountain Ranges of Colorado,"* Kenneth Segerstrom,
No. 215, September 1936, pp. 109-115, 1 Map.

Illustration, "A Bit of Weather on Mt. Quandary," J. Donald
McBride, No. 233, April 1938, p. 42.

"Free Wheeling in the Rockies or How to Lose 25 Pounds,"*
Stan Midgely, No. 318, June 1945, pp. 71-74.

"An Exagbination into Sundry Doings of the C.C.C.M.C.: First
Semester,"* Stanley Boucher, No. 351, March 1948, pp. 43-44.
"Correction," No. 352, April 1948, p. 51.
Note on title correction.

"Initiation," G. C. Kehmeier, No. 380, August 1950, p. 123.

"Snow Slide," Spencer Swanger, No. 626, February 1971, pp. 28-
30.

"The Rigors and Joys of Winter Climbing,"* Stan Stephan,
No. 643, July 1972, pp. 143-145.

"RAGGED PEAK", 12,641'   Elk Range   (Unnamed) Chair Mountain 1963
    Trail and Timberline
        "1873 Tells 1949,"* Louisa Ward Arps, No. 365, May 1949,
        pp. 68-70.

RALSTON BUTTES, 7,788'   Front Range   Ralston Buttes 1965
    Trail and Timberline
        "A Trip to Ralston," Dorothy Sethman, No. 299, November 1943,
        p. 143.

        "Guerilla Tactics Useful for Doggy Climbs: The Gentle Art of
        Freddy Peaking,"* Bob Michael, No. 689, May 1976, pp. 112-115.

"RECONNOITER PEAK", 12,960'   San Juan Mountains, Sneffels Range
                               (Unnamed) Mount Sneffels 1967
    American Alpine Journal
        "Southwestern Colorado Climbing Notes - 1933,"* Dwight G.
        Lavender, Vol. 2, 1934, p. 256.
        First ascent note, T. M. Griffiths, L. V. Giesecke, B. M.
        Souder, and Dwight G. Lavender.

    The Mountaineering Journal (British)
        "Correspondence,"* Dwight Lavender, Vol. 2, No. 1, December,
        January, February 1933-34, pp. 47-51.
        First ascent note, Dwight Lavender, Lewis V. Giesecke, T.
        Melvin Griffiths, and Byron Souder.
        Second ascent note, San Juan Mountaineers.

    Trail and Timberline
        "The 1933 Climbing Season in Colorado,"* Carleton C. Long,
        No. 184, February 1934, pp. 20-23.
        Possible first ascent note, San Juan Mountaineers.

        Illustration,* "Reconnoiter Peak (in Clouds) and Peak S-2 from
        Upper Blaine Basin," S.J.M., No. 185, March 1934, p. 31.

RED ELEPHANT MOUNTAIN, 11,569'   North Park Range   Davis Peak 1955
    Trail and Timberline
        "North Park and Mt. Zirkle,"* No. 202, August 1935, p. 95.

RED MOUNTAIN,   San Juan Mountains
    Trail and Timberline
        Illustration, "Fort Peabody and Red Mountain," Art Porter,
        No. 620, August 1970, p. 172.

RED MOUNTAIN, 11,605'   Never Summer Mountains, Rocky Mountain National Park
                         Mount Richthofen 1957
    Trail and Timberline
        "The Trips of the Outing,"* No. 37, October 1921, pp. 2-4.

RED MOUNTAIN, 12,974'   Sangre de Cristo Range   Howard 15M 1959
    Trail and Timberline
        "Sangre de Cristo Saga,"* Lester A. Michel, with Wilbur F.
        Arnold, No. 524, August 1962, pp. 123-126, 133.

RED MOUNTAIN, 13,908'   Culebra Range   Culebra Peak 1967
    Trail and Timberline
        "A Guide to Colorado's Almost-Fourteens,"* William A. Graves,
    No. 683, November 1975, pp. 225-227.

RED PEAK, 13,189'   Gore Range   Willow Lakes 1970
    Trail and Timberline
        "Notes on the Gore Range, Summer, 1942,"* Carl Melzer,
    No. 284, August 1942, pp. 103-106.

        "Rock Climbing in the Gore Range,"* Mark P. Addison, No. 457,
    January 1957, pp. 3-4, 13, 2 Maps.

REDCLIFF, 13,642'   San Juan Mountains   Wetterhorn Peak 1963
    Trail and Timberline
        "An Outing is Born,"* Allen W. Greene, No. 564, December 1965,
    pp. 245-249, 1 Illustration.

REDCLOUD PEAK, 14,034'   San Juan Mountains   Redcloud Peak 1964
    Appalachia
        "All the 14,000's,"* Carl Melzer, Vol. 22, December 1939,
    pp. 466-479.

        "Club Excursions: Colorado Excursion, 1951,"* Jean K. Kent,
    Vol. 28, December 1951, pp. 584-589, 1 Illustration.

    Mazama
        "Ramble Number 21,"* A. H. Marshall, Vol. 21, No. 12,
    December 1939, pp. 55-61.

    Trail and Timberline
        "Climbing 60,000 Feet in the San Juan,"* Carl Blaurock,
    No. 40, January 1922, pp. 2-3.

        "Junior Jottings,"* No. 371, November 1949, pp. 172-173.

        "Handies, Redcloud, and Sunshine,"* Katy Wilson, No. 398,
    February 1952, p. 24.

        "Report on the 1952 San Juan Outing,"* Robert Ellingwood,
    No. 407, November 1952, pp. 159-161.

        "The Lake City Fourteens,"* Robin Simmons, No. 490,
    October 1959, pp. 141-142.

RICHMOND MOUNTAIN, 12,501'   Ruby Range   Oh-Be-Joyful 1961
    Trail and Timberline
        "Some Took the High Road,"* Stan Shepard, No. 455,
    November 1956, pp. 165-167.

MT. RICHTHOFEN, 12,940'   Never Summer Range, Rocky Mountain National Park
                            Mount Richthofen 1957
    Summit
        "Ascending Two Giants,"* Vincent Prichard, Vol. 13, No. 4,
    May 1967, pp. 8-13, 1 Map.

Trail and Timberline
    Illustration, "Scouting Party Nearing Summit of Mt.
Richthofen," No. 30, March 1921, p. 5.

    Illustration, "Mount Richthofen," No. 33, June 1921, p. 3.

    "The Trips of the Outing,"* No. 37, October 1921, pp. 2-4.

    "The Mountain Ranges of Colorado,"* Kenneth Segerstrom,
No. 215, September 1936, pp. 109-115, 1 Map.

    "Mountain Climbing and Statistics in Rocky Mountain National
Park,"* John C. Whitnah and Robert C. Peterson, No. 343,
July 1947, pp. 116-117.

    "The Never Summers III - Richthofen," Esther Holt, No. 451,
July 1956, pp. 105-106.

    "Colorado Mountain Club History: William S. Cooper - Explorer
of the Needles and Grenadiers,"* William M. Bueler, No. 672,
December 1974, pp. 284-288.
First recorded ascent noted, William S. Cooper.

"RIDGE PEAK", 13,431'   Elk Range   (Unnamed) Capitol Peak 1960
    Trail and Timberline
    "The Snowmass-Capitol Ridge,"* Karl Gustafson, No. 404,
August 1952, pp. 119-121.
First ascent noted, Karl Gustafson and Bob Allen.

MT. RIDGWAY, 13,468'   San Juan Mountains, Sneffels Range
See "S2"   Mount Sneffels 1967

RITO ALTO PEAK, 13,794'   Sangre de Cristo Range   Electric Peak 15M 1959
    Trail and Timberline
    "New Maps of the Sangre de Cristo Range,"* John L. J. Hart,
No. 519, March 1962, pp. 32-33.

ROGERS PEAK, 13,391'   Front Range   Harris Park 1957
    Trail and Timberline
    Front cover illustration, "Snowshoe Climb Up Rogers Peak,"
Samuel Alfend, No. 675, March 1975.

ROLLING MOUNTAIN, 13,693'   San Juan Mountains   Ophir 1955
    American Alpine Journal
    "Southwestern Colorado Climbing Notes - 1932,"* Dwight G.
Lavender, Vol. 2, 1933, p. 129.
First ascent note of the lower or western summit, Miss Martha
Bloom and Dave Lavender.

    "Colorado Climbing Notes, 1935,"* Carleton C. Long, Vol. 2,
1936, p. 546.
First ascent and traverse note of the eastern or higher
summit, Kenneth Segerstrom.

Trail and Timberline
"Six First Ascents on the '32 Outing,"* Dwight G. Lavender,
No. 168, October 1932, pp. 139-140, 149-150.
First ascent noted of the lower western summit, Brookie Bloom
and Dave Lavender.

"Exploring Ice Lake Basin,"* Allen W. Greene, No. 474,
June 1958, pp. 75-76, 87.

"Silverton - Mountain Mecca,"* Art Porter, No. 620,
August 1970, pp. 169, 171-172.

MT. ROSA, 11,499'   Pikes Peak Region   Manitou Springs 1961
Trail and Timberline
"Climbing Mt. Rosa in Winter," Bert S. Elliott, No. 133,
November 1929, pp. 4-5.

RUBY PEAK, 12,644'   Ruby Range   Marcellina Mountain 1961
Trail and Timberline
"Some Took the High Road,"* Stan Shepard, No. 455,
November 1956, pp. 165-167.

"PEAK S", 12,857'   Gore Range   (Unnamed) Vail East 1970
    Chicago Mountaineering Club Newsletter
        "Ascents by Club Members,"* Stanley Midgely, Vol. 1, No. 3,
        September to December 1945, pp. 10-11.
        First ascent note, Stanley Midgely.

    Trail and Timberline
        "Free Wheeling in the Rockies or How to Lose 25 Pounds,"*
        Stan Midgely, No. 318, June 1945, pp. 71-74.
        First ascent noted, Stan Midgely.

"S2" (MOUNT RIDGWAY), 13,468'   San Juan Mountains, Sneffels Range
                                 (Unnamed) Mount Sneffels 1967
    The Mountaineering Journal (British)
        "Correspondence,"* Dwight Lavender, Vol. 2, No. 1, December,
        January, February 1933-34, pp. 47-51.
        Ascent note, Carleton Long.

    Trail and Timberline
        "The 1933 Climbing Season in Colorado,"* Carleton C. Long,
        No. 184, February 1934, pp. 20-23.
        Solo ascent note of the two summits, Carleton C. Long.

        Illustration,* "Reconnoiter Peak (in Clouds) and Peak S-2 from
        Upper Blaine Basin," S.J.M., No. 185, March 1934, p. 31.

"S3", 13,410'   San Juan Mountains, Sneffels Range
                 (Unnamed) Mount Sneffels 1967
    American Alpine Journal
        "Colorado Climbing Notes, 1934,"* Carleton C. Long, Vol. 2,
        1935, p. 416.
        Possible first ascent note, A. C. Bartelt, Robert Blair, and
        Mr. and Mrs. Fred Morath.

    Trail and Timberline
        "1934 Summer Outing Climbs,"* Everett C. Long, No. 192,
        October 1934, pp. 131-133.
        First ascent noted, A. C. Bartelt and Robert Blair.

"S5", 13,360'   San Juan Mountains, Sneffels Range
                 (Unnamed) Mount Sneffels 1967
    Trail and Timberline
        "1934 Summer Outing Climbs,"* Everett C. Long, No. 192,
        October 1934, pp. 131-133.

"S6", 13,441'   San Juan Mountains, Sneffels Range
                 (Unnamed) Mount Sneffels 1967
    American Alpine Journal
        "Colorado Climbing Notes, 1934,"* Carleton C. Long, Vol. 2,
        1935, p. 416.
        Possible first ascent note, Mr. and Mrs. Russel (Russell)
        Briggs, Philip Moore, Robert Blair, and Don McBride.

Trail and Timberline
   "1934 Summer Outing Climbs,"* Everett C. Long, No. 192,
   October 1934, pp. 131-133.
   First ascent note, Mr. and Mrs. Russell Briggs, Philip Moore,
   Robert Blair, and Donald McBride.

"THE SABER", 12,000'   Front Range, Rocky Mountain National Park
                 (Unnamed) McHenrys Peak 1957
American Alpine Journal
   "The Saber," Layton Kor, Vol. 13, 1963, p. 493.
   First ascent note, Dean Moore and Layton Kor.

Climbing
   "Basecamp: Rocky Mountain National Park,"* Nos. 22 and 23,
   Winter 1973-74, p. 36.
   New route note on spire to the right of The Saber, Duncan
   Ferguson and Mark Hesse.

ST. PETERS DOME, 8,704'   Pikes Peak Region   Mount Big Chief 1961
Climbing
   "Basecamp: Colorado,"* No. 4, November 1970, p. 2.
   Ascent note, "Swansong Dihedral", Steve Cheyney and Don
   Doucette.

   "'Swansong Dihedral', Aig de Saint Peter, Pikes Peak Massif,
   Colo.," No. 8, July-August 1971, p. 28.
   First ascent note, Pete Croff, Bob Stauch, and Steve Cheyney.
   Third ascent and first complete ascent note, Steve Cheyney,
   Pete Croff, and Bob Stauch.

Trail and Timberline
   "St. Peter's Dome," Mrs. H. J. Wagner, No. 309, September 1944,
   pp. 107-108, 1 Illustration.

ST. SOPHIA RIDGE, 13,040'   San Juan Mountains, Sneffels Range
                  Telluride 1955
American Alpine Journal
   "Southwestern Colorado Climbing Notes - 1932,"* Dwight G.
   Lavender, Vol. 2, 1933, p. 129.
   Traverse note of the entire ridge along the base of the
   pinnacles, San Juan Mountaineers.

The Mountaineering Journal (British)
   Illustration, "St. Sophia," T. M. Griffiths, Vol. 1, No. 4,
   June, July, August 1933, p. 246.

Trail and Timberline
   "Notes on the 1932 Climbing Season,"* Carleton C. Long,
   No. 171, January 1933, p. 10.
   Exploratory note, T. Melvin Griffiths, Don Bingham, Gordon
   Williams, and Joe Merhar.

   "First Ascent Criteria,"* Carleton C. Long and Dwight G.
   Lavender, No. 174, April 1933, pp. 48, 52-53.
   Reconnaissance noted, T. M. Griffiths and party.

"Report on the 1952 San Juan Outing,"* Robert Ellingwood,
No. 407, November 1952, pp. 159-161, 1 Illustration p. 167.

"Class E Flower Walk," Sam Alfend, No. 538, October 1963,
pp. 173-174, 1 Illustration.

Front cover illustration, "Saint Sophias Ridge," John F.
Bennett, No. 595, July 1968.

ST. VRAIN MOUNTAIN, 12,162'   Front Range, Indian Peaks   Allens Park 1957
Trail and Timberline
   "Our Indian Peaks,"* Karl E. Boehm, No. 497, May 1960, pp. 73-
74.

SAN BERNARDO MOUNTAIN, 11,861'   San Miguel Range   Mount Wilson 1953
Alpine Journal
   "Mountaineering in Southern Colorado,"* Percy W. Thomas,
Vol. 15, August 1891, pp. 480-490.

   "Alpine Notes: Rocky Mountain Sickness,"* Percy W. Thomas,
Vol. 17, May 1894, pp. 140-141.
Ascent note, Percy W. Thomas.

SAN LUIS PEAK, 14,014'   San Juan Mountains   Creede 15M 1959
American Alpine Journal
   "The Rocky Mountains of the United States,"* Howard Palmer,
Vol. 1, 1931, pp. 360-367.

Appalachia
   "The Call of Colorado,"* Edward W. Harnden, Vol. 16,
June 1925, pp. 158-164.

   "All the 14,000's,"* Carl Melzer, Vol. 22, December 1939,
pp. 466-479.

Mazama
   "Ramble Number 21,"* A. H. Marshall, Vol. 21, No. 12,
December 1939, pp. 55-61.

The Mountaineer
   "A Mountaineer in Colorado,"* Edward W. Harnden, Vol. 15,
December 15, 1922, pp. 47-53.

Trail and Timberline
   "Climbing San Luis, Elevation 14,146 Feet,"* George H. Harvey,
Jr., No. 125, March 1929, pp. 7, 9.

   "Climbing Notes,"* No. 144, October 1930, p. 9.
Ascent note, Hiking and Outing Club of Western State College.

   "Confessions of A Solo Climber or How I Recanted My Heresy,"*
Wilbur F. Arnold, No. 389, May 1951, pp. 51-55.

   "Stewart and San Luis in May,"* Jack L. Harry, No. 509,
May 1961, pp. 92-94.

SAWTOOTH MOUNTAIN, 12,304'   Front Range, Indian Peaks   Allens Park 1957
   Trail and Timberline
      "The Poudre Canyon Road and the Mountain Club,"* George
      McCormick, No. 99, December 1926, pp. 2-3, 1 Map.

      Front cover illustration, "Sawtooth Mountain Near Cameron
      Pass," R. T. Burdick, No. 149, March 1931.

      "Junior Jottings,"* No. 371, November 1949, pp. 172-173.

      "Our Indian Peaks,"* Karl E. Boehm, No. 497, May 1960, pp. 73-
      74.

SCHUYLKILL MOUNTAIN, 12,146'   Ruby Range   Oh-Be-Joyful 1961
   Trail and Timberline
      Front cover illustration, "Schuylkill Mountain from Pittsburgh
      Campsite," Glenn Gebhardt, No. 451, July 1956.

      "Some Took the High Road,"* Stan Shepard, No. 455,
      November 1956, pp. 165-167.

SENTINEL POINT, 12,527'   Pikes Peak Region   Pikes Peak 1951
   Iowa Mountaineers Journal
      "1963 Pikes Peak Crags Outing,"* Vol. 5, No. 5, 1965, p. 35.
      Ascent note.

      "Pikes Peak Crags Outing,"* Harvey and Annie T. Carter, Vol. 5,
      No. 5, 1965, pp. 54-59.

"MT. SEVEN", 13,297'   Sangre de Cristo Range   (Unnamed) Medano Pass 1967
   Trail and Timberline
      "New Names in Sangres,"* No. 621, September 1970, p. 206.

THE SHARKSTOOTH, 12,630'   Front Range, Rocky Mountain National Park
                           McHenrys Peak 1957
   American Alpine Journal
      "Colorado Climbing Notes, 1936,"* Kenneth Segerstrom, Vol. 3,
      1937, pp. 108-109.
      First ascent note, Warren Gorrell and Paul Hauk.

      "Sharkstooth, South Face," Layton Kor, Vol. 13, 1963, p. 492.
      First ascent note of the south face, Charlie Roskosz and
      Layton Kor.

   Chicago Mountaineering Club Newsletter
      "Shark's Tooth," Loren Jahn, Vol. 5, No. 5, November 1951,
      pp. 10-11, 1 Map p. 6.

   Climbing
      "Winter Climbing in Rocky Mountain National Park,"* Michael
      Covington, No. 37, July-August 1976, pp. 7-13.
      Winter ascent noted of the Left Gully route, Dean Ketchum and
      Michael Covington.

Off Belay
"Climbing at Rocky Mountain,"* Walt Fricke, No. 2, April 1972,
pp. 17-23, 1 Illustration, 2 Maps.

"More on National Parks: Rocky Mountain National Park,"*
No. 21, June 1975, pp. 39, 41.
Note on recorded ascents during the year.

Trail and Timberline
"First Ascent of the Cathedral Spire, 'Shark Tooth'," Warren
Gorrell, No. 215, September 1936, pp. 107-108, 1 Illustration,
Front cover illustration.
First ascent noted, Warren Gorrell and Paul Hauk.

"Climbing Notes,"* K. S., No. 215, September 1936, p. 108.
First ascent note, Warren Gorrell and Paul Hauk.

"Boulder Notes,"* Hope Leighton, No. 470, February 1958, p. 27.
Ascent note, Harold Walton and party.

"The South Face of the Shark's Tooth," Charlie Roskosz,
No. 533, May 1963, pp. 93-94, 1 Illustration.
First ascent noted of the south face, Charlie Roskosz and
Layton Kor.

"Seven Spires: A Story of Some Climbs in Rocky Mountain
National Park,"* Kent Keller, No. 651, March 1973, pp. 70-74,
1 Illustration.

SHAVANO PEAK, 14,225'   Sawatch Range   Poncha Springs 15M 1956
Appalachia
"An Ascent of Mt. Shavano," Charles E. Fay, Vol. 5,
December 1888, pp. 236-239.

"All the 14,000's,"* Carl Melzer, Vol. 22, December 1939,
pp. 466-479.

Trail and Timberline
"Denver Local Walks," No. 105, June 1927, p. 17.
Trip notice.

"Junior Outing,"* Anonymous, No. 227, October 1937, p. 107.

"A Conglomerate Review of the C.M.C. Summer Outing,
August 15-23, 1942 - Collegiate Range,"* Nancy Plowman, Eliot
Moses, Harold Brewer, Mary Wagner, No. 287, November 1942,
pp. 141-143, 1 Map p. 140.

"Shavano," Louise Roloff, No. 300, December 1943, p. 154.

"An Exagbination into Sundry Doings of the C.C.C.M.C.: First
Semester,"* Stanley Boucher, No. 351, March 1948, pp. 43-44.
"Correction," No. 352, April 1948, p. 51.
Note on title correction.

"Junior Jottings,"* No. 371, November 1949, pp. 172-173.

"Backpacking the Sawatch Range,"* Bud Boylard, No. 378, June 1950, pp. 83-85, 90-91.

"Giant Staircase - Shavano,"* Burgette Cahoon, No. 442, October 1955, pp. 166, 172.

SHAWNEE PEAK, 11,922'   Platte River Mountains   Shawnee 1945
    Trail and Timberline
        "The Mountain Ranges of Colorado,"* Kenneth Segerstrom, No. 215, September 1936, pp. 109-115, 1 Map.

SHEEP MOUNTAIN,
    American Alpine Journal
        "Club Activities: Colorado College Mountain Club,"* John W. Kuglin, Vol. 13, 1962, pp. 291-292.
        Second ascent note, James Dyson and John Auld, via new route on the southeast face.

SHEEP MOUNTAIN, 12,241'   Flattops   Trappers Lake 1977
    Trail and Timberline
        "The Mountain Ranges of Colorado,"* Kenneth Segerstrom, No. 215, September 1936, pp. 109-115, 1 Map.

SHEEP MOUNTAIN, 12,376'   Gore Range   Copper Mountain 1970
    Appalachia
        "News Flashes from Camp Hale: Still Going Strong,"* José M. Acebo, Vol. 24, June 1943, pp. 386-388.

    Trail and Timberline
        "Notes on the Gore Range, Summer, 1942,"* Carl Melzer, No. 284, August 1942, pp. 103-106.

SHEEP NOSE, 8,894'   Rampart Range   Westcreek 1956
    Climbing
        "Nostalgia/Part II Mundus Est Mons,"* Harvey T. Carter, No. 6, March-April 1971, pp. 3-5.
        First ascent noted.

MT. SHERMAN, 14,036'   Mosquito Range   Mount Sherman 1961
    Appalachia
        "All the 14,000's,"* Carl Melzer, Vol. 22, December 1939, pp. 466-479.

    Trail and Timberline
        "14,000 Feet,"* Russell Briggs, No. 246, June 1939, p. 77.

        "An Exagbination into Sundry Doings of the C.C.C.M.C.: First Semester,"* Stanley Boucher, No. 351, March 1948, pp. 43-44.
        "Correction," No. 352, April 1948, p. 51.
        Note on title correction.

SHIPLER MOUNTAIN, 11,317'   Never Summer Range, Rocky Mountain National Park
                             Fall River Pass 1958
   Trail and Timberline
      "The Trips of the Outing,"* No. 37, October 1921, pp. 2-4.

SHIPS PROW, 12,800'   Front Range, Rocky Mountain National Park
                       Longs Peak 1961
   American Alpine Journal
      "Ship's Prow," Stanley Shepard, Vol. 14, 1964, pp. 196-197.
      First ascent note, "The Portal" route, Bob Boucher and Stanley
      Shepard.
      First ascent note, the "Nexus Corner" route, James Burbank and
      Stanley Shepard.

   Climbing
      "View from Within: Colorado Rocky Mountain National Park,"*
      Michael Covington, No. 29, March-April 1975, p. 31.
      Free ascent note of the East Portal route, Harry Kent and
      Keith Lober.

"SHOSHONI PEAK", 12,967'   Front Range, Indian Peaks
                           (Unnamed) Monarch Lake 1958
   Alpine Journal
      "The Rockies of Colorado,"* Evelio Echevarría C., Vol. 71,
      May 1966, pp. 26-36, 1 Map, Bibliography.

   Trail and Timberline
      "Letter to the Editor: New Peak Names,"* Evelio Echevarría C.,
      No. 572, August 1966, p. 139.

MT. SILEX, 13,628'   Needle Mountains   Storm King Peak 1964
   Trail and Timberline
      "The Colorado Mountain Club Announces the Twenty-Eighth Annual
      Summer Outing,"* Henry Buchtel, Lewis Giesecke, Kenneth
      Segerstrom, No. 265, January 1941, pp. 9-14, 1 Map, Front cover
      sketch map.

      Illustration,* "The Guardian and Mt. Silex from the Vallecito
      Side," Ralph Rosenbaum, No. 608, August 1969, p. 146.

      "Letters to the Editor,"* Martin A. Etter, No. 610,
      October 1969, p. 187.
      North ridges note.

SILVER MOUNTAIN, 12,480'   La Plata Range   La Plata 1963
   Trail and Timberline
      Illustration, "Silver Mountain from Durango," Charles W.
      Halley, No. 694, October 1976, p. 192.

MT. SILVERHEELS, 13,822'   Front Range   Alma 1970
   Trail and Timberline
      "Silverheels," Esther Holt, No. 371, November 1949, pp. 168-
      169, 1 Illustration.

"MT. SILVERTHORNE", 13,357'   Gore Range   (Unnamed) Willow Lakes 1970
   Trail and Timberline
        "Backpacking in the Gore Range,"* Shirli Voigt, No. 667,
   July 1974, pp. 177-180, 1 Map.

SIMMONS PEAK, 12,051'   Sangre de Cristo Range   Howard 15M 1959
   Trail and Timberline
        "Sangre de Cristo Saga,"* Lester A. Michel, with Wilbur F.
   Arnold, No. 524, August 1962, pp. 123-126, 133.

"SLATE MOUNTAIN" (PURPLE MOUNTAIN), 12,958'   Ruby Range
                                      (Unnamed) Oh-Be-Joyful 1961
   Chicago Mountaineering Club Newsletter
        "Colorado's Elk Mountains,"* Weldon F. Heald, Vol. 13, No. 6,
   October 1959, pp. 1-5, Front cover map.

MT. SNEFFELS, 14,150'   San Juan Mountains, Sneffels Range
                        Mount Sneffels 1967
   Alpine Journal
        "The Rockies of Colorado,"* Evelio Echevarría C., Vol. 71,
   May 1966, pp. 26-36, 1 Map, Bibliography.

   American Alpine Journal
        "Climbing in the Mount Sneffels Region, Colorado,"* Dwight G.
   Lavender and T. Melvin Griffiths, Vol. 2, 1933, pp. 97-102,
   1 Map.
   First ascent noted of the north face and first traverse of the
   peak, Gordon Williams, Melvin Griffiths, and Dwight Lavender.

        "Southwestern Colorado Climbing Notes - 1932,"* Dwight G.
   Lavender, Vol. 2, 1933, p. 128.
   First complete ascent note of the north face, T. M. Griffiths,
   Gordon Williams, and Dwight G. Lavender.
   Modification of the older partial route of the north face,
   Dave Lavender, Miss Martha Bloom, and Dwight G. Lavender.

        "Southwestern Colorado Climbing Notes - 1933,"* Dwight G.
   Lavender, Vol. 2, 1934, p. 256.
   Ascent note of the northeast arete to base of the east arete
   to the summit, L. V. Giesecke, T. M. Griffiths, C. C. Long,
   and Dwight G. Lavender.
   Direct ascent note of the central portion of the north face,
   T. M. Griffiths, Dwight G. Lavender, Miss M. McClintock, and
   L. V. Giesecke, Dr. H. L. McClintock, F. McClintock.

        "Naming America's Mountains - The Colorado Rockies,"* Francis
   P. Farquhar, Vol. 12, 1961, pp. 319-346.
   First ascent noted, A. D. Wilson, F. Rhoda, F. M. Endlich, and
   Ford.

        "Club Activities: Colorado College Mountain Club,"* Jim
   McChristal and Steve Specht, Vol. 16, 1968, pp. 236-237.
   Ascent note.

"Club Activities: Simians," Peter Zvengrowski, Vol. 17, 1971,
p. 483.
Ski ascent note, Chuck Cooper, Laura Jasch, and Pete
Zvengrowski.

"Club Activities: Colorado College Mountain Club,"* Jim
McChristal, Vol. 19, 1974, pp. 229-230.
Winter ascent note.

Appalachia
"The San Juan Mountains," Frederick H. Chapin, Vol. 6,
December 1890, pp. 147-162.

"Alpina,"* K. A. H., Vol. 19, December 1933, p. 594.
First ascent note of the central portion of the south (north)
face.
First ascent note of the northeast ridge.

"Present-Day Rock Climbing in Colorado,"* Carleton C. Long,
Vol. 20, June 1934, pp. 132-134.

"All the 14,000's,"* Carl Melzer, Vol. 22, December 1939,
pp. 466-479.

Climbing
"Sneffels Kamikaze Style," Laura Jasch, No. 7, May-June 1971,
pp. 9-10, 27, 4 Illustrations.

Mazama
"Hither and Yon,"* A. H. Marshall, Vol. 14, No. 12,
December 1932, pp. 32-38.

The Mountaineering Journal (British)
"Outstanding Climbing Centres in the South-Western Colorado
Rockies,"* Dwight G. Lavender, Vol. 1, No. 4, June, July,
August 1933, pp. 238-248.
First complete ascent noted of the north face.

"Correspondence,"* Dwight Lavender, Vol. 2, No. 1, December,
January, February 1933-34, pp. 47-51.
Ascent note, Dwight Lavender.
Ascent note of the northeast arete to the east arete and to
the summit, Lewis V. Giesecke, Dwight Lavender, Carleton Long,
and T. Melvin Griffiths.
Ascent note of the central portion of the north face, T. Melvin
Griffiths, Dwight Lavender, Mary McClintock, and Lewis V.
Giesecke, Dr. McClintock, Frank McClintock.

Sierra Club Bulletin
"Notes and Correspondence: The Colorado Mountain Club,"* David
Rosendale, Vol. 18, No. 1, February 1933, pp. 123-124.
Ascent note of the north face.

Summit
Illustration, "Mount Sneffels," Vol. 7, No. 8, August 1961,
p. 15.

"Mount Sneffels in the San Juan," Dr. Thomas C. Emmel and
Michael K. Fosdick, Vol. 14, No. 1, January-February 1968,
pp. 12-13, 4 Illustrations.

Trail and Timberline
"Climbing Notes,"* Dwight Lavender, No. 156, October 1931,
    p. 165.
New route note via the north face and northeast ridge, T. M.
Griffiths, Charles Kane, Gordon Williams, and Dwight Lavender.

"The San Juan's Mightiest," D. G. Lavender, No. 157,
November 1931, pp. 175-176, 1 Sketch.
First ascent noted, Rhoda, Wilson, Endlich, and Ford, via
southwestern arete.
New route noted of the north face and northeast arete, T. M.
Griffiths, G. Williams, C. Kane, and D. G. Lavender.

"Mount Sneffels (14,170)," D. G. Lavender, No. 158,
December 1931, pp. 191-193, 2 Illustrations, 1 Sketch.
New route noted of the north face and northeast arete, D. G.
Lavender, Melvin Griffiths, Charles Kane, and Gordon Williams.

"Editorial Notes,"* David Rosendale, No. 166, August 1932,
    p. 120.
North face ascent note, Dwight Lavender, Melvin Griffiths, and
Gordon Williams.

"The North Face of Sneffels," Dwight G. Lavender, No. 169,
November 1932, pp. 159-160, Front cover illustration.
First direct ascent noted of the north face, Melvin Griffiths,
Gordon Williams, and Dwight Lavender.

Illustration, "The Lower Gendarmes of the Southwest Arete of
Mt. Sneffels," T. Melvin Griffiths, No. 171, January 1933,
    p. 7.

"Notes on the 1932 Climbing Season,"* Carleton C. Long,
No. 171, January 1933, p. 10.
Partial north face route note, Dwight Lavender, David Lavender,
and Brookie Bloom.

"High Altitude Camping," T. Melvin Griffiths, No. 178,
August 1933, pp. 107-109, 2 Illustrations.

"Editorial Notes," David Rosendale, No. 181, November 1933,
    p. 163, 1 Illustration p. 159.
Direct route note of the north face, Dwight G. Lavender,
Melvin Griffiths, Frank McClintock, and Mary McClintock (also
L. V. Giesecke and Dr. H. L. McClintock).

"The 1933 Climbing Season in Colorado,"* Carleton C. Long,
No. 184, February 1934, pp. 20-23.
New route note of the direct north face.
New ridge route note via the northeast arete to east arete and
to the summit.

"Winter Mountaineering in the San Juan,"* G. K. Williams and
T. M. Griffiths, No. 185, March 1934, pp. 31-33.

"1934 Summer Outing Climbs,"* Everett C. Long, No. 192,
October 1934, pp. 131-133.
Ascent noted via Blue Lakes pass and the south ridge, the
route of the first ascent party of Rhoda, Endlich, Wilson, and
Ford.

"The 1934 Climbing Season in Colorado,"* Carleton C. Long,
No. 196, February 1935, pp. 15-18.
(First) winter ascent note, San Juan Mountaineers.

Front cover illustration, "Spectacular Spire in the Mt.
Sneffels Group," Everett C. Long, No. 238, September-
October 1938.
Title information from T&T, No. 240, December 1938, p. 127.

"A Winter Climb on Sneffels," Melvin Griffith (Griffiths),
No. 251, November 1939, pp. 153-155, 157, 2 Illustrations.

"North Face of Mount Sneffels," Melvin Griffiths, No. 265,
January 1941, pp. 5-8, 2 Illustrations.
First direct ascent noted of the north face, Melvin Griffiths,
Dwight Lavender, Lewis Giesecke, Dr. H. L. McClintock, Mary
McClintock, and Frank McClintock.

"Confessions of A Solo Climber or How I Recanted My Heresy,"*
Wilbur F. Arnold, No. 389, May 1951, pp. 51-55.

Illustration, "The North Face of Mt. Sneffels," Lavender and
Griffiths, No. 401, May 1952, p. 87.

"Report on the 1952 San Juan Outing,"* Robert Ellingwood,
No. 407, November 1952, pp. 159-161, 2 Illustrations p. 167,
Front cover illustration.

"A New Approach to Sneffels: The Northwest Ridge of Mount
Sneffels," Henry L. McClintock, No. 473, May 1958, pp. 63-64,
Front cover illustration.
New route noted, Frank McClintock and David Lewis.

"On to the Summit," Frank A. McClintock, No. 473, May 1958,
pp. 64-66, 1 Illustration, Front cover illustration.
New route noted of the northwest ridge, Frank McClintock and
David Lewis.

Illustration,* "Looking Toward Matterhorn and Wetterhorn from
Uncompahgre, Mt. Sneffels in Background," Mike Sadusky,
No. 485, May 1959, p. 67.

"Mount Sneffels," Philip C. Settles, No. 507, March 1961,
pp. 43-48, 2 Illustrations, Bibliography.
First ascent noted, Franklin Rhoda, Wilson, Dr. Endlick
(Endlich), and Ford.

"Colorado's Most Beautiful Mountain," Ken Franzen and Russ Palmer, No. 512, August 1961, pp. 135-136, 1 Illustration.

"Organization Plus or Sneffels Will be No Snafu," Tad Frost, No. 533, May 1963, pp. 95-96.

"A Novice's View of the San Juans,"* David Slawson, No. 538, October 1963, pp. 171-172.

Illustration, "Mt. Sneffels," Charles Grover, No. 649, January 1973, p. 19.

MT. SNIKTAU, 13,234'   Front Range   Grays Peak 1958
   Trail and Timberline
      Front cover illustration, "Mt. Sniktau, from Loveland Pass Ski Area," Esther Holt, No. 182, December 1950.

SNOWDRIFT PEAK, 12,274'   Front Range, Rocky Mountain National Park
                           McHenrys Peak 1957
   Iowa Mountaineers Journal
      "Colorado's Rockies,"* Ruth Norman, Vol. 1, No. 10, February 1945, pp. 53-57.

   Trail and Timberline
      "Mountain Climbing and Statistics in Rocky Mountain National Park,"* John C. Whitnah and Robert C. Peterson, No. 343, July 1947, pp. 116-117.

SNOWMASS MOUNTAIN, 14,092'   Elk Range   Snowmass Mtn. 1960
   American Alpine Journal
      "Technical Climbing in the Mountains of Colorado and Wyoming,"* Albert Russell Ellingwood, Vol. 1, 1930, pp. 140-147.

      "Naming America's Mountains - The Colorado Rockies,"* Francis P. Farquhar, Vol. 12, 1961, pp. 319-346.

   Appalachia
      "The Call of Colorado,"* Edward W. Harnden, Vol. 16, June 1925, pp. 158-164, 2 Illustrations.

      "All the 14,000's,"* Carl Melzer, Vol. 22, December 1939, pp. 466-479.

      "Epilogue," Vol. 28, June 1950, p. 81.
      Accident note.

      "Excursions: Mountaineering and Hiking Trip to the Colorado Rockies,"* Wilbur W. Squire, Vol. 37, December 1968, p. 326.

   Chicago Mountaineering Club Newsletter
      "Colorado's Elk Mountains,"* Weldon F. Heald, Vol. 13, No. 6, October 1959, pp. 1-5, Front cover map.

   The Mountaineer
      "A Mountaineer in Colorado,"* Edward W. Harnden, Vol. 15, December 15, 1922, pp. 47-53, 1 Illustration.

The Mountaineering Journal (British)
    "American Notes: Climbing in the Snowmass Region of the Elk
Mountains of Colorado,"* Hubert M. Walters, Vol. 2, No. 2,
March, April, May 1934, p. 98.
First traverse noted of the Hagerman-Snowmass ridge. See T&T,
No. 228, November 1937, p. 126 for correct first traverse of
the Hagerman-Snowmass ridge by Harold Clark.

Summit
    "Colorado's High-Rising Elks,"* Weldon F. Heald, Vol. 8,
No. 11, November 1962, pp. 20-23.

    "Elk Range: The Living-Color Mountains," Bob Michael, Vol. 15,
No. 10, December 1969, pp. 13-15, 2 Illustrations.

Trail and Timberline
    "The Trips and the Country,"* Lucretia Vaile, No. 49,
October 1922, pp. 4-7, 1 Illustration.

    "More High Ones,"* No. 52, January 1923, pp. 12-13.

    Illustration,* "Snowmass and Capitol Peaks from Hagerman
Peak," Wm. H. Crisp, No. 114, April 1928, p. 5.

    "North Ridge," C. H. Jarret, No. 120, October 1928, p. 15,
1 Illustration p. 5, 1 Illustration p. 11.

    "Climbing Notes,"* No. 144, October 1930, p. 9.
Ascent note, Hiking and Outing Club of Western State College.

    "Snowmass and Hagerman,"* Harvey T. Sethman, No. 180,
October 1933, pp. 145-146, 1 Illustration, 1 Illustration
p. 140.
First recorded traverse noted of the Hagerman-Snowmass ridge.
See T&T, No. 228, November 1937, p. 126 for correct first
traverse of the Hagerman-Snowmass ridge by Harold Clark.

    "Clark Peak?"* Percy Hagerman, No. 228, November 1937, pp. 120,
126.
First traverse noted of the Hagerman-Snowmass ridge, Harold
Clark.

    "Junior Outing,"* Rex A. Young, No. 239, November 1938,
pp. 115-116.

    Front cover illustration, "Snowmass Peak and Lake," Peregrine,
No. 322, October 1945.

    "1873 Tells 1949,"* Louisa Ward Arps, No. 365, May 1949,
pp. 68-70, 1 Illustration following p. 70.

    "1949 Snowmass Outing was A Great Success,"* Karl T.
Neuberger, No. 370, October 1949, pp. 143, 152.

    "Hi-Peak Ascents of 1949 Summer Outing,"* Bob Steele, No. 371,
November 1949, pp. 164-165.

"Confessions of A Solo Climber or How I Recanted My Heresy,"*
Wilbur F. Arnold, No. 389, May 1951, pp. 51-55.

"The Snowmass-Capitol Ridge,"* Karl Gustafson, No. 404,
August 1952, pp. 119-121, Front cover illustration.

"Fish Fry at Snowmass," Bruce Sommers, No. 447, March 1956,
pp. 41-43.

Front cover illustration, "Snowmass Mountain from Pierre
Lakes," Wilbur Arnold, No. 503, November 1960, pp. 163-164.

"Snowmass or Snowmess? Take Your Choice," Mike Berman,
No. 567, March 1966, pp. 46-47.

Illustration, "Snowmass Mountain from Geneva Lake," Gwen
Toepfer, No. 591, March 1968, p. 55.

"Hikes and Climbs from Crystal,"* John Beyer, No. 598,
October 1968, pp. 224-229, 1 Illustration, 1 Map.

"Snowmass," John Wullshleger, No. 652, April 1973, pp. 102-103,
1 Illustration.

SNOWMASS PEAK, 13,600'   Elk Range   Snowmass Mtn. 1960
    Trail and Timberline
      "A New Snowmass," No. 598, October 1968, p. 229.

"MT. SOLITUDE", 13,075'   Gore Range   (Unnamed) Vail East 1970
See "PEAK 13,053'"   (Unnamed) Minturn 15M 1934, 13,053'

MT. SOPRIS, 12,953'   Elk Range   Mount Sopris 1961
    American Alpine Journal
      "Naming America's Mountains - The Colorado Rockies,"* Francis
      P. Farquhar, Vol. 12, 1961, pp. 319-346.

    Off Belay
      Illustration, "A Large Rock Glacier on the Northeast Side of
      Mount Sopris Near Aspen, Colorado," Jim Peterson, No. 17,
      October 1974, p. 6.

    Summit
      "Colorado's High-Rising Elks,"* Weldon F. Heald, Vol. 8,
      No. 11, November 1962, pp. 20-23, 1 Illustration.

    Trail and Timberline
      Illustration, "Early Morning Clouds. Mt. Sopris, Near
      Carbondale, Colo.," Wm. F. Ervin, No. 110, December 1927, p. 5.

      "1873 Tells 1949,"* Louisa Ward Arps, No. 365, May 1949,
      pp. 68-70, 1 Illustration following p. 70.

      Illustration, "Large Rock Glacier Heading in A Cirque on the
      Northeast Side of Mt. Sopris, Near Aspen, Colorado," Jim
      Peterson, No. 664, April 1974, p. 102.

SOUTH ARAPAHO PEAK, 13,397'   Front Range, Indian Peaks   Monarch Lake 1958
  Summit
        "Analysis of Mountaineering Accidents,"* Vol. 7, No. 7,
        July 1961, pp. 2-5.
        (From the American Alpine Club annual report).

        "Arapaho Glacier Country,"* Weldon F. Heald, Vol. 9, No. 10,
        November 1963, pp. 20-23.
        See the following corrections to the above article:
        "Letters," John M. Clark, Vol. 9, No. 11, December 1963, p. 31.
        "Letters," David Parkhurst, Vol. 10, No. 1, January-
        February 1964, p. 36.

        "An En-Lightening Experience," Wes Loder, Vol. 19, No. 5,
        June 1973, pp. 14-17, 1 Illustration, 1 Map.

  Trail and Timberline
        "Up the Arapahoes in January,"* No. 18, March 1920, p. 4.

        "Boulder Bunch Leads A Horde Up the Arapahoes,"* Frances
        Thompson, No. 35, August 1921, p. 6.

        Illustration,* "Arapahoe Peaks and Glacier," Geo. H. Harvey,
        Jr., No. 48, September 1922, p. 7.

        "Winter Climbing Notes,"* No. 158, December 1931, p. 188.
        Note on winter ascents, Carleton C. Long.

        Illustration, "The Gore Range from South Arapaho Peak," Ronald
        L. Ives, No. 204, October 1935, p. 116.

        "Our Indian Peaks,"* Karl E. Boehm, No. 497, May 1960, pp. 73-
        74.

        Illustration, "Face of South Arapaho Peak," Tom Hewitt,
        No. 694, October 1976, p. 201.

SOUTH LOOKOUT PEAK, 13,357'   San Juan Mountains   Ophir 1955
  American Alpine Journal
        "Southwestern Colorado Climbing Notes - 1932,"* Dwight G.
        Lavender, Vol. 2, 1933, p. 129.
        Attempt note of the northern summit, Charles Kendrick, Bob
        Scott, and Dwight G. Lavender.

  Trail and Timberline
        "Six First Ascents on the '32 Outing,"* Dwight G. Lavender,
        No. 168, October 1932, pp. 139-140, 149-150.
        First ascent noted, Lewis Giesecke and Dwight G. Lavender, and
        Brookie Bloom, Dudley Smith, and Dave Lavender. See T&T,
        No. 173, March 1933, p. 41 for first ascent correction.

        "Climbing Notes,"* D. G. L., No. 173, March 1933, p. 41.
        First ascent correction note.

        "Exploring Ice Lake Basin,"* Allen W. Greene, No. 474,
        June 1958, pp. 75-76, 87.

"SOUTH TRAVERSE PEAK", 13,041'   Gore Range   (Unnamed) Willow Lakes 1970
May also be known as "GRAND TRAVERSE PEAK".   See ADDENDA p. 258.
      Trail and Timberline
          "Backpacking in the Gore Range,"* Shirli Voigt, No. 667,
          July 1974, pp. 177-180, 1 Map.

SOUTH TWIN CONE PEAK ("KENOSHA CONE"), 12,323'   Kenosha Mountains
                                                  Mount Logan 1945
      Trail and Timberline
          "The Mountain Ranges of Colorado,"* Kenneth Segerstrom,
          No. 215, September 1936, pp. 109-115, 1 Map.

SOUTH TWIN PEAK, 13,534'   Sangre de Cristo Range   Twin Peaks 1965
      Trail and Timberline
          "Climbing in the Sangre de Cristo,"* Albert R. Ellingwood,
          No. 81, June 1925, pp. 1-5.

SOUTH TWIN THUMB, 13,320'   Needle Mountains   Storm King Peak 1964
See also TWIN THUMBS
      The Mountaineering Journal (British)
          "Correspondence,"* Dwight Lavender, Vol. 2, No. 1, December,
          January, February 1933-34, pp. 47-51.
          First ascent note, San Juan Mountaineers.

      Trail and Timberline
          "The Needle Mountains Expedition,"* Carleton C. Long, No. 181,
          November 1933, pp. 155-157, 166.
          Possible first ascent noted, San Juan Mountaineers.

          "The 1933 Climbing Season in Colorado,"* Carleton C. Long,
          No. 184, February 1934, pp. 20-23.
          Possible first ascent note, San Juan Mountaineers.

SPANISH PEAKS, Spanish Peaks   Spanish Peaks 1971
See also EAST SPANISH PEAK and WEST SPANISH PEAK
      Trail and Timberline
          "Huerfano Playgrounds,"* Thomas J. Everly, No. 248,
          August 1939, pp. 103-104.

          "Legend of Huajatolla," Louis Bernhardt Sporleder Sr., No. 297,
          September 1943, pp. 111-113, 1 Illustration.
          From "A Souvenir of Colorado's Mystic Mountain."

THE SPEARHEAD, 12,575'   Front Range, Rocky Mountain National Park
                          McHenrys Peak 1957
      American Alpine Journal
          "Colorado Climbing Notes, 1936,"* Kenneth Segerstrom, Vol. 3,
          1937, pp. 107-108.
          First ascent note, Charles Buckingham and Stan Midgeley
          (Midgely).

          "New Routes in Rocky Mountain National Park,"* Walter Fricke,
          Vol. 17, 1971, pp. 379-380.
          New route note, "The Barb" on the north face, Charlie Logan
          and Walter Fricke.

Chicago Mountaineering Club Newsletter
"Ascents by Club Members,"* Stanley Midgely, Vol. 1, No. 3,
September to December 1945, pp. 10-11.
First ascent note, Stanley Midgely (and Charles Buckingham).

"Chief's Head and Spear Head,"* Jerry Wolkoff, Vol. 5, No. 5,
November 1951, pp. 17-18, 1 Map p. 6.

Climbing
"View from Within: Colorado Rocky Mountain National Park,"*
No. 28, Winter 1974-75, p. 36.
First free ascent note of "The Barb", Daniel McClure and
Robert Gulley.
Second free ascent note of "The Barb", Chris Reveley and
George Hurley.

"Snatching Defeat from the Jaws of Victory," Ron Matous,
No. 37, July-August 1976, pp. 14-15, 4 Illustrations.

"Basecamp: Colorado,"* No. 38, September-October 1976, pp. 3-5.
New route note to the left of "Obviously Four Believers", Dave
Breashears and Mike Weiss.

Off Belay
"New Routes in Rocky Mountain National Park: Other Peaks and
Rocks," Walt Fricke, No. 1, January-February 1972, p. 40.
Ascent note of the East Buttress, Fil Sokol and Dick Erb.

"Climbing at Rocky Mountain,"* Walt Fricke, No. 2, April 1972,
pp. 17-23, 2 Maps.

Trail and Timberline
"Climbing Notes,"* No. 217, November 1936, p. 132.
First ascent note, Charles Buckingham and Stan Midgely.

"Spearhead - the Northeast Face," Stanley Shepard, No. 495,
March 1960, pp. 31-32, 36.

"Seven Spires: A Story of Some Climbs in Rocky Mountain
National Park,"* Kent Keller, No. 651, March 1973, pp. 70-74.

SPECIMEN MOUNTAIN, 12,489'   Front Range, Rocky Mountain National Park
                            Fall River Pass 1958
Appalachia
"The Peaks of Rocky Mountain National Park,"* Roger W. Toll,
Vol. 17, June 1929, pp. 252-260.

Trail and Timberline
"The Trips of the Outing,"* No. 37, October 1921, pp. 2-4,
1 Illustration.

SPREAD EAGLE PEAK, 13,431'   Sangre de Cristo Range
                            Electric Peak 15M 1959
Appalachia
"Club Excursions: Colorado, 1946,"* Emma Rutherford, Vol. 26,
December 1946, pp. 261-264.

Trail and Timberline
"The Sangre de Cristo Range,"* Eva and Bill Rathbun, No. 460,
April 1957, pp. 55-60, 64, 1 Map.

"Pikes Peak Doings,"* Katy Wilson, No. 492, December 1959,
p. 180.
Ascent note of unnamed portion of Spread Eagle Peak.

"New Maps of the Sangre de Cristo Range,"* John L. J. Hart,
No. 519, March 1962, pp. 32-33.

"Sangre de Cristo Saga,"* Lester A. Michel, with Wilbur F.
Arnold, No. 524, August 1962, pp. 123-126, 133, Front cover
illustration.

SPRING MOUNTAIN, 13,244'   Sangre de Cristo Range   Horn Peak 1959
Trail and Timberline
"Sangre de Cristo Saga,"* Lester A. Michel, with Wilbur F.
Arnold, No. 525, September 1962, pp. 139-142, 150, (Continued
from August 1962 T&T).

SQUARE TOP MOUNTAIN, 13,794'   Front Range   Montezuma 1958
Trail and Timberline
"Notes on Nomenclature,"* K. S., No. 178, August 1933, p. 109.

STAR PEAK, 13,521'   Elk Range   Pearl Pass 1961
Chicago Mountaineering Club Newsletter
"Colorado's Elk Mountains,"* Weldon F. Heald, Vol. 13, No. 6,
October 1959, pp. 1-5, Front cover map.

Climbing
Illustration,* "Colorado's Mount Hayden (13,561') in Ski
Country USA ... Star Peak is in the Background," Tom Merrill,
No. 5, January 1971, p. 3.

Trail and Timberline
"The Mountain Ranges of Colorado,"* Kenneth Segerstrom,
No. 215, September 1936, pp. 109-115, 1 Map.

"The Ascent of Star Peak, Colorado," Otto Eugene Schniebs,
No. 247, July 1939, pp. 87-88, 2 Illustrations.

"A Spring Outing in the Elk Mts. - 1939," F. Cranmer, No. 247,
July 1939, pp. 89-90, 1 Illustration.

Illustration, "Looking South from Star Peak Down East Brush
Creek," No. 363, March 1949, p. 47.

Front cover illustration, "Star Peak in the Elk Mountains,"
Margaret Chase, No. 445, January 1956.

"The Lighter Side,"* Hal Brewer, No. 478, October 1958,
pp. 135, 138, 1 Illustration p. 136.

"Floating Around with the Juniors - We Climb Star Peak,"
Maurine Hoge, No. 484, April 1959, p. 47.

STEAMBOAT ROCK, 6,074'   Northwest Colorado, Dinosaur National Monument
                         Canyon of Ladore South 1954
    American Alpine Journal
        "Colorado Climbing Notes, 1936,"* Kenneth Segerstrom, Vol. 3,
        1937, p. 109.
        Unclimbed note.

        "Steamboat Rock, Southeast Face, Dinosauer National Monument,"
        Layton Kor, Vol. 15, 1966, p. 146.
        First ascent note, Mike Covington, Brian Marts, and Layton Kor.

    Trail and Timberline
        "Scouting the Yampa-Ladore Region," H. M. Walters, No. 214,
        August 1936, pp. 91-92, 1 Illustration.

        "Climbing Notes,"* No. 217, November 1936, p. 132.
        Unclimbed note.

        "The Canyon of the Ladore - Yampa River Reconnaissance of
        1936," Richard Morris, No. 219, January 1937, pp. 3-4, 13-14,
        1 Illustration.
        "Correction," No. 220, February 1937, p. 24.
        Note on photograph correction.

        "Steamboat Rock," Chuck Pavlik, No. 409, January 1953, pp. 3,
        17, Front cover illustration.

        Illustration, "Steamboat Rock," No. 413, May 1953, p. 70.

        Front cover illustration, "Steamboat Rock Near Echo Park Dam
        Site," Airplane photo by Otto Roach, No. 423, March 1954.

        Illustration, "The Useless Green River Wastefully Flows by
        Steamboat Rock in Dinosauer National Monument," Harry L.
        Standley, No. 591, March 1968, p. 67.

STEWART PEAK, 13,983'   San Juan Mountains   Stewart Peak 1965
    Appalachia
        "The Call of Colorado,"* Edward W. Harnden, Vol. 16,
        June 1925, pp. 158-164.

        "All the 14,000's,"* Carl Melzer, Vol. 22, December 1939,
        pp. 466-479.

    Mazama
        "Ramble Number 21,"* A. H. Marshall, Vol. 21, No. 12,
        December 1939, pp. 55-61.

    The Mountaineer
        "A Mountaineer in Colorado,"* Edward W. Harnden, Vol. 15,
        December 15, 1922, pp. 47-53.

    Trail and Timberline
        "Climbing San Luis, Elevation 14,146 Feet,"* George H. Harvey,
        Jr., No. 125, March 1929, pp. 7, 9.
        Ascent noted of Stewart Peak.

"Confessions of A Solo Climber or How I Recanted My Heresy,"* Wilbur F. Arnold, No. 389, May 1951, pp. 51-55.

"Stewart and San Luis in May,"* Jack L. Harry, No. 509, May 1961, pp. 92-94.

"The Mystery of Stewart Peak," No. 556, April 1965, p. 79.

"The Growing and the Shrinking: One Less Fourteen," Hugh E. Kingery, No. 564, December 1965, pp. 260-261.

"A Guide to Colorado's Almost-Fourteens,"* William A. Graves, No. 683, November 1975, pp. 225-227.

STONES PEAK, 12,922'   Front Range, Rocky Mountain National Park
                        McHenrys Peak 1957
Appalachia
   "Exploration,"* F. O. Carpenter, Vol. 5, December 1888, p. 235.
   Ascent note, F. H. Chapin and W. L. Hallett.

Trail and Timberline
   "Mountain Climbing and Statistics in Rocky Mountain National
   Park,"* John C. Whitnah and Robert C. Peterson, No. 343,
   July 1947, pp. 116-117.

STONY MOUNTAIN, 12,698'   San Juan Mountains, Sneffels Range
                           Telluride 1955
Trail and Timberline
   "Yankee Boy Basin Revisited," H. B. Van Valkenburgh, No. 635,
   November 1971, p. 221.

STORM KING PEAK, 13,752'   Needle Mountains   Storm King Peak 1964
American Alpine Journal
   "Club Activities: Harvard Mountaineering Club,"* David S.
   Roberts, Vol. 14, 1964, pp. 243-244.
   First winter ascent note.

Appalachia
   Illustration,* "Grenadier Range, Colorado: Peaks Above Balsam
   Lake; East Trinity on Left, Storm King in Right Distance,"
   A. B. Fielding, Vol. 23, December 1941, Following p. 536.

Climbing
   "View from Within: The Grenadiers," No. 28, Winter 1974-75,
   p. 36.
   First ascent note of the north face, Bob Bliss and Don Jones.

Harvard Mountaineering
   "Climbing Notes, 1963: Colorado, Needle Mountains,"* Dave
   Roberts, No. 17, May 1965, pp. 55-56.
   (First) winter ascent note, Don Jensen and Dave Roberts.

Trail and Timberline
   "Some First Ascent Possibilities in Colorado,"* Kenneth
   Segerstrom, No. 165, July 1932, pp. 103-104, 1 Illustration.

"The Colorado Mountain Club Announces the Twenty-Eighth Annual Summer Outing,"* Henry Buchtel, Lewis Giesecke, Kenneth Segerstrom, No. 265, January 1941, pp. 9-14, 1 Map, Front cover sketch map.

"Garlic Gulch Episode,"* L. V. Giesecke, No. 274, October 1941, pp. 143-145.
First ascent noted on CMC outing.

"The Grenadiers in Winter,"* David S. Roberts, No. 547, July 1964, pp. 111-117.
First winter ascent noted, Dave Roberts and Don Jensen.

Illustration, "Storm King Peak, Colorado Needles," Don Jensen, No. 593, May 1968, p. 107.

"Trails of the Western Weminuche,"* William Weihofen, Ralph Rosenbaum, and Henri Navelet, No. 608, August 1969, pp. 144-147.

"Letters to the Editor,"* Martin A. Etter, No. 610, October 1969, p. 187.
North face note.

SUGARLOAF MOUNTAIN, 8,917'   Front Range   Gold Hill 1957
    Trail and Timberline
        "Foothill Climbs Near Longmont,"* Dave Taylor, No. 649, January 1973, pp. 3-5.

SULTAN MOUNTAIN, 13,368'   San Juan Mountains   Silverton 1955
    Trail and Timberline
        "Exploring Ice Lake Basin,"* Allen W. Greene, No. 474, June 1958, pp. 75-76, 87.

        "Silverton - Mountain Mecca,"* Art Porter, No. 620, August 1970, pp. 169, 171-172.

SUNLIGHT PEAK, 14,059'   Needle Mountains   Storm King Peak 1964
    American Alpine Journal
        "Technical Climbing in the Mountains of Colorado and Wyoming,"* Albert Russell Ellingwood, Vol. 1, 1930, pp. 140-147.

        "The Rocky Mountains of the United States,"* Howard Palmer, Vol. 1, 1931, pp. 360-367.

        "Colorado Climbing Notes, 1934,"* Carleton C. Long, Vol. 2, 1935, p. 416.
        Ascent note to establish San Juan Mountaineers survey station, John Nelson, Everett Long, and Carleton C. Long.

        "A.A.C. and C.M.C. Joint Outing, Needle Mountains, Colorado, July 19 - August 9, 1953,"* Henry L. McClintock, Vol. 9, 1954, pp. 169-171.
        New route note.

Appalachia

"All the 14,000's,"* Carl Melzer, Vol. 22, December 1939, pp. 466-479.

"Excursions: Colorado Trip,"* E. Folger Taylor and Walter D. Howe, Vol. 23, December 1940, pp. 257-259, 1 Illustration following p. 262.

"The Old and New West in the Needle Mountains,"* Duncan A. MacInnes, Vol. 23, June 1941, pp. 374-379.

Climbing

"Sunlight Peak (14,060 Ft.) and Window (sic) Peak (14,091 Ft.), Needle Range, San Juans, Colorado,"* No. 7, May-June 1971, p. 20.
First winter ascent note, Rick Nolting, Barry Nash, Floyd Frank, and Steve Lewis. Actual first winter ascent in 1966, Phil Schmuck, Don Monk, and Kermith Ross.

Illustration,* "Descent from Windom and Sunlight Col," No. 15, September-October 1972, p. 21.

Mazama

"Ramble Number 21,"* A. H. Marshall, Vol. 21, No. 12, December 1939, pp. 55-61, 2 Illustrations.

Trail and Timberline

"Where We Went and What We Climbed,"* No. 25, October 1920, pp. 8-11, 1 Illustration p. 13.

Illustration, "Summit of Sunlight Peak (14,053 Ft.)," Geo. C. Barnard, No. 103, April 1927, p. 2.

Illustration, "Near Summit - Sunlight Peak," Harvey Sethman, No. 104, May 1927, p. 2.

"Sunlight Peak," Naomi Anderson, No. 107, September 1927, p. 11.

"Four in One Day,"* Dr. Corwin S. Clarke, No. 107, September 1927, p. 18.

"The 1934 Climbing Season in Colorado,"* Carleton C. Long, No. 196, February 1935, pp. 15-18.
Ascent note, John Nelson, Everett Long, and Carleton C. Long. Ascent note from the north side, William P. House and Miss Elizabeth Woolsey.

Front cover illustration, "Sunlight Peak in the Needle Mountains," No. 222, April 1937.

"Needle Mountain Notes,"* David Lavender, No. 225, July 1937, pp. 80-81.
Windom Peak to Sunlight Peak traverse noted.

"Outing Ridge Work,"* Forest Greenfield, No. 227,
October 1937, pp. 102-103, 105.
Traverse noted of ridge from Jupiter - Windom - Sunlight - to
start of Needle Ridge, Jack Heeney and party.

"The Colorado Mountain Club Announces the Twenty-Eighth Annual
Summer Outing,"* Henry Buchtel, Lewis Giesecke, Kenneth
Segerstrom, No. 265, January 1941, pp. 9-14, 1 Illustration.

"Reaching the High Spots,"* George J. Kubricht, No. 325,
January 1946, pp. 3-4.

"Noname Prospects,"* Mel Griffiths, No. 340, April 1947,
pp. 56-59.

"Climbers Guide to Noname,"* No. 342, June 1947, pp. 97-98,
1 Map, 1 Illustration p. 94.

"Climber's Guide from Noname Creek,"* Henry Buchtel, No. 345,
September 1947, pp. 143-144, Front cover illustration.

"Confessions of A Solo Climber or How I Recanted My Heresy,"*
Wilbur F. Arnold, No. 389, May 1951, pp. 51-55.

"We Started at the Top,"* Virginia Copeland, No. 395,
November 1951, pp. 145-147, 1 Illustration.

Illustration,* "Upper Basin of No-Name Creek - Peaks from Left
to Right: Jagged Mtn., Peak 10, Knifepoint, and North Ridge of
Sunlight Peak," No. 419, November 1953, p. 156.

"A Rugged Ten-Day Outing,"* Neil Wernette, No. 426, June 1954,
pp. 83-84.

"Denver Junior Summer Outing,"* Louise Jackson, No. 443,
November 1955, pp. 190-191.

"The Needles, June 1957,"* Gene White, No. 471, March 1958,
pp. 31-35.

"Fifty-Two in '52,"* Dwight Hamilton, No. 482, February 1959,
pp. 25-26.

"Climber's Paradise,"* Lester Michel, No. 496, April 1960,
pp. 60-62.

"Revised Climbers' Guide from Noname Creek,"* William E.
Davis, No. 502, October 1960, pp. 149-154, 1 Illustration,
1 Map.

"Chicago Basin Expedition,"* Al Ossinger, No. 559, July 1965,
pp. 131-133, 1 Illustration.

Front cover illustration,* "Needle Mountains - Sunlight and
Windom," William Searcy, No. 607, July 1969.

"Chicago Basin Grand Slam,"* Carl C. Hinrichs, No. 659, November 1973, pp. 291-294, 2 Illustrations.

"SUNLIGHT SPIRE", 13,995'   Needle Mountains
                              (Unnamed) Storm King Peak 1964
American Alpine Journal
"Ascents in the San Juan Needles,"* George I. Bell, Vol. 13, 1962, pp. 230-231.
First ascent note, David Michael, John Marshall, and George I. Bell.

Trail and Timberline
"Some Ascents in the San Juan Needles,"* George Bell, No. 518, February 1962, pp. 19-21, 1 Illustration.
First ascent noted, George Bell, David Michael, and John Marshall.

SUNSHINE MOUNTAIN, 12,930'   San Miguel Range   Mount Wilson 1953
Alpine Journal
"Mountaineering in Southern Colorado,"* Percy W. Thomas, Vol. 15, August 1891, pp. 480-490.

"Alpine Notes: Rocky Mountain Sickness,"* Percy W. Thomas, Vol. 17, May 1894, pp. 140-141.

Trail and Timberline
"San Miguel Mountains,"* Dwight Lavender, No. 137, March 1930, p. 3.

"Outing Impressions,"* Evelyn Runnette, No. 156, October 1931, pp. 152-157.

SUNSHINE PEAK, 14,001'   San Juan Mountains   Redcloud Peak 1964
Appalachia
"All the 14,000's,"* Carl Melzer, Vol. 22, December 1939, pp. 466-479.

"Club Excursions: Colorado Excursion, 1951,"* Jean K. Kent, Vol. 28, December 1951, pp. 584-589, 2 Illustrations.

Mazama
"Ramble Number 21,"* A. H. Marshall, Vol. 21, No. 12, December 1939, pp. 55-61.

Trail and Timberline
"Climbing 60,000 Feet in the San Juan,"* Carl Blaurock, No. 40, January 1922, pp. 2-3.

"Junior Jottings,"* No. 371, November 1949, pp. 172-173.

"Handies, Redcloud, and Sunshine,"* Katy Wilson, No. 398, February 1952, p. 24.

"Report on the 1952 San Juan Outing,"* Robert Ellingwood, No. 407, November 1952, pp. 159-161.

"The Lake City Fourteens,"* Robin Simmons, No. 490,
October 1959, pp. 141-142.

"T0", 13,735'   San Juan Mountains, Sneffels Range
                 (Unnamed) Telluride 1955
    American Alpine Journal
        "Southwestern Colorado Climbing Notes - 1933,"* Dwight G.
        Lavender, Vol. 2, 1934, p. 256.
        First ascent note, T. M. Griffiths.

        "Colorado Climbing Notes, 1934,"* Carleton C. Long, Vol. 2,
        1935, p. 416.
        Second ascent note, A. C. Bartelt and Robert Blair.
        Third ascent note, A. C. Bartelt and party.

    The Mountaineering Journal (British)
        "Correspondence,"* Dwight Lavender, Vol. 2, No. 1, December,
        January, February 1933-34, pp. 47-51.
        First ascent note, T. Melvin Griffiths.

    Trail and Timberline
        "The 1933 Climbing Season in Colorado,"* Carleton C. Long,
        No. 184, February 1934, pp. 20-23, 1 Illustration p. 19.
        Probable first ascent note.

        "1934 Summer Outing Climbs,"* Everett C. Long, No. 192,
        October 1934, pp. 131-133.
        Second ascent noted, A. C. Bartelt and Robert Blair.

"T1" ("GILPIN BLOCK TOPS"), 13,408'#   San Juan Mountains, Sneffels Range
See also "GILPIN BLOCK TOPS"   (Unnamed) Telluride 1955
    American Alpine Journal
        "Colorado Climbing Notes, 1934,"* Carleton C. Long, Vol. 2,
        1935, p. 416.
        First ascent note, Everett Long and Caye Corr Breitenstein.

    Trail and Timberline
        "1934 Summer Outing Climbs,"* Everett C. Long, No. 192,
        October 1934, pp. 131-133.
        First ascent noted, Catherine Corr and Everett Long.

"T2" ("GILPIN BLOCK TOPS"), 13,553'+   San Juan Mountains, Sneffels Range
See also "GILPIN BLOCK TOPS"   (Unnamed) Telluride 1955
    American Alpine Journal
        "Colorado Climbing Notes, 1934,"* Carleton C. Long, Vol. 2,
        1935, p. 416.
        First ascent note of all three summits, east, center, west,
        Everett Long and Caye Corr Breitenstein.

    Trail and Timberline
        "1934 Summer Outing Climbs,"* Everett C. Long, No. 192,
        October 1934, pp. 131-133.
        First ascent noted, Catherine Corr and Everett Long.

#Elevation figure from the American Alpine Journal.

+Elevation figure from the American Alpine Journal.

"T3" ("GILPIN BLOCK TOPS"), 13,528'[#]   San Juan Mountains, Sneffels Range
See also "GILPIN BLOCK TOPS"   (Unnamed) Telluride 1955
    American Alpine Journal
        "Colorado Climbing Notes, 1934,"* Carleton C. Long, Vol. 2,
        1935, p. 417.
        First ascent note, William Nagel, Robert Blair, Orval Settles,
        and Robert Thallon.

    Trail and Timberline
        "1934 Summer Outing Climbs,"* Everett C. Long, No. 192,
        October 1934, pp. 131-133.
        (First) ascent noted, William Nagel, Robert Blair, Orval
        Settles, and Robert Thallon.

"T4" ("GILPIN BLOCK TOPS"), 13,533'[+]   San Juan Mountains, Sneffels Range
See also "GILPIN BLOCK TOPS"   (Unnamed) Telluride 1955
    American Alpine Journal
        "Colorado Climbing Notes, 1934,"* Carleton C. Long, Vol. 2,
        1935, p. 416.
        First ascent note, Dwight Lavender, Charles Kendrick, Jack
        Seerley, and Bob Thallon.

    Trail and Timberline
        "1934 Summer Outing Climbs,"* Everett C. Long, No. 192,
        October 1934, pp. 131-133.
        First ascent noted, John Seerley, Robert Thallon, Dwight
        Lavender, and Charles Kendrick.

"T5", 13,436'   San Juan Mountains, Sneffels Range
                (Unnamed) Telluride 1955
    Trail and Timberline
        Illustration, "Unnamed Point (T5): One of the Summits of
        Gilpin Peak," T. Melvin Griffiths, No. 171, January 1933, p. 7.

TABEGUACHE PEAK, 13,908' (14,155')   Sawatch Range   Garfield 15M 1940
    Appalachia
        "All the 14,000's,"* Carl Melzer, Vol. 22, December 1939,
        pp. 466-479.

    Trail and Timberline
        "Club Notes," No. 149, March 1931, p. 35.
        Note on new 14,000' peak.

        "Junior Outing,"* Anonymous, No. 227, October 1937, p. 107.

        "A Conglomerate Review of the C.M.C. Summer Outing,
        August 15-23, 1942 - Collegiate Range,"* Nancy Plowman, Eliot
        Moses, Harold Brewer, Mary Wagner, No. 287, November 1942,
        pp. 141-143, 1 Map p. 140.

[#]Elevation figure from the American Alpine Journal.

[+]Elevation figure from the American Alpine Journal.

"An Exagbination into Sundry Doings of the C.C.C.M.C.: First
Semester,"* Stanley Boucher, No. 351, March 1948, pp. 43-44.
"Correction," No. 352, April 1948, p. 51.
Note on title correction.

"Junior Jottings,"* No. 371, November 1949, pp. 172-173.

"Backpacking the Sawatch Range,"* Bud Boylard, No. 378,
June 1950, pp. 83-85, 90-91.

Front cover illustration, "CMC'ers - Mt. Tabeguache," Esther
Holt, No. 381, September 1950.

"Giant Staircase - Shavano,"* Burgette Cahoon, No. 442,
October 1955, pp. 166, 172.
Ascent noted of Tabeguache Peak.

TABLE MOUNTAIN, 8,830'   Front Range   Trail Mountain 1957
    Appalachia
        "Exploration,"* F. O. Carpenter, Vol. 5, December 1888, p. 234.
        Ascent note, F. H. Chapin.

"THE TAJ MAHAL", 9,748'#   Rampart Range   (Unnamed) Devils Head 1954
See also DEVILS HEAD
    Trail and Timberline
        "The Taj Mahal," Larry Griffin, No. 647, November 1972,
        pp. 228-229, 1 Illustration, Front cover illustration.
        New route noted, "Inside Taj Mahal", Lee Gilman, Sandy Kline,
        Janie Griffin, and Larry Griffin.
        New route noted, "Genectic Impressions", Lee and Mike White.

TANIMA PEAK, 12,420'   Front Range, Rocky Mountain National Park
                        Isolation Peak 1958
    Trail and Timberline
        "The Wild Basin Outing,"* Elinor Eppich Kingery, No. 298,
        October 1943, pp. 123-126.

"TARRYALL TOWER", 9,964'   Tarryall Mountains
                            (Unnamed) McCurdy Mountain 1956
    Trail and Timberline
        "The Sinks - A New Area for Mountaineers,"* Don Howe and Dick
        Slusser, No. 512, August 1961, pp. 142-144, 1 Map.

        "A Climb of Tarryall Tower," Dick Yeatts, No. 593, May 1968,
        pp. 108-109, 1 Illustration.

TAYLOR MOUNTAIN, 13,657'   Sawatch Range   Garfield 15M 1940
    Chicago Mountaineering Club Newsletter
        "Sneaking Up on Colorado Peaks by Way of Texas,"* Groves
        Kilbourn, Vol. 17, No. 1, February 1964, pp. 4-5.

—————
#Elevation of Devils Head.

TAYLOR PEAK, 13,153'   Front Range, Rocky Mountain National Park
                        McHenrys Peak 1957
American Alpine Journal
    "Taylor Peak, East Face," Michael Covington, Vol. 20, 1976,
    pp. 459-460.
    New route note on the east face, Doug Scott, Doug Snively, and
    Michael Covington.

Appalachia
    "The Peaks of Rocky Mountain National Park,"* Roger W. Toll,
    Vol. 17, June 1929, pp. 252-260, 1 Illustration.

Chicago Mountaineering Club Newsletter
    "Flattop, Hallett, Otis, and Taylor Peaks,"* Barbara Heiberg,
    Vol. 5, No. 5, November 1951, pp. 9-10, 1 Map p. 6.

Climbing
    "Winter Climbing in Rocky Mountain National Park,"* Michael
    Covington, No. 37, July-August 1976, pp. 7-13,
    3 Illustrations.
    Ascent noted of the east face, Doug Scott, Doug Snively, and
    Michael Covington.

Iowa Mountaineers Journal
    "Colorado's Rockies,"* Ruth Norman, Vol. 1, No. 10,
    February 1945, pp. 53-57.

Trail and Timberline
    "Some Wild Garden Climbs," Kenneth Segerstrom, No. 246,
    June 1939, pp. 75-76, 1 Illustration.

TAYLOR PEAK, 13,435'   Elk Range   Pearl Pass 1961
Chicago Mountaineering Club Newsletter
    "Colorado's Elk Mountains,"* Weldon F. Heald, Vol. 13, No. 6,
    October 1959, pp. 1-5, Front cover map.

Trail and Timberline
    "The Lighter Side,"* Hal Brewer, No. 478, October 1958,
    pp. 135, 138, 1 Illustration p. 137.

    "Pearl Pass, Castle, and Taylor,"* Paul Stewart, No. 478,
    October 1958, p. 143, 1 Illustration p. 137.

    "'F' is for Fun, Friends and Fiasco,"* Dick Walker, No. 676,
    April 1975, pp. 73, 75.

TEAKETTLE MOUNTAIN, 13,819'   San Juan Mountains, Sneffels Range
                               Mount Sneffels 1967
American Alpine Journal
    "Climbing in the Mount Sneffels Region, Colorado,"* Dwight G.
    Lavender and T. Melvin Griffiths, Vol. 2, 1933, pp. 97-102,
    1 Map.
    Second ascent noted, T. M. Griffiths, Dwight G. Lavender, and
    Gordon Williams.
    First ascent noted, Alonzo Hartman and Charles Rolfe.

"Southwestern Colorado Climbing Notes - 1932,"* Dwight G.
Lavender, Vol. 2, 1933, p. 128.
Second ascent note, T. M. Griffiths, Dwight G. Lavender, and
Gordon Williams.
First ascent note, Alonzo Hartman and Charles Rolfe.

The Mountaineering Journal (British)
"Outstanding Climbing Centres in the South-Western Colorado
Rockies,"* Dwight G. Lavender, Vol. 1, No. 4, June, July,
August 1933, pp. 238-248, 1 Illustration.

Trail and Timberline
"Editorial Notes,"* David Rosendale, No. 166, August 1932,
p. 120, 1 Illustration p. 118, Front cover illustration.
First ascent note, Dwight Lavender, Melvin Griffiths, and
Gordon Williams. See T&T, No. 173, March 1933, p. 41 for
correct first ascent by Charles Rolfe and Alonzo Hartman.

"Climbing Notes," D. G. L., No. 173, March 1933, p. 41.
First ascent note, Charles Rolfe and Alonzo Hartman.

"First Ascent Criteria,"* Carleton C. Long and Dwight G.
Lavender, No. 174, April 1933, pp. 48, 52-53.

"Teakettle," Dorr H. Burns, No. 407, November 1952, pp. 161-
163, 1 Illustration.

"New Route on Teakettle," R. A. Schluter, No. 477,
September 1958, p. 126.

Front cover illustration,* "Cirque Peak, Teakettle and Potosi
from Cirque Shoulder," Sam Alfend, No. 539, November 1963.

TELLURIDE PEAK, 13,509'   San Juan Mountains   Ironton 1955
Trail and Timberline
"Silverton - Mountain Mecca,"* Art Porter, No. 620,
August 1970, pp. 169, 171-172.

TENMILE PEAK ("PEAK 2"), 12,933'   Tenmile Range   Frisco 1970
Trail and Timberline
"Ten Mile Range Traverse,"* Carl Melzer, No. 326,
February 1946, pp. 19-23.

TEOCALLI MOUNTAIN, 13,208'   Elk Range   Gothic 1961
Chicago Mountaineering Club Newsletter
"Colorado's Elk Mountains,"* Weldon F. Heald, Vol. 13, No. 6,
October 1959, pp. 1-5, Front cover map.

Trail and Timberline
"1873 Tells 1949,"* Louisa Ward Arps, No. 365, May 1949,
pp. 68-70.

TERRA TOMAH MOUNTAIN, 12,718'   Front Range, Rocky Mountain National Park
                                 Trail Ridge 1957
    Trail and Timberline
        "Forest Canon," Joe Mills, No. 32, May 1921, pp. 2-5,
        1 Illustration.

        Illustration, "Terra Tomah Peak," Geo. C. Barnard, No. 163,
        May 1932, p. 71.

        "Terra Tomah Mountain," Louisa Ward Arps, No. 558, June 1965,
        pp. 110-111.

THATCHTOP, 12,668'   Front Range, Rocky Mountain National Park
                      McHenrys Peak 1957
    Appalachia
        "The Peaks of Rocky Mountain National Park,"* Roger W. Toll,
        Vol. 17, June 1929, pp. 252-260.

    Trail and Timberline
        "Group Activities: Denver Group,"* Evelyn Runnette, No. 215,
        September 1936, p. 118.
        Ascent note.

"THIRSTY PEAK", 13,217'   Sangre de Cristo Range
                           (Unnamed) Electric Peak 15M 1959
    Trail and Timberline
        "New Names in Sangres,"* No. 621, September 1970, p. 206.

THORODIN MOUNTAIN, 10,540'   Front Range   Tungsten 1972
    Off Belay
        "Lightening Strikes Rappeler (sic)," No. 5, October 1972, p. 41.
        Fatality note.

    Trail and Timberline
        "Private Property: No Trespassing!"* Sally Richards, Nos. 679-
        680, July-August 1975, pp. 148-150.

        "Guerilla Tactics Useful for Doggy Climbs: The Gentle Art of
        Freddy Peaking,"* Bob Michael, No. 689, May 1976, pp. 112-115.

THE THREE APOSTLES, Sawatch Range   Mt. Harvard 15M 1955
See also ICE MOUNTAIN
    Trail and Timberline
        "The High Peaks of the La Plata Mining Region,"* John L. J.
        Hart, No. 159, January 1932, pp. 3-4, 14, 1 Map.

        Front cover illustration,* "The Three Apostles, Ice Mountain
        in the Center," Gale Kehmeier, No. 463, July 1957.

        Illustration, "The Three Apostles from Near Camp," No. 468,
        December 1957, p. 185.

        Illustration, "The Three Apostles," Margaret Bivans, No. 544,
        April 1964, p. 71.

THREE NEEDLES, 13,481'   San Juan Mountains   Telluride 1955
   American Alpine Journal
      "Colorado Climbing Notes, 1935,"* Carleton C. Long, Vol. 2,
      1936, p. 546.
      First ascent note of the two highest pinnacles, Harry Kane and
      Kenneth Segerstrom.

   Trail and Timberline
      "The San Juan Ho!"* Dwight Lavender, No. 142, August 1930,
      pp. 5-6.

"THE THUMB", 13,100'#   San Juan Mountains, Sneffels Range
                          (Unnamed) Mount Sneffels 1967
   American Alpine Journal
      "Southwestern Colorado Climbing Notes - 1933,"* Dwight G.
      Lavender, Vol. 2, 1934, p. 256.
      First ascent note, T. M. Griffiths, L. V. Giesecke, and Dwight
      G. Lavender.

   The Mountaineering Journal (British)
      "Outstanding Climbing Centres in the South-Western Colorado
      Rockies,"* Dwight G. Lavender, Vol. 1, No. 4, June, July,
      August 1933, pp. 238-248.

      "Correspondence,"* Dwight Lavender, Vol. 2, No. 1, December,
      January, February 1933-34, pp. 47-51.
      First ascent note, Dwight Lavender, T. Melvin Griffiths, and
      Lewis V. Giesecke.

   Trail and Timberline
      Illustration,* "Aiguilles Northwest of Mt. Sneffels,
      Photographed from Blaine Peak," D. G. Lavender, No. 171,
      January 1933, p. 10.

      "The 1933 Climbing Season in Colorado,"* Carleton C. Long,
      No. 184, February 1934, pp. 20-23.
      First ascent note, San Juan Mountaineers.

"THUNDER MOUNTAIN", 13,932'   Elk Range   (Unnamed) Maroon Bells 1960
   Trail and Timberline
      "Peak 13,932, Elk Mountains," Spencer Swanger, No. 621,
      September 1970, p. 184.
      Probable first ascent noted, Spencer Swanger and party.

      "A Guide to Colorado's Almost-Fourteens,"* William A. Graves,
      No. 683, November 1975, pp. 225-227.

THUNDERBOLT, 11,938'   Front Range, Indian Peaks   Monarch Lake 1958
   Trail and Timberline
      "Our Indian Peaks,"* Karl E. Boehm, No. 497, May 1960, pp. 73-
      74.

#Elevation figure from the American Alpine Journal.

"TIJERAS PEAK", 13,604'   Sangre de Cristo Range
                            (Unnamed) Crestone Peak 1967
    Trail and Timberline
        "New Names in Sangres,"* No. 621, September 1970, p. 206.

MT. TOLL ("PAIUTE HORN"), 12,979'   Front Range, Indian Peaks
                                       Monarch Lake 1958
    Alpine Journal
        "The Rockies of Colorado,"* Evelio Echevarría C., Vol. 71,
        May 1966, pp. 26-36, 1 Map, Bibliography.
        First ascent noted, Dr. Arnold Emch.

    American Alpine Journal
        "Technical Climbing in the Mountains of Colorado and Wyoming,"*
        Albert Russell Ellingwood, Vol. 1, 1930, pp. 140-147.

    Chicago Mountaineering Club Newsletter
        "Club Outing in the Arapahoes,"* Ray J. Gatz, Vol. 4, No. 5,
        November 1950, pp. 8-9.

    Trail and Timberline
        Illustration, "Paiute Horn from Valley of Mitchell and Blue,"
        Ernest D. Hull, No. 211, May 1936, p. 50.

        "Peak Named for Roger Toll," No. 265, January 1941, p. 17.

        "The Long Lake Region,"* A. Gayle Waldrop, No. 281, May 1942,
        pp. 69-70, Front cover illustration.

        "Our Indian Peaks,"* Karl E. Boehm, No. 497, May 1960, pp. 73-
        74.

        "Adventure, Culture and Prunes,"* Susan Gibbs, No. 555,
        March 1965, pp. 58-59.

TOMBSTONE RIDGE, 11,722'   Front Range, Rocky Mountain National Park
                              Trail Ridge 1957
    Trail and Timberline
        "Undiscovered Jewels of Rocky Mountain National Park,"* R. D.
        Martin, No. 618, June 1970, pp. 132-134.

TORREYS PEAK, 14,267'   Front Range   Grays Peak 1958
    Alpine Journal
        "The Rockies of Colorado,"* Evelio Echevarría C., Vol. 71,
        May 1966, pp. 26-36, 1 Map, Bibliography.

    Appalachia
        "All the 14,000's,"* Carl Melzer, Vol. 22, December 1939,
        pp. 466-479.

    Trail and Timberline
        Illustration, "Torrey's Peak (14,336 Ft.)," No. 46, July 1922,
        p. 8.

Illustration,* "Grays (14,341 Ft.) and Torreys (14,336 Ft.) Peaks from Near Clear Creek Camp," Geo. H. Harvey, Jr., No. 48, September 1922, p. 9.

"Mountain Registers,"* Carl Blaurock, No. 52, January 1923, p. 6.

Illustration,* "Grays and Torreys Peaks - Climb from Camp July 4th," Geo. H. Harvey, Jr., No. 56, May 1923, p. 16.

"Boulder Group Activities,"* John D. McLucas, No. 156, October 1931, p. 162.
North face ascent note.

"Torreys Peak in May," Carleton C. Long, No. 166, August 1932, pp. 119-120.

"First Ascent Criteria,"* Carleton C. Long and Dwight G. Lavender, No. 174, April 1933, pp. 48, 52-53.

"The Gray and Torrey Reunion Fable,"* Erl H. Ellis, No. 301, January 1944, pp. 6-7.
Reprinted from The Colorado Magazine.

"Junior Jottings,"* Dorothy Sethman, No. 308, August 1944, p. 94.

"The Tale,"* No. 310, October 1944, pp. 117-121.

"The Colorado Mountaineer: CMC Winter Mountaineering School,"* Gregg Blomberg, No. 542, February 1964, pp. 28-29, 1 Illustration.

"The Four Fourteen Foible,"* William L. Myatt, No. 545, May 1964, pp. 87-88.

"Climbing Torreys' Northeast Ridge," Thomas N. (M.) Jenkins, No. 681, September 1975, pp. 171-172, 1 Illustration.

TREASURE MOUNTAIN, 13,528'   Elk Range   Snowmass Mtn. 1960
    Trail and Timberline
    "Hikes and Climbs from Crystal,"* John Beyer, No. 598, October 1968, pp. 224-229, 1 Map.

TREASURY MOUNTAIN, 13,462'   Elk Range   Snowmass Mtn. 1960
    Trail and Timberline
    "1873 Tells 1949,"* Louisa Ward Arps, No. 365, May 1949, pp. 68-70, 1 Illustration following p. 70.

    "Hikes and Climbs from Crystal,"* John Beyer, No. 598, October 1968, pp. 224-229, 1 Illustration, 1 Map.

"MT. TRIDENT" ("PEAK Q"), 13,230'   Gore Range   (Unnamed) Vail East 1970
See also "PEAK Q"
   Trail and Timberline
     "Backpacking in the Gore Range,"* Shirli Voigt, No. 667,
     July 1974, pp. 177-180, 1 Map.

TRINCHERA PEAK, 13,517'   Culebra Range   Trinchera Peak 1967
   Alpine Journal
     "The Rockies of Colorado,"* Evelio Echevarría C., Vol. 71,
     May 1966, pp. 26-36, 1 Map, Bibliography.

   Trail and Timberline
     "Huerfano Playgrounds,"* Thomas J. Everly, No. 248,
     August 1939, pp. 103-104.

     "An Amateur Climbs Trinchera Peak," Paul Krier, No. 271,
     July 1941, pp. 102-103.

TRINITY PEAKS, Needle Mountains   Storm King Peak 1964
See also EAST TRINITY PEAK, MIDDLE TRINITY PEAK, WEST TRINITY PEAK
   Climbing
     "'Mass Gyration', Trinity North Saddle, San Juans, Colo.,"
     No. 11, January-February 1972, p. 28.
     First ascent note, Henry Barber and Tom Stimson.

   Trail and Timberline
     "Needle Mountaimania,"* Dave Lavender, No. 265, January 1941,
     pp. 3-4, 14-15, 1 Illustration, Front cover sketch map.

TRURO PEAK, 13,282'   Sawatch Range   New York Peak 1960
   Climbing
     "'Newspaper Route', Truro Peak, Northface, Elk Mountains,
     Colorado," No. 5, January 1971, p. 21.
     First ascent note, Fritz Stammberger and Bill Dunaway.

     "Truro Peak/North Face Premiere," William R. Dunaway, No. 6,
     March-April 1971, pp. 15, 17, 1 Illustration.
     First ascent noted of the north face, William R. Dunaway and
     Fritz Stammberger.

     "'West Face', Truro Peak (13,282'), Aspen Area, Colo.," No. 14,
     July-August 1972, p. 36.
     Possible first ascent note, Bill Dunaway and Fritz Stammberger.

     "Basecamp: Colorado,"* No. 38, September-October 1976, pp. 3-5.
     Direct variation note of the north face route, Mike Kennedy and
     Chris Landry.

"TURKSHEAD PEAK", 12,734'   San Juan Mountains   (Unnamed) Silverton 1955
   Trail and Timberline
     "First Ascent Criteria,"* Carleton C. Long and Dwight G.
     Lavender, No. 174, April 1933, pp. 48, 52-53.

TURRET NEEDLES (PEAK FIFTEEN, PEAK SIXTEEN, LITTLE FINGER ["PEAK
          SEVENTEEN"])
          Needle Mountains   Snowdon Peak 1964
See also PEAK FIFTEEN, PEAK SIXTEEN, LITTLE FINGER ["PEAK SEVENTEEN"]
     Trail and Timberline
          "Letters to the Editor,"* Martin A. Etter, No. 610,
          October 1969, p. 187.
          Note on north ridges.

TURRET PEAK, 13,835'   Needle Mountains   Snowdon Peak 1964
     American Alpine Journal
          "Technical Climbing in the Mountains of Colorado and Wyoming,"*
          Albert Russell Ellingwood, Vol. 1, 1930, pp. 140-147.

          "Colorado Climbing Notes, 1937,"* Carl Blaurock, Vol. 3, 1938,
          p. 218.
          Ascent note, Elwyn Arps and party.

     Appalachia
          "Colorado Climbs, 1931,"* Winthrop Means, Vol. 18,
          December 1931, pp. 357-364, 1 Illustration.
          (Second) ascent noted, Carleton Long, Marjorie Hurd, Dean
          Peabody, Jr., Florence Peabody, Payson Newton, and Winthrop Means.

          "Colorado,"* Alice R. Allan, Vol. 18, December 1931, pp. 483-485.

          "The Old and New West in the Needle Mountains,"* Duncan A.
          MacInnes, Vol. 23, June 1941, pp. 374-379, 1 Illustration.

     Harvard Mountaineering
          "Climbing Notes, 1964: Colorado Needles,"* Matt Hale, No. 17,
          May 1965, pp. 59-60.
          Ascent note, partial north face, Matt Hale and Dave Roberts.

     The Mountaineering Journal (British)
          Illustration,* "View Southwards from Point Pun in the
          Grenadiers," Carleton C. Long, Vol. 1, No. 4, June, July,
          August 1933, p. 242.

     Trail and Timberline
          Illustration,* "Turret and Pigeon from Emerald Lake," Dr. Wm.
          C. Crisp, No. 25, October 1920, p. 18.

          Illustration,* "Mts. Pigeon and Turret, Seen from Emerald
          Lake, Near Camp on 1927 Annual Outing," William F. Ervin,
          No. 103, April 1927, p. 3.

          Front cover illustration,* "Ridge North of Pigeon and Turret,"
          Wm. F. Ervin, courtesy American Alpine Journal, No. 153,
          July 1931.

          "The Second Ascent of Turret Peak,"* Carleton C. Long, No. 156,
          October 1931, p. 166.
          Second ascent noted, Dr. and Mrs. Peabody, Payson Newton,
          Marjorie Hurd, Winthrop Means, and Carleton C. Long.
          First ascent noted, A. R. Ellingwood and Barton Hoag.

"First Ascent Criteria,"* Carleton C. Long and Dwight G.
Lavender, No. 174, April 1933, pp. 48, 52-53.
Second ascent noted.

Illustration,* "Mt. Eolus (Left), Turret Peak (Center), and
Pigeon Peak (Right)," Percy Hagerman, No. 178, August 1933,
p. 110.

Front cover illustration,* "Pigeon and Turret Peaks from
Emerald Lake," No. 223, May 1937.

Illustration,* "Turret and Pigeon Peaks from Animas Mtn.,"
Everett C. Long, No. 223, May 1937, p. 57.

"San Juan Testimony,"* Harvey Sethman, No. 224, June 1937,
pp. 68-70.

"Pigeon and Turret Trip,"* Elwyn Arps, No. 227, October 1937,
p. 104, 1 Illustration.
First ascent noted, Ellingwood and Haug (Hoag).
Second ascent noted, Appalachian Club and Carleton Long.
Third ascent noted, Gordon Williams.
Fourth ascent noted, Joe Buswell, Whitney Boreland (Borland),
Bob Blair, and Elwyn Arps.

"Noname Prospects,"* Mel Griffiths, No. 340, April 1947,
pp. 56-59, 1 Illustration.

"Climbers Guide to Noname,"* No. 342, June 1947, pp. 97-98,
1 Map.

"Pigeon and Turret or the Fly Camp of 1947,"* Louise Roloff,
No. 345, September 1947, pp. 144-145.

"Pigeon, Turret, Peak 12, Etc. or the Fly Camp of '53."*
William E. Davis, No. 419, November 1953, pp. 155-158.

"Revised Climbers' Guide from Noname Creek,"* William E.
Davis, No. 502, October 1960, pp. 149-154, 1 Map, Front cover
illustration.

"TURRET RIDGE", 12,260'   San Juan Mountains
                          (Unnamed) Courthouse Mountain 1963
    The Mountaineering Journal (British)
        "Outstanding Climbing Centres in the South-Western Colorado
        Rockies,"* Dwight G. Lavender, Vol. 1, No. 4, June, July,
        August 1933, pp. 238-248.

"TUTT"S PINNACLE", 12,100'(?)   Elk Range   (Unnamed) Maroon Bells 1960
    Climbing
        "'Incarnate', Tutt's Pinnacle, Pyramid Peak, Elk Mountains,
        Colorado," No. 6, March-April 1971, p. 21.
        First ascent note, Harvey T. Carter and Tom Merrill.

TWILIGHT PEAK, 13,158'   West Needle Mountains   Snowdon Peak 1964
    Trail and Timberline
        "The Mountain Ranges of Colorado,"* Kenneth Segerstrom,
        No. 215, September 1936, pp. 109-115, 1 Map.

TWIN SISTERS, 13,087'   Sangre de Cristo Range   Howard 15M 1959
    Trail and Timberline
        "New Maps of the Sangre de Cristo Range,"* John L. J. Hart,
        No. 519, March 1962, pp. 32-33.

        "Sangre de Cristo Saga,"* Lester A. Michel, with Wilbur F.
        Arnold, No. 524, August 1962, pp. 123-126, 133.

TWIN SISTERS, 13,432'   San Juan Mountains   Ophir 1955
    Trail and Timberline
        "Exploring Ice Lake Basin,"* Allen W. Greene, No. 474,
        June 1958, pp. 75-76, 87.

TWIN SISTERS PEAKS, 11,428'   Front Range, Rocky Mountain National Park
                               Longs Peak 1961
    Appalachia
        "The Peaks of Rocky Mountain National Park,"* Roger W. Toll,
        Vol. 17, June 1929, pp. 252-260.

    Trail and Timberline
        Front cover illustration, "Rappelling Off the Crags Near Twin
        Sisters Peak," Robert W. Beatty, No. 537, September 1963.

TWIN THUMBS, Needle Mountains   Storm King Peak 1964
See also NORTH TWIN THUMB and SOUTH TWIN THUMB
    American Alpine Journal
        "Southwestern Colorado Climbing Notes - 1933,"* Dwight G.
        Lavender, Vol. 2, 1934, p. 257.
        First ascent note of both needles, San Juan Mountaineers.

        "A.A.C. and C.M.C. Joint Outing, Needle Mountains, Colorado,
        July 19 - August 9, 1953,"* Henry L. McClintock, Vol. 9, 1954,
        pp. 169-171.
        New route note.

    The Mountaineering Journal (British)
        Illustration,* "View Southwards from Point Pun in the
        Grenadiers," Carleton C. Long, Vol. 1, No. 4, June, July,
        August 1933, p. 242.

    Trail and Timberline
        Illustration, "Twin Thumbs, the Needle Mts.," Everett C. Long,
        No. 223, May 1937, p. 58.

        "San Juan Testimony,"* H. L. McClintock, No. 224, June 1937,
        p. 68.

        "Climbers Guide to Noname,"* No. 342, June 1947, pp. 97-98,
        1 Map.

"Denver Junior Summer Outing,"* Louise Jackson, No. 443, November 1955, pp. 190-191.

"Revised Climbers' Guide from Noname Creek,"* William E. Davis, No. 502, October 1960, pp. 149-154, 1 Map.

"PEAK U" ("WEST PARTNER PEAK"), 13,041'   Gore Range
                                    (Unnamed) Vail East 1970
                                    (Unnamed) Minturn 15M 1934, 13,021'
    Trail and Timberline
        "Names on the Gores,"* William Bird Mounsey, No. 568,
        April 1966, pp. 63-65, 1 Illustration, 1 Map.

UNCOMPAHGRE PEAK, 14,309'   San Juan Mountains   Uncompahgre Peak 1963
    American Alpine Journal
        "Technical Climbing in the Mountains of Colorado and Wyoming,"*
        Albert Russell Ellingwood, Vol. 1, 1930, pp. 140-147.

        "Naming America's Mountains - The Colorado Rockies,"* Francis
        P. Farquhar, Vol. 12, 1961, pp. 319-346.
        First ascent noted, Wilson, Rhoda, and Endlich.

    Appalachia
        "All the 14,000's,"* Carl Melzer, Vol. 22, December 1939,
        pp. 466-479.

        "Climbs and Trips by Members: A Colorado Vacation,"* Edmund
        Bassett, Vol. 24, December 1942, pp. 257-258, 1 Illustration
        following p. 268.

        "Club Excursions: Colorado Excursion, 1951,"* Jean K. Kent,
        Vol. 28, December 1951, pp. 584-589, 1 Illustration.

    Chicago Mountaineering Club Newsletter
        "A 'Cook's Tour' of Aspen Wonderland,"* Groves Kilbourn,
        Vol. 13, No. 2, March 1959, pp. 13-15.

    Mazama
        "Ramble Number 21,"* A. H. Marshall, Vol. 21, No. 12,
        December 1939, pp. 55-61, 1 Illustration.

    The Mountaineering Journal (British)
        "Outstanding Climbing Centres in the South-Western Colorado
        Rockies,"* Dwight G. Lavender, Vol. 1, No. 4, June, July,
        August 1933, pp. 238-248.

    Trail and Timberline
        "Climbing 60,000 Feet in the San Juan,"* Carl Blaurock,
        No. 40, January 1922, pp. 2-3.

        Illustration, "Uncompahgre Peak," W. I. Hutchinson, No. 72,
        September 1924, p. 5.

        Illustration, "Uncompahgre, the Highest Peak of the San Juan
        to be Climbed During the Summer Outing, 1929," No. 125,
        March 1929, p. 8.

        "Uncompahgre," Grace M. Harvey, No. 132, October 1929, p. 5.

        "Climbing Notes,"* No. 144, October 1930, p. 9.
        Ascent note, Hiking and Outing Club of Western State College.

"An American Alpine Adventure," Melvin Griffiths, No. 155,
September 1931, pp. 135-140.

"The Mountain Ranges of Colorado,"* Kenneth Segerstrom,
No. 215, September 1936, pp. 109-115, 1 Map.

"American Flats,"* Whitney Borland, No. 272, August 1941,
pp. 115-117, 122-123, 1 Illustration.

Front cover illustration, "Uncompahgre, the Highest Peak of
the San Juan," No. 368, August 1949.

"Report on the 1952 San Juan Outing,"* Robert Ellingwood,
No. 407, November 1952, pp. 159-161.

Front cover illustration, "Uncompahgre Peak from Top of
Wetterhorn," W. C. Eggleston, No. 441, September 1955.

"The Lake City Fourteens,"* Robin Simmons, No. 490,
October 1959, pp. 141-142.

Illustration, "Peaks in the Upper Cimarron Area: Uncompahgre
Peak," No. 557, May 1965, p. 94.

"Fly Camps on the Yankee Boy Outing,"* Barbara Evert, No. 635,
November 1971, pp. 222-223.

U. S. GRANT PEAK, 13,767'   San Juan Mountains   Ophir 1955
American Alpine Journal
    "Southwestern Colorado Climbing Notes - 1932,"* Dwight G.
    Lavender, Vol. 2, 1933, p. 129.
    First ascent note, party of eight led by Father H. M. Walters.

Trail and Timberline
    "1932 Summer Outing,"* Jack Kendrick, No. 162, April 1932,
    pp. 47, 57-58.

    "Six First Ascents on the '32 Outing,"* Dwight G. Lavender,
    No. 168, October 1932, pp. 139-140, 149-150, 1 Illustration
    p. 145.
    First ascent noted, party of eight led by Mike Walters.

    "Exploring Ice Lake Basin,"* Allen W. Greene, No. 474,
    June 1958, pp. 75-76, 87.

"PEAK V" ("EAST PARTNER PEAK"), 13,057'   Gore Range
See also "EAST PARTNER PEAK"   (Unnamed) Vail East 1970
                                            (Unnamed) Minturn 15M 1934, 13,019'
    Trail and Timberline
        "Names on the Gores,"* William Bird Mounsey, No. 568,
        April 1966, pp. 63-65, 1 Map.

"V2", 13,309'   San Juan Mountains   (Unnamed) Ophir 1955
    Trail and Timberline
        "Exploring Ice Lake Basin,"* Allen W. Greene, No. 474,
        June 1958, pp. 75-76, 87.
        Greene probably mistakenly identified "V2" as "V4".

"V4", 13,520'   San Juan Mountains   (Unnamed) Ophir 1955
    American Alpine Journal
        "Southwestern Colorado Climbing Notes - 1932,"* Dwight G.
        Lavender, Vol. 2, 1933, p. 129.
        First ascent note, Bob Scott and L. Giesecke.

    Trail and Timberline
        "Six First Ascents on the '32 Outing,"* Dwight G. Lavender,
        No. 168, October 1932, pp. 139-140, 149-150.
        First ascent noted, Lewis Giesecke and Bob Scott.

"V5", 13,156'   San Juan Mountains   (Unnamed) Ophir 1955
    American Alpine Journal
        "Southwestern Colorado Climbing Notes - 1932,"* Dwight G.
        Lavender, Vol. 2, 1933, p. 129.
        First ascent note, L. Giesecke and Dwight G. Lavender.

    Trail and Timberline
        "Six First Ascents on the '32 Outing,"* Dwight G. Lavender,
        No. 168, October 1932, pp. 139-140, 149-150.
        First ascent noted, Lewis Giesecke and Dwight G. Lavender.

        Illustration, "Clear Lake and the Outing Peaks (Photo from Top
        of Peak No. V-5 to East of Clear Lake)," D. G. Lavender,
        No. 169, November 1932, p. 164.

VALLECITO MOUNTAIN, 13,428'   Needle Mountains   Storm King Peak 1964
    Trail and Timberline
        "Letters to the Editor,"* Martin A. Etter, No. 610,
        October 1969, p. 187.
        Note on north face, east end.

        "San Juan Pack Trip," Ed Bach, No. 635, November 1971,
        pp. 224-225.

VASQUEZ PEAK, 12,947'   Front Range   Byers Peak 1957
    The Mountaineering Journal (British)
        "High Altitude Ski-ing," Carleton C. Long, Vol. 1, No. 5,
        Sept., Oct., Nov. 1933, pp. 294-293.
        Ascent note, David Rosendale and Donald ------ (McBride).

Trail and Timberline
   Illustration,* "Vasquez Peak and Byers Peak from the Oberland
   in April," Erl Ellis, No. 151, May 1931, p. 70.

   "The 1933 Climbing Season in Colorado,"* Carleton C. Long,
   No. 184, February 1934, pp. 20-23.
   Ascent note partially by skis, David Rosendale and Donald
   McBride.

VENABLE PEAK, 13,352'   Sangre de Cristo Range   Electric Peak 15M 1959
   Trail and Timberline
   "The Sangre de Cristo Range,"* Eva and Bill Rathbun, No. 460,
   April 1957, pp. 55-60, 64, 1 Map.

   "New Maps of the Sangre de Cristo Range,"* John L. J. Hart,
   No. 519, March 1962, pp. 32-33.

VERMILLION PEAK, 13,894'   San Juan Mountains   Ophir 1955
   American Alpine Journal
   "Southwestern Colorado Climbing Notes - 1932,"* Dwight G.
   Lavender, Vol. 2, 1933, p. 129.
   Northeast arete ascent note, L. Giesecke and Dwight G.
   Lavender.

   Trail and Timberline
   "Climbing Vermillion Peak," Dwight Lavender, No. 155,
   September 1931, pp. 141-142.

   "1932 Summer Outing,"* Jack Kendrick, No. 162, April 1932,
   pp. 47, 57-58.

   Illustration, "Vermillion Peak from the West," No. 163,
   May 1932, p. 69.

   "Opportunities for Climbing Afforded by the Ice Lake Basin
   Outing,"* D. G. Lavender, No. 164, June 1932, p. 91.

   Illustration, "On Summit of Vermillion," No. 168,
   October 1932, p. 145.

   "Exploring Ice Lake Basin,"* Allen W. Greene, No. 474,
   June 1958, pp. 75-76, 87.

   "Silverton - Mountain Mecca,"* Art Porter, No. 620,
   August 1970, pp. 169, 171-172.

   "Colorado Mountain Club History: William S. Cooper - Explorer
   of the Needles and Grenadiers,"* William M. Bueler, No. 672,
   December 1974, pp. 284-288.

VESTAL PEAK, 13,664'   Needle Mountains   Storm King Peak 1964
   American Alpine Journal
   "Club Activities: Harvard Mountaineering Club,"* David S.
   Roberts, Vol. 14, 1964, pp. 243-244.
   First winter ascent note.

Appalachia
"Alpina: Colorado,"* John A. Woodworth, Vol. 39,
December 1972, p. 143.
Accident note.

Chicago Mountaineering Club Newsletter
"Grenadiers 1962,"* John C. Ohrenschall, Vol. 17, No. 2,
April 1963, pp. 1-4.
First recorded ascent via north face, John C. Ohrenschall and
Doug Ward.

"The Trinity Peaks and Vestal Peak,"* Frank Babb, Vol. 24,
No. 1, March 1970, pp. 13-14, 1 Illustration p. 7,
1 Illustration p. 15.

Climbing
Inside front cover illustration,* "Glacier-Polished Quartzite
Slabs, Wham Ridge of Vestal Peak and Arrow Peak," Steve Miller,
No. 15, September-October 1972.

Illustration, "Approaching Wham Ridge Vestal Peak," No. 15,
September-October 1972, p. 20.

Illustration, "Approaching Vestal Peak from Ten Mile Creek,"
No. 15, September-October 1972, p. 23.

Harvard Mountaineering
"Climbing Notes, 1963: Colorado, Needle Mountains,"* Dave
Roberts, No. 17, May 1965, pp. 55-56.
First winter ascent note of the west ridge, Matt Hale and
Steve Pomerance.
First winter ascent note of the southeast ridge, Don Jensen
and Dave Roberts.

The Mountaineering Journal (British)
Illustration,* "View North from Heisspitz," Carleton C. Long,
Vol. 1, No. 4, June, July, August 1933, p. 241.

Summit
"Climbing in the Grenadiers,"* Larry Kline, Vol. 17, No. 1,
January-February 1971, pp. 22-25, 2 Illustrations.

Trail and Timberline
"Some First Ascent Possibilities in Colorado,"* Kenneth
Segerstrom, No. 165, July 1932, pp. 103-104.

Illustration, "Wham Ridge, the Startling North Arete of Vestal
Peak," J. E. Nelson, No. 169, November 1932, p. 157.

Illustration,* "Arrow Peak (Left) and Vestal Peak (Right) from
An Unnamed Peak 13,500 Feet High About One Mile North of
Leviathan Peak," Percy Hagerman, No. 178, August 1933, p. 110.

"The Mountain Ranges of Colorado,"* Kenneth Segerstrom,
No. 215, September 1936, pp. 109-115, 1 Map.

"Needle Mountaimania,"* Dave Lavender, No. 265, January 1941, pp. 3-4, 14-15, 1 Illustration, Front cover sketch map.

"The Colorado Mountain Club Announces the Twenty-Eighth Annual Summer Outing,"* Henry Buchtel, Lewis Giesecke, Kenneth Segerstrom, No. 265, January 1941, pp. 9-14, 3 Illustrations, 1 Map, Front cover sketch map.

"A First Ascent of Wham Ridge," Rit Burrows and Werner Schnackenberg, No. 274, October 1941, p. 141, 1 Illustration p. 142, Front cover illustration.
First ascent noted of the Wham Ridge, Rit Burrows, Werner Schnackenberg, and Jim Patterson.

"Garlic Gulch Episode,"* L. V. Giesecke, No. 274, October 1941, pp. 143-145.
First ascent noted of the Wham Ridge.

"The Grenadiers, 1962,"* John C. Ohrenschall, No. 534, June 1963, pp. 107-109.
First recorded ascent noted of the north face, John C. Ohrenschall and Doug Ward.

"The Grenadiers in Winter,"* David S. Roberts, No. 547, July 1964, pp. 111-117, 1 Illustration.
First winter ascent noted of the west ridge, Matt Hale and Steve Pomerance.
First winter ascent noted of the southeast ridge, Don Jensen and Dave Roberts.

"A Winter Ascent of the Wham Ridge," Arthur Mears, No. 601, January 1969, pp. 4-7, 1 Illustration.
First winter ascent noted of the Wham Ridge, Arthur Mears, Dan Vasicek, Steve Tandy, John Pinamont, and Tom Ruwitch.

"Letters to the Editor: East Face of Vestal Peak," Martin A. Etter, No. 610, October 1969, p. 187.
Probable first ascent note of the east face, Bo Shelby and Martin A. Etter.

"Colorado Mountain Club History: William S. Cooper - Explorer of the Needles and Grenadiers,"* William M. Bueler, No. 672, December 1974, pp. 284-288.
First ascent noted, William S. Cooper and John V. Hubbard.

MT. VIGIL, 10,073'   Pikes Peak Region   Mount Big Chief 1961
American Alpine Journal
"Mount Vigil, Southwest Face," Gary Ziegler, Vol. 17, 1971, p. 380.
First ascent note of the southwest face, Molly Higgins, Chuck Berensmier (Behrensmeyer), and Gary Ziegler.

Climbing
"'Emaculate Conception', Mt. Virgel (sic)," No. 3, September 1970, p. 23.
First ascent (winter) note, Gary Ziegler and Chuck Behrensmeyer.

VIRGINIA PEAK, 13,088'   Sawatch Range   Mt. Harvard 15M 1955
    Trail and Timberline
      "Climbing Winfield and Virginia,"* Philip Settles, No. 468,
    December 1957, p. 181.

"PEAK W", 12,775'   Gore Range   (Unnamed) Vail East 1970
    Trail and Timberline
        "Names on the Gores,"* William Bird Mounsey, No. 568,
        April 1966, pp. 63-65, 1 Map.

WASATCH MOUNTAIN, 13,555'   San Juan Mountains   Telluride 1955
    Trail and Timberline
        "The San Juan Ho!"* Dwight Lavender, No. 142, August 1930,
        pp. 5-6.

        "Climbing Notes,"* Dwight Lavender, No. 156, October 1931,
        p. 165.
        Ascent note via the western ridge, R. L. Phillippi, David
        Lavender, and Dwight Lavender.

WAVERLY MOUNTAIN, 13,309'   Sawatch Range   Mt. Harvard 15M 1955
    Trail and Timberline
        "The High Peaks of the La Plata Mining Region,"* John L. J.
        Hart, No. 159, January 1932, pp. 3-4, 14, 1 Map.

        "Some Trails of the La Plata Mining Region,"* Bruce and
        Elisabeth MacCannon, No. 159, January 1932, pp. 5-6.

        "Surveying the La Plata Mining Region,"* Ronald L. Ives,
        No. 192, October 1934, p. 139, 1 Map.
        "A Correction," No. 196, February 1935, p. 22.
        Map correction.

"WEST DALLAS PEAK", 13,741'   San Juan Mountains, Sneffels Range
                              (Unnamed) Telluride 1955
    American Alpine Journal
        "Colorado Climbing Notes, 1934,"* Carleton C. Long, Vol. 2,
        1935, p. 416.
        Probable first ascent note, A. C. Bartelt and Robert Blair.
        Second ascent note, A. C. Bartelt and party.

    Trail and Timberline
        Illustration,* "Blue Lakes from the Summit of Mt. Sneffels:
        Peaks on the Skyline are, from Left to Right, Dallas Peak,
        Dallas Hump, West Dallas, and Peak T-0," H. L. McClintock,
        No. 184, February 1934, p. 19.

        "1934 Summer Outing Climbs,"* Everett C. Long, No. 192,
        October 1934, pp. 131-133.
        First ascent noted, A. C. Bartelt and Robert Blair.

WEST ELK PEAK, 13,035'   West Elk Range   West Elk Peak 1965
    Trail and Timberline
        "The Mountain Ranges of Colorado,"* Kenneth Segerstrom,
        No. 215, September 1936, pp. 109-115, 1 Map.

WEST NEEDLE MOUNTAINS, West Needle Mountains   Snowdon Peak 1964
    Trail and Timberline
        Illustration, "West Needles Near Molas Lake, San Juans,"
        Monarch Air Lines, No. 369, September 1949, p. 131.

Illustration, "West Needles Near Molas Lake, San Juans,"
Monarch Air Lines, No. 534, June 1963, p. 114.

WEST SPANISH PEAK, 13,626'   Spanish Peaks   Spanish Peaks 1971
See also SPANISH PEAKS
    Trail and Timberline
        "The Legend of Wahatoyeh,"* Janet Chatin, No. 142,
        August 1930, pp. 8-9, 1 Illustration.

        "The Spanish Peaks,"* Leola Crump, No. 248, August 1939,
        pp. 106-107, 1 Illustration.

        "The Mystic Huajatolla,"* Frances P. Evans, No. 271,
        July 1941, pp. 107-108.

        Front cover illustration, "West Spanish Peak from Cuchara Camp
        Road," Walsenburg World-Independent, No. 315, March 1945.

        "Reaching the High Spots,"* George J. Kubricht, No. 325,
        January 1946, pp. 3-4.

        "The Mystic Huajatolla,"* Frances P. Evans, No. 476,
        August 1958, p. 103, Front cover illustration.
        Reprinted in condensed form from July 1941 T&T.

        "Wahatoyah,"* Irma Zanoni, No. 476, August 1958, p. 104,
        Front cover illustration.

        "First Climb," Janet Chatin, No. 476, August 1958, pp. 105,
        109, Front cover illustration.

        "Assorted Notes on Miscellaneous Routes: West Spanish Peak,"
        Art Porter, No. 628, April 1971, p. 97.

WEST TRINITY PEAK, 13,765'   Needle Mountains   Storm King Peak 1964
See also TRINITY PEAKS
    American Alpine Journal
        "Club Activities: Harvard Mountaineering Club,"* David S.
        Roberts, Vol. 14, 1964, pp. 243-244.
        First winter ascent note.

    Appalachia
        "Climbs and Trips by Members: Up Tenmile Creek to the
        Grenadiers in Colorado," Grace L. Pennock, Vol. 23,
        December 1941, pp. 535-537, 1 Map.

    Chicago Mountaineering Club Newsletter
        "Grenadiers 1962,"* John C. Ohrenschall, Vol. 17, No. 2,
        April 1963, pp. 1-4.

        "The Trinity Peaks and Vestal Peak,"* Frank Babb, Vol. 24,
        No. 1, March 1970, pp. 13-14.

    Climbing
        Illustration, "Northwest Ridge of West Trinity Peak," No. 15,
        September-October 1972, p. 24.

Harvard Mountaineering
"Climbing Notes, 1963: Colorado, Needle Mountains,"* Dave
Roberts, No. 17, May 1965, pp. 55-56.
First winter ascent note, Dave Roberts and Steve Pomerance.

Summit
"Climbing in the Grenadiers,"* Larry Kline, Vol. 17, No. 1,
January-February 1971, pp. 22-25, 2 Illustrations.

Trail and Timberline
"The Colorado Mountain Club Announces the Twenty-Eighth Annual
Summer Outing,"* Henry Buchtel, Lewis Giesecke, Kenneth
Segerstrom, No. 265, January 1941, pp. 9-14, 1 Map, Front cover
sketch map.

"Garlic Gulch Episode,"* L. V. Giesecke, No. 274,
October 1941, pp. 143-145.
First ascent noted on CMC outing.

"The Grenadiers, 1962,"* John C. Ohrenschall, No. 534,
June 1963, pp. 107-109.

"The Grenadiers in Winter,"* David S. Roberts, No. 547,
July 1964, pp. 111-117.
First winter ascent noted, Steve Pomerance and Dave Roberts.

WETTERHORN PEAK, 14,015'   San Juan Mountains   Wetterhorn Peak 1963
American Alpine Journal
"Technical Climbing in the Mountains of Colorado and Wyoming,"*
Albert Russell Ellingwood, Vol. 1, 1930, pp. 140-147.

"Wetterhorn Peak, North Face," Jeff Lowe, Vol. 20, 1975,
p. 139.
First ascent note of the north face, Paul Hogan and Jeff Lowe.

Appalachia
"All the 14,000's,"* Carl Melzer, Vol. 22, December 1939,
pp. 466-479.

"Club Excursions: Colorado Excursion, 1951,"* Jean K. Kent,
Vol. 28, December 1951, pp. 584-589.

Mazama
"Ramble Number 21,"* A. H. Marshall, Vol. 21, No. 12,
December 1939, pp. 55-61, 2 Illustrations.

The Mountaineering Journal (British)
"Outstanding Climbing Centres in the South-Western Colorado
Rockies,"* Dwight G. Lavender, Vol. 1, No. 4, June, July,
August 1933, pp. 238-248, 1 Illustration.

Trail and Timberline
Illustration,* "Wetterhorn, Matterhorn and Coxcomb Peaks, All
to be Climbed During the 1929 Summer Outing," U.S. Forest
Service, No. 127, May 1929, p. 7.

"Wetterhorn, My First Peak," Geo. C. Barnard, No. 130,
August 1929, pp. 5-7, 1 Illustration.
First ascent noted, Dr. (Rev.) Dave Utter, Dr. Will P. Smedley,
Clyde Smedley, and George C. Barnard.

Illustration, "Near Summit of Wetterhorn," No. 132,
October 1929, p. 2.

"American Flats,"* Whitney Borland, No. 272, August 1941,
pp. 115-117, 122-123, 1 Illustration, Front cover illustration.

Illustration,* "Wetterhorn and Matterhorn in Uncompahgre
National Forest, Colorado," U.S. Forest Service, No. 368,
August 1949, p. 119.

Back cover illustration, "'American Wetterhorn'," U.S. Forest
Service, No. 368, August 1949.

"Report on the 1952 San Juan Outing,"* Robert Ellingwood,
No. 407, November 1952, pp. 159-161, 1 Illustration p. 166.

Illustration,* "Looking Toward Matterhorn and Wetterhorn from
Uncompahgre, Mount Sneffels in Background," Mike Sadusky,
No. 485, May 1959, p. 67.

"The Lake City Fourteens,"* Robin Simmons, No. 490,
October 1959, pp. 141-142, Front cover illustration.

"The San Juan Fly Camps,"* Wilma Epp, No. 538, October 1963,
pp. 175-177.

Illustration, "Peaks in the Upper Cimarron Area: Wetterhorn
Peak," No. 557, May 1965, p. 94.

"An Outing is Born,"* Allen W. Greene, No. 564, December 1965,
pp. 245-249, Front cover illustration.

"Fly Camps on the Yankee Boy Outing,"* Barbara Evert, No. 635,
November 1971, pp. 222-223.

WHETSTONE MOUNTAIN, 12,516'   Ruby Range   Crested Butte 1961
    Trail and Timberline
        "Pittsburgh on the Slate,"* Louisa Ward Arps, No. 450,
    June 1956, pp. 87-90.

WHITE DOME, 13,627'   San Juan Mountains   Storm King Peak 1964
    Chicago Mountaineering Club Newsletter
        "White Dome, Via Mine," Paul Hartsuch, Vol. 24, No. 1,
    March 1970, p. 10.

        "White Dome," Lee Orear, Vol. 24, No. 1, March 1970, p. 12.

WHITE ROCK MOUNTAIN, 13,520'   Elk Range   Gothic 1961
    Chicago Mountaineering Club Newsletter
        "Colorado's Elk Mountains,"* Weldon F. Heald, Vol. 13, No. 6,
    October 1959, pp. 1-5, Front cover map.

Trail and Timberline
   "1873 Tells 1949,"* Louisa Ward Arps, No. 365, May 1949,
   pp. 68-70.

   "Pittsburgh on the Slate,"* Louisa Ward Arps, No. 450,
   June 1956, pp. 87-90.

"WIGWAM TOWER",   Tarryall Range
   American Alpine Journal
      "Club Activities: Colorado College Mountain Club,"* John W.
      Kuglin, Vol. 13, 1962, pp. 291-292.
      First ascent note.

MT. WILCOX, 13,408'   Front Range   Montezuma 1958
   American Alpine Journal
      "Various Notes: Colorado Mountain Club,"* Evelyn Runnette,
      Vol. 7, September 1949, pp. 347-348.
      Ascent and naming ceremonies note.

   Appalachia
      "Western Mountains: The Naming of Mount Wilcox, Colorado,"
      Vol. 27, December 1948, p. 253.

   Trail and Timberline
      "Naming Mount Wilcox," Benjamin Draper, No. 355, July 1948,
      p. 102, 1 Illustration.

WILD MOUNTAIN, 6,382'   Pikes Peak Region   Mount Pittsburg 1961
   Trail and Timberline
      "Wild Mountain," Julia E. Wagner, No. 344, August 1947, p. 133.

WILDHORSE PEAK, 13,266'   San Juan Mountains   Wetterhorn Peak 1963
   Trail and Timberline
      "The 1934 Climbing Season in Colorado,"* Carleton C. Long,
      No. 196, February 1935, pp. 15-18.
      Winter ascent note, Gordon Williams and Melvin Griffiths.

      "If You Know the Name - Name It," Kenneth Segerstrom, No. 285,
      September 1942, pp. 121-122.
      First ascent noted, Eli Stanton, Frank H. Stanton, and William
      Killen.

      "Wildhorse Peak and American Flats," Everly N. Berry, No. 490,
      October 1959, pp. 134, 146, 1 Illustration p. 138.

      "Letters to the Editor: NE Face (the Cliff Side) of Wildhorse
      Peak," Martin A. Etter, No. 610, October 1969, p. 186.
      Probable first ascent note, Greg Simmons, John McDermott,
      Henry Barker, and Martin A. Etter.

WILLIAMS PEAK, 11,619'   Williams Fork Mountains   Ute Peak 15M 1933
   Trail and Timberline
      "New Regions,"* No. 140, June 1930, p. 16.

MT. WILSON, 14,246'   San Miguel Range   Mount Wilson 1953
  Alpine Journal
      "The Rockies of Colorado,"* Evelio Echevarría C., Vol. 71,
      May 1966, pp. 26-36, 1 Map, Bibliography.

  American Alpine Journal
      "Technical Climbing in the Mountains of Colorado and Wyoming,"*
      Albert Russell Ellingwood, Vol. 1, 1930, pp. 140-147.

      "American Rockies - Notes, 1929,"* J. L. J. Hart, Vol. 1,
      1930, p. 242.
      Ascent note, Colorado Mountain Club party.

      "The Rocky Mountains of the United States,"* Howard Palmer,
      Vol. 1, 1931, pp. 360-367.

      "Naming America's Mountains - The Colorado Rockies,"* Francis
      P. Farquhar, Vol. 12, 1961, pp. 319-346.
      First ascent noted, Allen D. Wilson, Franklin Rhoda, and
      Frederick M. Endlich.

  Appalachia
      "Colorado Climbs, 1931,"* Winthrop Means, Vol. 18,
      December 1931, pp. 357-364.

      "All the 14,000's,"* Carl Melzer, Vol. 22, December 1939,
      pp. 466-479.

      "Accidents: Accident on Mt. Wilson, Colorado," B. G. Ferris,
      Jr., Vol. 30, December 1955, p. 593.

  Mazama
      "Ramble Number 21,"* A. H. Marshall, Vol. 21, No. 12,
      December 1939, pp. 55-61.

  The Mountaineering Journal (British)
      "Outstanding Climbing Centres in the South-Western Colorado
      Rockies,"* Dwight G. Lavender, Vol. 1, No. 4, June, July,
      August 1933, pp. 238-248.

  Sierra Club Bulletin
      "Notes and Correspondence: The Colorado Mountain Club,"* David
      Rosendale, Vol. 17, No. 1, February 1932, pp. 109-110.
      Ascent note during CMC summer outing.

  Trail and Timberline
      "Climbing 60,000 Feet in the San Juan,"* Carl Blaurock,
      No. 40, January 1922, pp. 2-3, 1 Illustration.

      "Mount Wilson Trip, July 4th to 7th,"* L. R. Kendrick, No. 130,
      August 1929, pp. 9, 12, 2 Illustrations.

      "San Miguel Mountains,"* Dwight Lavender, No. 137, March 1930,
      p. 3, 1 Illustration p. 4.

Back cover illustration, "Mount Wilson from El Diente," D. Lavender, No. 143, September 1930.

"The 1931 Outing Country,"* Dwight G. Lavender, No. 151, May 1931, pp. 63-66, 1 Sketch.

Illustration, "Mount Wilson from El Diente," D. Lavender, No. 154, August 1931, p. 115.

"The Mountain Ranges of Colorado,"* Kenneth Segerstrom, No. 215, September 1936, pp. 109-115, 1 Map.

"'The Tooth' and Its Companion,"* Hugh W. Hetherington, No. 283, July 1942, pp. 91-93, 1 Illustration, Front cover illustration.

"San Miguels 1949,"* W. F. Arnold, No. 382, October 1950, pp. 147-148.

"Report on the 1952 San Juan Outing,"* Robert Ellingwood, No. 407, November 1952, pp. 159-161, 1 Illustration p. 167.

"Fifty-Two in '52,"* Dwight Hamilton, No. 482, February 1959, pp. 25-26.

"The San Juan Fly Camps,"* Wilma Epp, No. 538, October 1963, pp. 175-177, 1 Illustration.

"The High Ones: A San Miguel Adventure,"* Raoul Bates and Bob Stuemky, No. 586, October 1967, pp. 179-180.

"Navajo High Capades,"* Wilma Epp, No. 586, October 1967, pp. 184-185.

Front cover illustration,* "CMC Group on Wilson-El Diente Ridge," Sam Alfend, No. 632, August 1971.

"Fly Camps on the Yankee Boy Outing,"* Barbara Evert, No. 635, November 1971, pp. 222-223.

Illustration,* "Mark Stanton, Mike Ruckhaus, Dave Harmon and Robbie Dubin on Wilson-El Diente Ridge," Glenn Ruckhaus, No. 676, April 1975, p. 71.

Front cover illustration,* "Window on Lizard Head and Mt. Wilson," Richard H. Balay, No. 693, September 1976.

WILSON PEAK, 14,017'   San Miguel Range   Mount Wilson 1953
  American Alpine Journal
    "American Rockies - Notes, 1929,"* J. L. J. Hart, Vol. 1, 1930, p. 242.
    Ascent note, Colorado Mountain Club party.

  Appalachia
    "All the 14,000's,"* Carl Melzer, Vol. 22, December 1939, pp. 466-479.

The <u>Mountaineering Journal</u> (British)
"Outstanding Climbing Centres in the South-Western Colorado Rockies,"* Dwight G. Lavender, Vol. 1, No. 4, June, July, August 1933, pp. 238-248.

<u>Sierra Club Bulletin</u>
"Notes and Correspondence: The Colorado Mountain Club,"* David Rosendale, Vol. 17, No. 1, February 1932, pp. 109-110. Ascent note during CMC summer outing.

<u>Trail and Timberline</u>
"Climbing 60,000 Feet in the San Juan,"* Carl Blaurock, No. 40, January 1922, pp. 2-3, 1 Illustration.

"Mount Wilson Trip, July 4th to 7th,"* L. R. Kendrick, No. 130, August 1929, pp. 9, 12, 1 Illustration.

"San Miguel Mountains,"* Dwight Lavender, No. 137, March 1930, p. 3.

"Climbing in the San Miguels,"* Dwight Lavender, No. 143, September 1930, pp. 3-4.

"The 1931 Outing Country,"* Dwight G. Lavender, No. 151, May 1931, pp. 63-66, 1 Sketch.

"Outing Impressions,"* Evelyn Runnette, No. 156, October 1931, pp. 152-157, 1 Illustration p. 151.

"San Miguels 1949,"* W. F. Arnold, No. 382, October 1950, pp. 147-148.

"Report on the 1952 San Juan Outing,"* Robert Ellingwood, No. 407, November 1952, pp. 159-161, 1 Illustration p. 167.

"The End of the Climbing Season," Gene White, No. 459, March 1957, p. 41.

"Fifty-Two in '52,"* Dwight Hamilton, No. 482, February 1959, pp. 25-26.

"The San Juan Fly Camps,"* Wilma Epp, No. 538, October 1963, pp. 175-177.

"The High Ones: A San Miguel Adventure,"* Raoul Bates and Bob Stuemky, No. 586, October 1967, pp. 179-180.

"Navajo High Capades,"* Wilma Epp, No. 586, October 1967, pp. 184-185.

"Wilson Peak Last Summer," Sue Waddington, No. 616, April 1970, p. 87.

WINDOM PEAK, 14,082'   Needle Mountains   Columbine Pass 1973
   <u>American Alpine Journal</u>
      "Technical Climbing in the Mountains of Colorado and Wyoming,"*
      Albert Russell Ellingwood, Vol. 1, 1930, pp. 140-147.

   <u>Appalachia</u>
      "Colorado Climbs, 1931,"* Winthrop Means, Vol. 18,
      December 1931, pp. 357-364.

      "All the 14,000's,"* Carl Melzer, Vol. 22, December 1939,
      pp. 466-479.

      "Excursions: Colorado Trip,"* E. Folger Taylor and Walter D.
      Howe, Vol. 23, December 1940, pp. 257-259, 1 Illustration
      following p. 262.

      "The Old and New West in the Needle Mountains,"* Duncan A.
      MacInnes, Vol. 23, June 1941, pp. 374-379.

   <u>Chicago Mountaineering Club Newsletter</u>
      "1959 'Big Hike' in the Needles Mountain Area of Colorado,"*
      Charles I. Pierce, Vol. 14, No. 1, February 1960, pp. 3-6.

   <u>Climbing</u>
      "Sunlight Peak (14,060 Ft.) and Window (sic) Peak (14,091 Ft.),
      Needle Range, San Juans, Colorado,"* No. 7, May-June 1971,
      p. 20.
      First winter ascent note, Rick Nolting, Barry Nash, Floyd
      Frank, and Steve Lewis. Actual first winter ascent in 1966,
      Phil Schmuck, Don Monk, and Kermith Ross.

      Illustration, "Windom Peak," No. 15, September-October 1972,
      pp. 18-19.

      Illustration,* "Descent from Windom and Sunlight Col," No. 15,
      September-October 1972, p. 21.

   <u>Mazama</u>
      "Ramble Number 21,"* A. H. Marshall, Vol. 21, No. 12,
      December 1939, pp. 55-61.

   <u>Trail and Timberline</u>
      "Where We Went and What We Climbed,"* No. 25, October 1920,
      pp. 8-11, 1 Illustration.

      Illustration, "Chairman Harvey T. Sethman of the 1927 Annual
      Outing Committee Seen Leading Party Up Glacial Snowbank,
      Nearing Summit of Mt. Windom (14,091 Ft.) on 1920 Outing,"
      Geo. H. Harvey, Jr., No. 105, June 1927, p. 14.

      "The Highest of All," No. 107, September 1927, p. 12,
      1 Illustration, 1 Illustration p. 2.

      "Four in One Day,"* Dr. Corwin S. Clarke, No. 107,
      September 1927, p. 18, 1 Illustration p. 2.

"The Mountain Ranges of Colorado,"* Kenneth Segerstrom,
No. 215, September 1936, pp. 109-115, 1 Map.

"Needle Mountain Notes,"* David Lavender, No. 225, July 1937,
pp. 80-81.
Windom Peak to Sunlight Peak traverse noted.

"Outing Ridge Work,"* Forest Greenfield, No. 227,
October 1937, pp. 102-103, 105, 1 Illustration.
Traverse noted of ridge from Jupiter - Windom - Sunlight - to
start of Needle Ridge, Jack Heeney and party.

Illustration, "Nearing Summit of Windom - 1920," No. 280,
April 1942, p. 40.

"Reaching the High Spots,"* George J. Kubricht, No. 325,
January 1946, pp. 3-4.

"Noname Prospects,"* Mel Griffiths, No. 340, April 1947,
pp. 56-59.

"Climbers Guide to Noname,"* No. 342, June 1947, pp. 97-98,
1 Map.

"Climber's Guide from Noname Creek,"* Henry Buchtel, No. 345,
September 1947, pp. 143-144, Front cover illustration.

"Confessions of A Solo Climber or How I Recanted My Heresy,"*
Wilbur F. Arnold, No. 389, May 1951, pp. 51-55.

"We Started at the Top,"* Virginia Copeland, No. 395,
November 1951, pp. 145-147, 1 Illustration.

"San Juan Idyll,"* Jose W. Miller, No. 430, October 1954,
pp. 131-133, 139.

"Denver Junior Summer Outing,"* Louise Jackson, No. 443,
November 1955, pp. 190-191.

"The Needles, June 1957,"* Gene White, No. 471, March 1958,
pp. 31-35.

"Fifty-Two in '52,"* Dwight Hamilton, No. 482, February 1959,
pp. 25-26.

"Climber's Paradise,"* Lester Michel, No. 496, April 1960,
pp. 60-62.

"Revised Climbers' Guide from Noname Creek,"* William E.
Davis, No. 502, October 1960, pp. 149-150, 1 Map.

"Chicago Basin Expedition,"* Al Ossinger, No. 559, July 1965,
pp. 131-133, 1 Illustration.

Front cover illustration,* "Needle Mountains - Sunlight and
Windom," William Searcy, No. 607, July 1969.

"Chicago Basin Grand Slam,"* Carl C. Hinrichs, No. 659,
November 1973, pp. 291-294, 1 Illustration.

WINFIELD PEAK, 13,077'   Sawatch Range   Mt. Harvard 15M 1955
   Trail and Timberline
      "Climbing Winfield and Virginia,"* Philip Settles, No. 468,
   December 1957, p. 181.

WOLCOTT MOUNTAIN, 13,041'   San Juan Mountains, Sneffels Range
                            Mount Sneffels 1967
   American Alpine Journal
      "Southwestern Colorado Climbing Notes - 1933,"* Dwight G.
   Lavender, Vol. 2, 1934, p. 256.
   First ascent note, L. V. Giesecke.

      "Colorado Climbing Notes, 1934,"* Carleton C. Long, Vol. 2,
   1935, pp. 416, 417.
   Second ascent note, Carleton Long and party.
   Third ascent note, Don McBride and party.

   The Mountaineering Journal (British)
      "Correspondence,"* Dwight Lavender, Vol. 2, No. 1, December,
   January, February 1933-34, pp. 47-51.
   First ascent note, Lewis V. Giesecke.

   Trail and Timberline
      "The 1933 Climbing Season in Colorado,"* Carleton C. Long,
   No. 184, February 1934, pp. 20-23.
   Probable first ascent note, San Juan Mountaineers.

      Front cover illustration,* "Looking Up Blue Lakes Fork of
   Dallas Creek Towards Dallas Peak (Center) and Wolcott Peak
   (Right)," S.J.M., No. 185, March 1934.

      "1934 Summer Outing Climbs,"* Everett C. Long, No. 192,
   October 1934, pp. 131-133.
   Second ascent noted, Carleton Long and party.
   First ascent noted, Lewis Giesecke.
   (Third) ascent noted, Donald McBride and party.

"WOLF TOOTH", 12,400'#   San Juan Mountains, Sneffels Range
                         (Unnamed) Mount Sneffels 1967
   American Alpine Journal
      "Southwestern Colorado Climbing Notes - 1933,"* Dwight G.
   Lavender, Vol. 2, 1934, p. 256.
   First ascent and traverse note, C. C. Long, L. V. Giesecke,
   T. M. Griffiths, and Dwight G. Lavender.

      "Colorado Climbing Notes, 1934,"* Carleton C. Long, Vol. 2,
   1935, pp. 416, 417.
   Second ascent note.
   Third ascent note.
   Fourth ascent note.

―――――――
#Elevation figure from the American Alpine Journal.

Appalachia
  "Present-Day Rock Climbing in Colorado,"* Carleton C. Long,
  Vol. 20, June 1934, pp. 132-134.

The Mountaineering Journal (British)
  "Outstanding Climbing Centres in the South-Western Colorado
  Rockies,"* Dwight G. Lavender, Vol. 1, No. 4, June, July,
  August 1933, pp. 238-248.

  "Correspondence,"* Dwight Lavender, Vol. 2, No. 1, December,
  January, February 1933-34, pp. 47-51.
  First ascent and traverse note, Dwight Lavender, T. Melvin
  Griffiths, Lewis V. Giesecke, and Carleton Long.

Trail and Timberline
  "The 1933 Climbing Season in Colorado,"* Carleton C. Long,
  No. 184, February 1934, pp. 20-23.
  First ascent and traverse note, San Juan Mountaineers.

  "1934 Summer Outing Climbs,"* Everett C. Long, No. 192,
  October 1934, pp. 131-133, 1 Illustration.

"WOODS PEAK", 13,123'   San Miguel Range   (Unnamed) Dolores Peak 1953
  Trail and Timberline
    "The 1931 Outing Country,"* Dwight G. Lavender, No. 151,
    May 1931, pp. 63-66.

"WULSTEN" BALDY PEAK, 12,829'   Sangre de Cristo Range
                                 Electric Peak 15M 1959
  Trail and Timberline
    "New Names in Sangres,"* No. 621, September 1970, p. 206.

"PEAK X", 13,085'   Gore Range   (Unnamed) Vail East 1970
                                   (Unnamed) Minturn 15M 1934, 13,055'

Trail and Timberline
    "Names on the Gores,"* William Bird Mounsey, No. 568,
    April 1966, pp. 63-65, 1 Map.

"PEAK Y", 12,960'   Gore Range   (Unnamed) Vail East 1970
    Trail and Timberline
        "Names on the Gores,"* William Bird Mounsey, No. 568,
        April 1966, pp. 63-65, 1 Map.

MT. YALE, 14,194'   Sawatch Range   Mt. Harvard 15M 1955
    American Alpine Journal
        "Naming America's Mountains - The Colorado Rockies,"* Francis
        P. Farquhar, Vol. 12, 1961, pp. 319-346.
        First ascent noted, Professor Josiah Dwight Whitney, Professor
        William Henry Brewer, William Morris Davis, S. F. Sharpless,
        and Robert Moore.

        "Club Activities: Simian Climbing Club,"* Peter Zvengrowski,
        Vol. 16, 1969, pp. 479-480.
        Ascent note via the northwest ridge.

    Appalachia
        "All the 14,000's,"* Carl Melzer, Vol. 22, December 1939,
        pp. 466-479.

    Trail and Timberline
        "Junior Outing,"* Anonymous, No. 227, October 1937, p. 107.

        "A Conglomerate Review of the C.M.C. Summer Outing,
        August 15-23, 1942 - Collegiate Range,"* Nancy Plowman, Eliot
        Moses, Harold Brewer, Mary Wagner, No. 287, November 1942,
        pp. 141-143, 1 Map p. 140.

        "Reaching the High Spots,"* George J. Kubricht, No. 325,
        January 1946, pp. 3-4.

        "Backpacking the Sawatch Range,"* Bud Boylard, No. 378,
        June 1950, pp. 83-85, 90-91.

        "First Overnight,"* Esther Holt, No. 382, October 1950,
        pp. 151-152.

        "Wetcliffe," Stan Justice, No. 567, March 1966, p. 50,
        1 Illustration.

        "Anniversary Climbs - Mt. Harvard, Mt. Yale - August 1969,"*
        Anne Sharples Frantz, No. 632, August 1971, pp. 168-170,
        1 Illustration.

YPSILON MOUNTAIN, 13,514'   Mummy Range, Rocky Mountain National Park
                             Trail Ridge 1957
    Appalachia
        "Ypsilon Peak," Frederick H. Chapin, Vol. 5, December 1888,
        pp. 175-183, 2 Illustrations.

        "Exploration,"* F. O. Carpenter, Vol. 5, December 1888, p. 234.
        Ascent note, F. H. Chapin.

        "The Peaks of Rocky Mountain National Park,"* Roger W. Toll,
        Vol. 17, June 1929, pp. 252-260.

Climbing
"Winter Climbing in Rocky Mountain National Park,"* Michael
Covington, No. 37, July-August 1976, pp. 7-13.
First winter ascent noted of the Blitzen Ridge, Dakers Gowan
(Gowans).

"Basecamp: Colorado,"* No. 39, November-December 1976, pp. 3-5.
Accident note.

Mountain
"Information: Rocky Mountains,"* No. 36, June 1974, p. 9.
First winter ascent note of the Blitzen Ridge, Dakers Gowan
(Gowans).

Summit
"Exploring New Routes in Rocky Mountain National Park,"*
Philip C. Ritterbush, Vol. 5, No. 2, February 1959, pp. 10-13,
20-21, 1 Illustration, 1 Map.
First ascent noted of the Blitzen Ridge, Charles Ehlert,
Clinton Brooks, James Walker, David Fedson, and Philip C.
Ritterbush.

"Letters,"* Gary Neptune, Vol. 14, No. 10, December 1968,
p. 34.
Solo east face ascent note, Gary Neptune.

Trail and Timberline
"The East Face of Ypsilon," Moritz Krieg, No. 263,
November 1940, pp. 167-168, 2 Illustrations, Front cover
illustration.
Ascent noted of the rock rib between the arms of the Y, Elwyn
Arps, Roy Murchison, and Louisa Ward.
Ascent noted of the left arm of the Y, Dudley Smith and party.

"PEAK Z", 13,245'   Gore Range   (Unnamed) Willow Lakes 1970
   Trail and Timberline
      "Names on the Gores,"* William Bird Mounsey, No. 568,
      April 1966, pp. 63-65, 1 Map.

MT. ZIRKEL, 12,180'   North Park Range   Mount Zirkel 1955
   Alpine Journal
      "The Rockies of Colorado,"* Evelio Echevarría C., Vol. 71,
      May 1966, pp. 26-36, 1 Map, Bibliography.

   Summit
      "Mount Zirkel," Charles K. Cranston, Vol. 10, No. 1, January-
      February 1964, pp. 14-15, 35, 1 Map.

   Trail and Timberline
      "Some First Ascent Possibilities in Colorado,"* Kenneth
      Segerstrom, No. 165, July 1932, pp. 103-104.

      "North Park and Mt. Zirkle,"* No. 202, August 1935, p. 95.

      "Group Activities: Denver Group,"* No. 203, September 1935,
      p. 106.
      Exploratory note.

      "Exploring the Mount Zirkel - Dome Peak Wild Area,"* Margaret
      B. Chase, No. 464, August 1957, pp. 111-113, Back cover
      illustration, 1 Map following p. 116.

      "Let's Go to the Zirkel Outing," Gertrude Pierce, No. 509,
      May 1961, pp. 87-88, 1 Illustration.

      "Highlights of the Outing,"* Janet M. Johnson, No. 514,
      October 1961, pp. 171-173, Front cover illustration.

      "Why Plan?" Kathy Krysiuk, No. 514, October 1961, p. 174,
      Front cover illustration.

"ZODIAC SPIRES", 12,550'#   Gore Range   (Unnamed) Willow Lakes 1970
   Trail and Timberline
      "Rock Climbing in the Gore Range,"* Mark P. Addison, No. 457,
      January 1957, pp. 3-4, 13, 2 Maps.
      Probable first ascent noted of Cancer Spire, Mark P. Addison
      and Don Brown.
      Probable first ascents noted of Gemini Twins, Taurus Spire,
      Scorpio Spire, Libra Spire, and Sagittarius Spire, Mark P.
      Addison, Don Brown, and Joe Prow.

"MT. ZWISCHEN", 12,006'   Sangre de Cristo Range
                       (Unnamed) Medano Pass 1967
   Trail and Timberline
      "New Names in Sangres,"* No. 621, September 1970, p. 206.

#Elevation of ridge point.

MISCELLANEOUS

BOOKLETS

<u>Trail and Timberline</u>
"The Colorado Fourteens: A Condensed Guide," Ray Phillips,
No. 582, June 1967, pp. 103-118, 3 Illustrations, 1 Map,
Front cover sketch.

"Sawatch Range - Eastern Slope," Helen J. Stiles, No. 595,
August 1968, 5 Illustrations, 1 Map, Front cover illustration.
CMC Trail Guide Series S-1.

"Sawatch Range - Chalk Creek Area," Helen J. Stiles, No. 608,
August 1969, 10 Illustrations, 2 Maps, Bibliography, Front
cover illustration.
CMC Trail Guide Series S-2.

"Sawatch Range - Cottonwood Area," Helen J. Stiles, No. 632,
August 1971, pp. 174A-174P, 8 Illustrations, 2 Maps,
Bibliography, Front cover illustration.
CMC Trail Guide Series S-3.

"Front Range - Indian Peaks," Jim Petrie, E. R. Weiner, and
Hugh Kingery, No. 646, October 1972, pp. 216A-216P,
6 Illustrations, 2 Maps, Front cover illustration.
CMC Trail Guide Series F-1.

MISCELLANEOUS

GENERAL ARTICLES

<u>American Alpine Journal</u>
"Flight Over the Colorado Rockies," Carl Blaurock, Vol. 5, 1945, pp. 363-365.
Flight noted along the Continental Divide and over the fifty highest peaks.

<u>Trail and Timberline</u>
"Condensed Guide to Colorado's 14,000-Foot Peaks," No. 331, July 1946, pp. 109-116, 1 Map.

"Growing Pains," No. 341, May 1947, p. 81.
Note on elevation changes among sixteen 14,000 foot peaks.

"All the 14,000 Foot Peaks in One Day!" No. 386, February 1951, p. 20.
Note on plane trip flying around all Colorado 14,000 foot peaks.

"A Plane Trip Around the 14,000 Ft. Peaks," H. B. Van Valkenburgh, III, No. 393, September 1951, pp. 110-112, 4 Illustrations.

"The Fourteens by Air," Martha Anderson, No. 393, September 1951, pp. 115-116.

"Early Morning Flight Over Colorado's Fourteens Huge Success," G. C. Kehmeier, No. 489, September 1959, p. 119.

"Elevations of 14,000' Peaks in Colorado (September, 1961)," Jack Reed, No. 522, June 1962, pp. 96-98.

"The Non-Shining Mountains," Elwyn and Louisa Arps, No. 529, January 1963, pp. 3-4, 16, 4 Illustrations.
Ascents noted of forty seven of the fifty three 14,000 foot peaks in celebration of the 50th anniversary of the Colorado Mountain Club.

"A Bird's Eye View of the Fourteens," G. C. Kehmeier, No. 529, January 1963, pp. 5-6, 1 Illustration.

"Revised List of 14,000-Foot Peaks," Jack Reed, No. 556, April 1965, pp. 78-79.

"14,000 Foot Mountains," William A. Graves, No. 590, February 1968, pp. 30-34, 2 Illustrations, 1 Illustration p. 36, Front cover illustration.
Proposals noted for criteria used in measuring 14,000 foot peaks.

"14,000 Foot Mountains," Raymond E. Hill, No. 593, May 1968, pp. 118-120, 1 Illustration.
Proposals noted for criteria used in measuring 14,000 foot peaks.

"100 Highest Summits in Colorado," compiled by William Graves, No. 593, May 1968, pp. 121-122.

"Mountains in Rocky Mountain National Park," R. D. Martin, No. 607, July 1969, pp. 128-130, 1 Illustration.

"Mountains of the Southern Sawatch," R. D. Martin, No. 627, March 1971, pp. 65-67, 2 Illustrations.

"What is A 14,000-Foot Mountain?" John Carpenter, No. 627, March 1971, pp. 68-69.
Proposals noted for criteria used in measuring 14,000 foot peaks.

"Glenn Porzak's Recipe: The Ninety-Eight Peaks in the Rocky Mountain National Park," H. S., No. 672, December 1974, p. 305, 1 Illustration p. 304.
First climber noted to climb all the 98 named summits above 11,000' in Rocky Mountain National Park, Glenn Porzak.

"Super Hike in Boulder Foothills Answers Riddle ... What has 16 Summits and 16,000 Feet Vertical Rise, Takes 20 Hours and Goes Three Miles?" Gerard Roach, No. 682, October 1975, pp. 202-204.

"Join the 43 Club by Climbing ... Colorado County Summits," Robert C. Michael, No. 688, April 1976, p. 95.

MISCELLANEOUS

CLIMBERS OF FOURTEEN THOUSAND FOOT MOUNTAINS

Climbing

"Basecamp: Fourteeners," No. 10, November-December 1971, p. 3.
Note on Rich Riefenberg climbing all 54 14,000 foot mountains in 54 days.

Trail and Timberline

"Group Activities: Denver Group,"* No. 192, October 1934, p. 141.
Note on Mary Cronin, first woman to climb all 51 14,000 foot mountains.

"All the 14,000-Footers," E. J. Settles, No. 309, September 1944, p. 104.
Note on Ruth and Paul Gorham, first couple to climb all 51 14,000 foot mountains.

"Club 52 (or 54 or 53)," Evelyn Runnette, No. 590, February 1968, pp. 34-35.

"Men and Women Who Climbed Them All," No. 590, February 1968, pp. 35-36.

"Addendum - Men and Women Who Have Climbed Them All," No. 601, January 1969, p. 12.

"The Hundreth Climber," No. 613, January 1970, p. 18.

"Addendum - Men and Women Who Climbed Them All," No. 613, January 1970, p. 18.

"Letters to the Editor," Bruce Stewart, No. 613, January 1970, pp. 18-19.
Note on Bruce Stewart climbing seven 14,000 foot mountains in one day.

"Editor's Note," Hugh E. Kingery, No. 613, January 1970, p. 19.
Note on Cleve McCarty climbing 54 14,000 foot mountains in 54 days.
Note on Steve Gaskill climbing nine 14,000 foot mountains in 24 hours.
Note on Phil Settles and Dick Walker climbing Crestone Peak, Crestone Needle, Kit Carson, and Humboldt in one day.

"Addendum - Men and Women Who Have Climbed Them All," No. 625, January 1971, p. 14.

"Men and Women Who Have Climbed Them All," No. 636, December 1971, p. 248.

"Men and Women Who Have Climbed Them All," No. 654, June 1973, p. 169.

"Men and Women Who Have Climbed Them All," No. 660,
December 1973, p. 329.

"Men and Women Who Have Climbed Them All," No. 663, March 1974,
p. 72.

"Ossinger Lone '106 Club' Member," No. 671, November 1974,
p. 260.
Note on Al Ossinger climbing all 14,000 foot mountains twice.

"Men and Women Who Have Climbed Them All," No. 671,
November 1974, p. 272.

"Letters to the Editor," George N. Smith, No. 673, January 1975,
p. 15.
Note on George, Flint, Quade, Cody, and Tyle Smith climbing all
14,000 foot mountains twice.

"Letters to the Editor," Jim Gehres, No. 677, May 1975, p. 96.
Note on Jim Gehres climbing all 14,000 foot mountains for the
third time.

"Men and Women Who Have Climbed Them All," No. 678, June 1975,
p. 136.

"Men and Women Who Have Climbed Them All," No. 682, October 1975,
p. 201.
Also note on Jim Gehres climbing all 14,000 foot mountains for
the fourth time.

"Men and Women Who Have Climbed Them All," No. 685, January 1976,
p. 11.

"The Fourteeners," Bill Bueler, No. 690, June 1976, p. 130.
Note on Carl Blaurock and William Ervin, first to climb all
then recognized 46 14,000 foot mountains in 1923.
Note on Albert Ellingwood, second to climb all 14,000 foot
mountains.

"Men and Women Who Have Climbed Them All," No. 695,
November 1976, p. 217.

MISCELLANEOUS

HISTORICAL NOTES ON INDIVIDUAL CLIMBERS

American Alpine Journal
"Albert R. Ellingwood, 1888-1934," J. L. J. H., Vol. 2, 1935,
pp. 388-390.
First ascents noted of Crestone Peak (1916); Crestone Needle
(1916); Kit Carson Peak (1916); Lizard Head (1920); Pigeon
(second ascent) (1920); Turret (1920); Bishop Rock in Platte
Canyon (1924).
New routes noted of Pagoda, west ridge (1916); Blanca, east
face and north ridge (1916); Maroon, south ridge (1919); North
Maroon, east ridge (1919); Evans, north face (1920); North
Maroon, south ridge (1922); Maroon, north ridge (1922);
Crestone Needle, east ridge (1925); Little Bear, west ridge
(1925); Crestone, north ridge (1925); Longs Peak, east face
(1927); Mt. Evans, snowshoes (1916).

"Dwight Garrigues Lavender," C. C. L., Vol. 2, 1935, pp. 390-391.
Ascents noted of the north face of Mt. Sneffels.
Discovery, naming, and ascent of the westernmost 14,000 ft.
peak in Colorado - El Diente.
First ascent noted of Jagged Mountain.

Trail and Timberline
"Albert R. Ellingwood," J. L. J. H., No. 188, June 1934, pp. 81,
85.

"Dwight G. Lavender," T. M. G., No. 192, October 1934, pp. 134-
135.

"CMC History - Colorado's Man of the Mountains: Carl Blaurock,"
William M. Bueler, No. 669, September 1974, pp. 212-218,
1 Illustration, Front cover illustration.
First ascents noted of Lone Eagle Peak, north face of Capitol
Peak, north face of Navajo, and east ridge of Blanca.
First to climb all 14,000 foot mountains with William Ervin.
Ascents noted of the east face of Longs Peak - 18 via
Alexander's Chimney, one of the North Chimney.

"Historical Note on James W. Alexander," William M. Bueler,
No. 681, September 1975, p. 178.
First ascent note of Alexanders Chimney on the east face of
Longs Peak. Second ascent note of Alexanders Chimney with Jack
Moomaw.
First ascents of the southwest ridge and the northwest
(keyhole) ridge.

"Historical Note on Percy W. Thomas," William M. Bueler, No. 681,
September 1975, p. 193.
First ascent note of El Diente, (with N. G. Douglass).
Attempt note of the Lizard Head, with N. G. Douglass.

"Historical Notes on Mountaineering: Chapin, Frederick H.;
Fay, Charles; Franklin Spalding," William M. Bueler, No. 685,
January 1976, pp. 28-29.

"Mountaineering History: A. D. Wilson," William M. Bueler,
No. 687, March 1976, p. 75.

"Mountain History: Isabella Bird," Bill Bueler, No. 688,
April 1976, p. 86.
Ascent note of Longs Peak.

"Werner Zimmerman," Bill Bueler, No. 688, April 1976, p. 103.
Ascent note of the east face of Longs Peak by a route on or
near Alexanders Chimney in 1919.

"Who Was Enos Mills?" William Bueler, No. 689, May 1976, p. 109.

"Historical Note: Hayden and Wheeler Surveys," William M.
Bueler, No. 693, September 1976, pp. 178-179.
Partial list of the peaks climbed by the two surveys.

ADDENDA

MT. DEFIANCE, 13,250'
    <u>Climbing</u>
       "Nostalgia/Part II Mundus Est Mons,"* Harvey T. Carter, No. 6,
        March-April 1971, pp. 3-5.
       First ascent noted of the Mount Defiance Wall.

MT. GARFIELD, TORRENT TOWER, 13,675'
    <u>Climbing</u>
       "Nostalgia/Part II Mundus Est Mons,"* Harvey T. Carter, No. 6,
        March-April 1971, pp. 3-5.
       First ascent noted of the Torrent Tower of Mt. Garfield.

"GRAND TRAVERSE PEAK", 13,041'   Gore Range   (Unnamed) Willow Lakes 1970
May also be known as "SOUTH TRAVERSE PEAK"
    <u>Trail and Timberline</u>
       "Boulder Notes,"* Hope Leighton, No. 467, November 1957,
        pp. 174-175.
       First ascent note, Stan Midgely.
       Ascent note, Harold Walton and party.

MT. MORRISON, 7,881'   Front Range   Morrison 1965
    <u>Trail and Timberline</u>
       "Geological Excursion to Mount Morrison," Prof. George L.
        Cannon, No. 38, November 1921, pp. 2-5, 1 Illustration.

"THE SPIDER", 12,692'   Gore Range   (Unnamed) Vail East 1970
See "PEAK I"

"MT. VALHALLA", 13,180'   Gore Range   (Unnamed) Willow Lakes 1970
See also "PEAK 13,200'"   (Unnamed) Dillon 15M 1929, 13,200'
    <u>Trail and Timberline</u>
       "Boulder Notes,"* Hope Leighton, No. 467, November 1957,
        pp. 174-175.
       First ascent note, Stan Midgely.
       Second ascent note, Harold Walton and party.